# Multiple Voices

# Multiple Voices

*Narrative in Systemic Family Psychotherapy*

edited by

Renos K. Papadopoulos
John Byng-Hall

KARNAC

Reprinted 2001by Karnac Books
6 Pembroke Buildings
London NW10 6RE
Tel. (0)20 8969 4454
Fax. (0)20 8969 5585

First published in 1997 by
Gerald Duckworth & Co. Ltd.

Library of Congress Cataloguing-in-Publication Data
Multiple voices: narrative in systemic family psychotherapy / edited by Renos K.
Papadopoulos and John Byng-Hall
1. Family psychotherapy. 2. Personal construct theory
3. Storytelling - Therapeutic use I. Papadopoulos, Renos K.
II. Byng-Hall, John
RC488.5.M85 1998
616.89'156--dc21                                         97-44057
                                                          CIP

ISBN: 185575 995 0

Typeset by Ray Davies

www.karnacbooks.com

Printed and bound in Great Britain by Antony Rowe Ltd, Eastbourne

01      09066

# Contents

# Preface

Since it was founded in 1920, the Tavistock Clinic has developed a wide range of psychotherapeutic approaches to community mental health which have always been strongly influenced by psychoanalysis. In the last thirty years it has also developed systemic family therapy as a new theoretical model and clinical approach. The Clinic has become the largest training institution in Britain for work of this kind, providing post-graduate and qualifying courses in social work, psychology, psychiatry, child, adolescent and adult psychotherapy and, latterly, in nursing. It trains about 1200 students each year in over 45 courses.

The Clinic's philosophy has been one of influencing mental health work toward therapeutic and humane methods and has, as an aim, the dissemination of training, clinical expertise and research throughout Britain and the rest of the world. This major new book series is designed to make available the extensive experience that the work of the Clinic represents, covering all its departments, specialist workshops and research seminars. The series seeks to be accessible to a wide audience by presenting new approaches and developments in a clear, readable style and at reasonable prices. It will enable the Clinic to describe many aspects both of its established clinical work and of current growing points and innovations in the practice, theory and research of experts.

In this book members of the Systems Group of the Tavistock Clinic address various aspects of the narrative approach to psychotherapy. The recent increased interest in this perspective to psychotherapy has created a rather confused field with different meanings, definitions and directions. This book offers a coherent approach based on clinical research and therapeutic work; the chapters address theoretical issues and clinical applications to a variety of contexts, including narratives in families with physical illness, fostering and adoption, divorce, bilingualism and refugees. The editors are Renos K. Papadopoulos and John Byng-Hall.

Nicholas Temple and Margot Waddell
Series Editors

# Acknowledgements

We would like to acknowledge and express our appreciation for the permissions given to reproduce previously published material in this book, specifically to:

Susan Sontag for a quote from her book *Illness as Metaphor* (1991) as well as to Penguin UK and Wylie Agency.

John Berger for quoting his poem 'Migrant Words' in *Pages of the Wound* (1996) as well as to Bloomsbury Publishing.

Italo Calvino for excerpts from *If on a Winter's Night Traveller* (1981) as well as to Martin Secker & Warburg Ltd, and Reed Consumer Books.

Edwina Welham at Routledge for permissions to reproduce extracts from *Special Care Babies and Their Developing Relationships* (1994).

# Foreword

This book is alive with the current practice and creativity in the field of family psychotherapy. Its immediacy and freshness stems from the first-hand experience of all its contributors. Whether they are writing from an historical, theoretical, clinical or research perspective, their involvement with their subject matter is palpable, a quality enriched by the Editors' request that contributors should include some reference to their own personal stories relating to their background relevant to their subject.

Another strength of this book is that the book's 'multiple voices' on narrative are from contributors coming from the same group working together in one (originally psychoanalytic) institution, the Tavistock Clinic. As the exploration of narrative in their various areas of work unfolds, their combined story seems almost isomorphic to the history of the systems group within the clinic. This is particularly evident in the chapters on step-families, adoption and fostering families and refugee families. Sebastian Kraemer suggests in his chapter that the early struggles of the systems group was influenced by the strong gravitational pull of the prevailing theories, and that this influence was just too strong to allow for radical change. This regrettably led to polarisation of the two theoretical stances, psychoanalytic and systems. But over the last two decades this polarisation has given way to a 'one country – two systems' approach, allowing the value of diversity to emerge and an alternative to the dominant narrative to be heard. This does not predicate the desirability of integrating psychoanalytic and systems theory, but 'to encourage the putting together of the fractured story of therapy'. Through this it is hoped that the mutual debt they owe each other will be acknowledged. The Tavistock Clinic now describes itself as both psychoanalytic and systemic, which is an important step in this process.

This book contains many, often differing, views and the multiplicity of contexts allows for compatible but distinct voices to be heard. It is remarkable that so much richness and diversity has come from one

ix

group of people working together in one institution. The theoretical papers in Part One are thoughtful, at times provocative. They stimulate the reader to begin thinking about his or her position in the debate. Part Two will be of great value to experienced clinicians, especially those working with a narrative approach in a variety of challenging arenas, such as physical illness, step-families and refugee families.

In the Preface it is explained that this book is one of the first of a series to be written by members of the departments of the Tavistock Clinic. In recent years the Tavistock has formed a Tavistock Society of Psychotherapists for all staff and trainees, past and present. At a recent conference of the society with presentations by its departments (in June of this year) we learnt that it is the intention of the Royal College of Psychiatrists to include a measure of systemic input in its future training of Consultant Adult Psychotherapists. This is just one example of how family therapy has become recognised as an integral part of the mental health and child care fields both inside and outside the Tavistock Centre.

As focus on the narrative interaction has occurred in both the psychoanalytic and family therapy fields, and since attachment theory is pertinent to both and features in several of the chapters, I believe that there is an important place for this book in training for both family therapists and individual psychotherapists, as well as for students within mental health and child care.

As one of the original members (from 1972 to 1990) with John Byng-Hall of the Family Systems Group at the Tavistock, I have been interested to see how unusually steady and consistent the membership of the group has remained over the years. It has had an outstanding influence on the development of family therapy, both in the UK and abroad over the past twenty five years and this excellent book testifies to its continued vitality and creativity. It is a great tribute to all current members of the group.

Rosemary Whiffen

# Contributors

*The editors and all contributors are systemic family psychotherapists coming from a variety of professional backgrounds and work at the Child and Family Department of the Tavistock Clinic as clinicians and trainers. All belong to research teams involved on a long-term basis with research into aspects of narrative in family psychotherapy within the Family Systems Group at the Tavistock Clinic.*

**Jenny Altschuler** is a consultant Clinical Psychologist at the Tavistock, previously employed in in-patient and liaison work at the Royal Free Hospital. She has published several papers as well as a book on *Working with Chronic Illness* (1996).

**Charlotte Burck** is a Senior Clinical Lecturer in Social Work. She has been involved in researching the process of change in family therapy. She has a particular interest in addressing the societal and cultural context in therapy, and has written on gender and family therapy. Her research on bilingual experience and their implications for therapy is in its early stages.

**John Byng-Hall** is a Consultant Child and Family Psychiatrist at the Tavistock Clinic. He is a member, and past Chair, of the Institute of Family Therapy in London. He has published widely on subjects such as family myths, stories, legends and scripts; the implications of attachment theory for family therapy; adolescence, supervision and illness in the family. His last book was *Rewriting Family Scripts* (1995). Research topics include: attachment in the family; developing instruments for assessing process and change using videotape of family therapy sessions; studying the interfaces between interaction, intrapsychic and transgenerational factors; and the influence of attachments on family care of the chronically ill.

**David Campbell** is a Consultant Clinical Psychologist who has worked at the Tavistock Clinic since 1973. He is currently the Chair of the Systems Team (The Family Therapy Team) in the Child and Family Department. He is the co-organiser of the MSc Family Therapy Course jointly run between the Tavistock and the University of East London. His research interests are in the field of family therapy outcome and supervision and teaching practices. He also works as an Organisational Consultant to organisations in the public and private sector and is the author of several books on this subject. He is also a co-editor of a 22 book series entitled *Systemic Teaching and Practice* published by Karnac Books.

**Barbara Dale** is a Senior Clinical Lecturer in Social Work, Trainer and Member of the Institute of Family Therapy. Current research and writing on chronic illness and on life-threatening illness and its effect on adults who are parents.

**Emilia Dowling** is a Consultant Clinical Psychologist. She is Head of Child Psychology in the Child and Family Department and Visiting Professor in the Psychology Department, Birkbeck College (University of London). Her research interests include systemic work with families and schools and she is currently investigating the children's perspective in divorcing families. She has published widely and co-edited with the late Elsie Osborne *The Family and The School: A Joint Systems Approach to Problems with Children* (1994, 2nd ed.)

**Stephen Frosh** is a Consultant Clinical Psychologist in the Child and Family Department, Tavistock Clinic, and Reader in Psychoanalytical Psychology at Birkbeck College, University of London. He is the author of numerous academic papers and several books, including *Sexual Difference* (1994), *Identity Crisis* (1991), *Politics of Psychoanalysis* (1987), *For and against Psychoanalysis* (1997). He has recently edited, with Anthony Elliott, *Psychoanalysis in Contexts* (1995).

**Gill Gorell Barnes** works as a Senior Clinical Lecturer at the Tavistock Clinic. She acts as Consultant for Training at the Institute of Family Therapy in London. She has worked with families for over 20 years in a variety of settings. She is now writing up some innovative research into the child's experience of step-families (*Growing up in Stepfamilies*: in press, Oxford University Press, with colleagues outside the Tavistock Clinic). This complements the work described in this chapter developed over the last three years in which the focus has been on the transitional processes in families following divorce, and the differential effects for mothers, fathers and children.

**Judy Hildebrand** is a Senior Clinical Lecturer in Social Work and for may years was Clinical Director of the Institute of Family Therapy, where she was a teacher and supervisor. She teaches both in the UK and abroad on a variety of topics, consults to professional teams. She has published widely and appeared in several media productions; her interests include child sexual abuse, bereavement in the family, mediation, group work supervision, couples work, personal and professional development.

**Sebastian Kraemer** studied medicine after a first degree in philosophy specialising in paediatrics and later in psychiatry. Since 1980 he has been Consultant Child and Adolescent Psychiatrist at the Tavistock Clinic and at the Whittington Hospital, London. His principal interests and publications are in family therapy, psychosomatic disorders, the training of psychiatrists, and the origins and roles of fatherhood.

**Caroline Lindsey** is a Consultant Child Psychiatrist and Family Therapist at the Tavistock Clinic and currently Chair of its Child and Family Department. She has been involved in training child psychiatrists and family therapists for many years. She runs a fostering and adoption consultation and treatment service. She has recently developed a course on systemic approaches in medical general practice. She had published in various areas of systemic applications to child and adolescent psychiatry, and her co-authored book on 'systemic supervision' is in press.

**Anne McFadyen** is a Senior Lecturer and Consultant in Child and Adolescent Psychiatry at the Royal Free Hospital School of Medicine and the Tavistock Clinic. As a clinician she works primarily in the field of infant mental health and learning disability. She is also involved in the training of a number of disciplines and has an active research life. Her academic writings include: *Special Care Babies and Their Developing Relationships* (1994).

**Renos K. Papadopoulos** is a Consultant Clinical Psychologist at the Tavistock Clinic, Professor of Analytical Psychology at the University of Essex, and a Training Jungian Analyst. He has worked with survivors in Soweto, Chernobyl and the former Yugoslavia and for the last few years has been working with a group of Bosnian ex camp prisoners who were brought to Britain as medical evacuees. His last book is *C.G. Jung: Critical Assessments* (1992), a four-volume edited work.

# Introduction

*Renos K. Papadopoulos and John Byng-Hall*

Family Therapists are intrigued by the influence and richness of narrative. We are not alone. Psychotherapy, whether with individuals, families or groups, is based primarily and almost exclusively on the verbal medium, hence the expression 'the talking cure'. In fact, it was a patient who first coined this term and not a therapist; it was Anna O., Dr Breuer's famous patient, who used it (in English) to refer to her activity of putting 'into words her freshly constructed phantasies' (Freud, 1909, p. 13). The central activities of the 'talking cure' are the patients' narratives which they construe about themselves and the therapists' responses to them. Jung, influenced by his early researches into the Word Association Test, examined the implications of appreciating the importance of the simple fact that the 'associations' patients offer (in connection with feelings, images, ideas, etc.) are, essentially, associations within the medium of language, in the context of a verbal interaction. This led him to emphasise the 'dialectical' nature of psychotherapy which highlights both its verbal medium as well as its interactional character: 'Dialectic was originally the art of conversation among ancient philosophers ... A person is a psychic system which, when it affects another person, enters into reciprocal reaction with another psychic system', hence, psychotherapy was for Jung 'a kind of dialectical process, a dialogue or discussion between two persons' (1935, p. 3), or, to use current terminology, an interactional exchange of narratives.

Throughout its relatively recent history, psychotherapy has focused on the various aspects of its language dimension (McLeod, 1997); this has ranged from emphasis on the symbolic and metaphorical facets of therapy as reflected in language interaction (Riikonen and Smith, 1997), to the appreciation of therapy in the context of discourse theories (Shotter, 1993). Movements such as structuralism and semiotic analysis (David, 1983; Ricoeur, 1984-5), post-structuralism and ecol-

1

ogy (Anderson and Goolishian, 1988), post-modernism and constructivism (McNamee and Gergen, 1992) have all contributed their own perspective to this dimension. In addition, psychology and the social sciences have also been preoccupied with the various narrative theories (Bruner, 1990; Gilligan, 1982; Gilligan, Lyons and Hanmer 1990; Gilligan, Rogers and Tolman, 1991; Howard, 1989; Jameson, 1981; Mair, 1988; Polkinghorne, 1988; Riessman, 1993). Essentially, once the archaeology model of psychotherapy was challenged (Spence, 1982), the emphasis has gradually been shifting from the accent on 'historical truth' (to be uncovered by the therapist) to that on 'narrative truth' (to be co-constructed by both therapist and patient).

According to Zimmerman and Dickerson (1994), the movement from First to Second-Order cybernetics enabled family therapists to understand more clearly the implications of moving away from causality and from the primacy of the therapists' experience (now valuing more the client's experiences); moreover, it increased their appreciation that their theories are nothing but 'useful metaphors' (p. 234). The same authors further argued that by developing a narrative approach to therapy, family therapists could focus on 'effects instead of causes' (p. 235) allowing narratives to be fluid in terms of their evolution through time; in addition, therapists could appreciate more fully therapeutic interactions as 'experience' rather than as 'information'. Inevitably, this has led to the invention of new roles for therapists, 'inviting clients to make meaning out of other aspects of their experience' apart from the 'problem-filled' stories. This development allows therapists to increase their role as providers of conditions within which clients can re-story their problems within the perspective of a wider life context.

One important observation which needs to be made is that the focus on the narrative interaction has occurred both in the psychoanalytic as well as family therapy fields. This is of particular relevance to this book which is produced by members of the Systems Group within the Tavistock Clinic, an institution which has a long tradition of encompassing both the psychoanalytic as well as the systemic approaches to therapy.

The current interest on 'narrative' and on 'stories' in family systems therapy seems to have spread widely (Epston, 1989; Epston and White, 1992; Parry, 1996; Parry and Doan, 1994; Roberts, 1994; Sluzki, 1992; White, 1989 and 1995; White and Epston, 1991), almost acquiring the proportion of a fashion. Inevitably, there has been a great deal of confusion about the precise meaning of what these terms refer to. Indeed, it would be very tempting for us to develop an elaborate classification of the different uses and applications of 'the narrative' and 'stories' in therapy and finally offer our own definitions of them. However, such didactic enthusiasm, on our part, would spoil the richness which the variability of the following chapters provide. Each contribution in this book develops its own unique way of understanding and applying these terms and the reader should be allowed to enjoy the diversity of these issues unfolding.

However, one clarification may be useful: 'narrative' seems to be used in at least two different ways — the first is to analyse any therapeutic material in terms of a narrative approach, and the second is to propose new kinds of therapeutic interventions which are in fact called 'narrative therapy' (Freedman and Coombs, 1996). This book is not aimed at offering an example of a 'narrative therapy' as such; instead, it espouses the view that narrative, *de facto*, is part of any form of psychotherapy. It may be argued that the very name 'narrative therapist' may be a mistake of logical typing, confusing subclass with class. All therapists who use talking are, of course, narrative therapists. To call one group of therapists 'narrative' implies that the others do not use narrative. It would be similar if a group of dentists defined themselves as the 'tooth dentists', implying that all other dentists do not work with teeth. Thus, all therapists may benefit from appreciating the function of narrative elements in their own therapeutic style even if they do not belong to the movement which calls itself 'narrative therapy'. Moreover, this book endeavours to demonstrate that for family psychotherapists it is imperative to become aware of the multiplicity of contexts which influence the narratives of their own work.

Family therapy seems to have limited the application of *stories* and the *narrative* almost exclusively to the context of therapy itself; in other words, it has been focusing on how to facilitate families to develop alternatives to the dominant narrative. Thus, insufficient attention has been placed on how stories develop within the domain of therapists' own theoretical, clinical and professional contexts. The innovation which this book brings is to examine the narrative from a variety of different perspectives including the therapists' own domain; this is possible because of the wide range of diversity within the Systems Group of the Tavistock Clinic. More specifically, it attempts to examine how stories develop and in turn affect the clinical work in relation to four interconnected domains: (a) the therapists' own personal stories about their background and training, (b) the story of the institutional setting which provides the context within which they work, (c) the narrative of the actual therapeutic or research material, and (d) in the background, the general theoretical paradigms and sociopolitical stories and myths of the time. In effect, this book offers a 'case study' on how different stories from the multiplicity of contexts actually affect the development of narratives used by various therapists within one institution.

The specific nature of the Systems Group of the Tavistock Clinic (as is shown below) offers fruitful ground for the examination of the complexities of interconnecting stories because of its following characteristic features: the Team is composed of clinicians from different disciplines (psychiatry, psychology, social work), from diverse cultural, linguistic and ethnic backgrounds, and from different theoretical traditions (post-Milan systemic, structural/systemic, script and attachment theory, Freudian, Jungian, etc.) who have been working together, and in parallel to the predominant psychoanalytic orientation of the Tavistock Clinic.

### Origins of the Book

For a long time the members of the Systems Group wanted to become involved in some joint project in order to learn more from each other and experience both our similarities and diversity. A few years ago, realising that we were channelling our creativity exclusively into our clinical work, supervision and teaching, we felt the need to actively create the conditions for more research work. This led to the establishment of several research groups which combined under one theme a research project, clinical work, and supervision of our post-graduate students. Later, when these projects reached either their conclusion or an advanced state of completion, we felt that it would be a good idea to produce them together in a book form, in order to place them in the wider public and professional domain hoping to benefit from the feedback we will receive.

However, we did not feel that it would be appropriate to just bundle together disparate writings and in a series of special meetings we embarked on a search for common themes. It gradually emerged that the 'narrative' approach to therapy was indeed a common thread through all our work. We then spent some time exploring the ways in which we related to this theme. During those meetings we developed a shared language through which we could address these issues. We hope that despite the diversity of the chapters, the reader will be able to discern our shared story.

Attention was also given to our personal stories. We felt that we as

4

authors should include a story from our own personal experience (past or present) which resonated with the theme of our work as presented in each chapter. The intention was that the individual stories would provide a more explicit personal narrative which would offer an additional dimension to the research project thus enriching the overall story of each contribution.

## The Story of the Systems Group at the Tavistock Clinic

### Early History

The Tavistock Clinic was one of the first places in the world to have introduced family therapy, in fact Bowlby (1949) wrote one of the earliest papers on family therapy. It remains a fascinating read. It conveyed all the excitement of a young man who had discovered the power of working with the family to produce change. He used family sessions to deal with impasses in individual therapy. Bowlby considered making family therapy his main approach but as a scientist decided to focus on the dyad as something more researchable (Bowlby, personal communication). If he had decided otherwise, it is interesting to speculate whether the Tavistock might have become one of the foremost pioneering institutions of family therapy, alongside the American ones. As it happens, it was Bowlby's work which influenced John Bell (1951) who, in turn, became a pioneer in the development of family therapy in the USA (see Byng-Hall, 1991, for a discussion of this).

Ronald Laing was on the staff of the Clinic in the 1960s, and made a world-wide impact on professional and cultural ways of thinking about families and had a significant influence on the early development of family therapy. However, despite their enormous popularity, his theories and work did not contribute directly to the articulation of specific techniques in family therapy. It is beyond the scope of this introduction to elaborate on this rather puzzling observation. Perhaps, Laing's approach became entangled with such powerful (counter) cultural ideologies that did not allow for specific clinical applications in family therapy.

In 1962 Freda Martin and J. Knight published an important paper about seeing the whole family as a group within the context of routine assessments of disturbed children. Freda was to become an important part of the story. There had been increasing conflict and discontent within the multidisciplinary teams at the Tavistock in the late sixties around whether or not family therapy should be used for cases that had

5

been referred. A minority wanted to offer family therapy but were frequently outvoted by those who wanted to provide individual work. Freda Martin became Chair of the Department of Children and Parents in the early 70s and she reorganised the Department into self selected groups who wanted to practice the same way. The Family Therapy Programme was born out of this scheme, in 1972, with Freda as its head.

John Byng-Hall joined the Family Therapy Group at its inception in 1972. He had been a senior registrar at Hill End Adolescent Unit in St. Albans and at the Adolescent Department of the Tavistock since 1969 where he had played a part in establishing a family therapy group. This group continued to develop a psychoanalytic object relations family therapy approach (Box et al., 1981), while the Family Therapy Programme went on to explore a number of alternative ways of working. Rosemary Whiffen was also one of the first members of the programme. She had worked in New York and had some training at the Ackerman Family Institute. She brought invaluable ideas from, and contacts with, America where family therapy had been pioneered. Freda Martin, however, returned to Canada in 1976 and Rosemary Whiffen and John Byng-Hall became Co-Chairs of the Family Therapy Programme which later became known as the Systems Group.

## The Tavistock Ethos that Supported Family Work

American family therapists are often amazed that a 'systems family therapy' group should have emerged and flourished within the Tavistock, the pillar of British psychoanalysis. By and large the history in the USA was of family therapists leaving analytic institutions, rubbishing all that they stood for, and starting anew. Why was our history different?

The Tavistock Clinic has had a long tradition of working with social systems and grappling with the effects of social upheaval. The Clinic itself was set up in 1920 to deal with the aftermath of the First World War and its shell shocked victims, and Tavistock Staff were involved in developing group therapy during and following the Second World War. By the time the Family Therapy Programme started in the 1970's, the Tavistock (Clinic and Institute) already had a long history of working with the concept of social systems in groups, communities, and industry. Henry Dicks had pioneered the idea of mutuality within the couple (Dicks, 1967), and in his history of the Clinic (1970) wrote, 'The concept of family therapy, of regarding the family as a unit and patient's difficulties in no small measure related to the interpersonal nexus with the parents, runs with great continuity through the theoretical base on which the Tavistock Clinic ... was developing' (p. 53). Concepts such as projective identification, shared fantasy, and Bion's group basic assumptions allowed for thinking about groups, and how members of a group were recruited into roles within a group process that was more than the sum of its parts; a central tenet of systems theory.

## The Ethos of Valuing Varied Approaches

In 1972 Robin Skynner brought together the London based teaching of family therapy under the umbrella of the Institute of Group Analysis, and in 1977 established the Institute of Family Therapy (IFT). He recruited staff with various approaches and disciplines from as wide a range of Institutions as possible. Several of us were part of the original group. It was very enriching. The Tavistock group also became influential within IFT, for instance Gill Gorell Barnes became Director of Training, Rosemary Whiffen, and Judy Hildebrand were Clinical Directors, and John Byng-Hall took over the Chair when Robin Skynner retired, while many members of the group have become IFT staff members.

Influenced by IFT, the Systems Group developed an ethos of each member of the group practising and developing his or her own approaches rather than following one 'Tavistock Systems' approach. This was also supported by the Tavistock's tradition that each staff member was expected to innovate and develop new ways of working, although this was usually within the psychoanalytic framework. Bowlby set a tradition of using many disciplines such as ethology to conceptualise his subject matter, although he remained a psychoanalyst. Despite all this, the move to establish systems-thinking as the primary framework for conceptualising our clinical work was a major departure, and it did not happen easily. As systems theory would predict, negative feedback loops were set up in an attempt to reduce such deviant behaviour. What was remarkable, however, was the fact that sufficient support was given for us to flourish despite this reaction. Success in the outside world helped, and the Tavistock Clinic now describes itself as 'psychoanalytic and systems' in its Prospectus. The value of diversity is recognised.

Most of the staff of the Systems Group bring an interest in psychodynamic thinking from their past as well as expertise from other approaches and theories. These include, amongst others: general systems theory, group analysis, attachment theory, feminism, Jungian and Psychoanalytic analysis, object relations theory, social constructionism, script theory, historical approaches, structural, Milan and post-Milan systemic therapy. Different themes have been explored and researched, these include: gender issues, illness and the family, links with schools, divorce, refugees, attachments, consultation, evaluation of family process and outcome. The bridge between object relations and family scripts has also been explored (Byng-Hall, 1986) thus keeping a link with the rest of the Clinic. The ongoing dialogue between psychoanalytic and systems thinking has been possible, although at times each side appears to speak with different tongues.

## Development of the Systems Group

Much of the early history of the Systems Group was making contact with, and learning from, most of the major pioneers in family therapy. First came Salvador Minuchin in 1972 when he spent a sabbatical year at our Clinic writing his famous book *Families and Family Therapy* (1974). We were a little too early in our development to take on structural family therapy ideas from him, but he sowed a seed and later Marianne Walters and Harry Aponte came and added to our expertise. Some members of our group also visited Philadelphia. An important input came from the Ackerman Family Institute in New York which was one major family-therapy institute that had kept links with psychoanalysis, and so was more readily assimilated by us. In 1975 we ran a joint Ackerman-Tavistock week-long intense experiential conference in London. We learned how to do family sculpts from Peggy Papp, genograms from Don Bloch and Olga Silverstein, and did 'systems exercises'. It was very exciting and proved seminal for family therapy in Britain. Interest and practice exploded all over the country. Another Ackerman-Tavistock conference followed the next year followed by three residential conferences in Cambridge. Well-known figures such as Lynn Hoffman, Harry Aponte and Fred and Bunny Duhl joined the staff in these conferences. In the mid 1970s Rosemary Whiffen and John Byng-Hall made contact in Brussels with the Milan group in particular Luigi Boscolo and Gianfranco Cecchin, who became regular visitors to the Clinic over the years and David Campbell, Caroline Lindsey and Ros Draper became well-known teachers and trainers in the field, establishing a parallel family therapy training course based on the Milan Approach (Draper et al., 1991; Campbell et al., 1991; Campbell and Draper, 1985).

# Introduction

## Development of Training and Practice

Training became an increasing preoccupation. We started the first full family therapy training in England in 1975. It was focused on training future trainers; this was an important decision as a high percentage of UK teachers were trained here. We developed techniques of live supervision. In 1979 we ran an International Training Conference with many leading family-therapists from all over the world attending. A book on family-therapy supervision came out of the conference (Whiffen and Byng-Hall, 1982), the first in the field.

We started the first Masters and Doctoral Courses in this area and today the Tavistock family therapy trainings include a comprehensive range of courses from introductory and intermediate level to two-year advanced family therapy training and an additional two year doctorate, all of which receive academic accreditation from the University of East London. A parallel four-year Clinical PhD in Child and Family Psychology, based at Birkbeck College (University of London), has a major input from members of the systems group. In addition, there are courses in family therapy, supervision, family-therapy observation, systemic approaches for general medical practitioners, systemic approaches for managers in the Health Service as well as courses on 'Illness and the Family', and on 'Working with Refugee Families'.

\*

It was not possible to include in the following chapters all the systemic approaches which were developed by members of our Group. It is worth mentioning at least two of those which are missing: the first is the work on the interconnecting systems of school-family-professionals which was developed by Elsie Osborne and Emilia Dowling and which influenced significantly educational and clinical practice (Dowling and Osborne, 1994) and the second is the pioneering application of systemic thinking to consultation work in various contexts (Campbell, 1994 and 1995; Huffington and Brunning, 1994).

## References

Anderson, H. and Goolishian, H.A. (1988) 'Human Systems as Linguistic Systems: preliminary and evolving ideas about the implications for clinical theory', *Family Process*, 27: 271-383.

Bell, J.E. (1951) *Family Group Therapy*, Public Health Monograph No. 64, U.S. Dept of Health, Education and Welfare.

Bowlby, J. (1949) 'The Study and Reduction of Group Tensions in the Family', *Human Relations*, 2, 123.

Box, S.; Copley, B.; Magagna, J. and Moustaki, E. (1981) *Psychotherapy with Families: an Analytic Approach*, London: Routledge.

Bruner, J. (1990) *Acts of Meaning*, Cambridge: Harvard University Press.

Byng-Hall, J. (1986) 'Family Scripts: a concept which can bridge child psychotherapy and family therapy thinking', *Journal of Child Psychotherapy*, 12:2, 3-13.

—— (1991) 'An Appreciation of John Bowlby: his significance for family therapy', *Journal of Family Therapy*, 13:1 5-16.

Campbell, D. (1994) *Systemic Work with Organisations*, London: Karnac Books.

—— (1995) *Learning Consultation*, London: Karnac Books.

Campbell, D. and Draper, R. (eds) (1985) *Applications of Systemic Family Therapy: the Milan approach*, London: Grune and Stratton.

Campbell, D. et al. (1991) *Teaching Systemic Thinking*, London: Karnac Books.

David, R.C. (ed.) (1983) *Lacan and Narration: the psychoanalytic difference in narrative theory*, Baltimore: Johns Hopkins University Press.

Dicks, H.V. (1967) *Marital Tensions: clinical studies towards a psychological theory of interaction*, New York: Basic Books.

—— (1970) *Fifty Years of the Tavistock Clinic*, London: Routledge and Kegan Paul.

Dowling, E. and Osborne, E. (eds) (1985) *The Family and the School: a joint systems approach to problems with children*, London: Routledge.

Draper, R. et al.. (1991) *Teaching Family Therapy*, London: Karnac Books.

Epston, D. (1989) *Collected Papers*, Adelaide, Australia: Dulwich Centre Publications.

Epston, D. and White, M. (1992) *Experience, Contradiction, Narrative and Imagination*, Adelaide, Australia: Dulwich Centre Publications.

Freedman, J. and Coombs, G. (1996) *Narrative Therapy*, New York: Norton.

Freud, S. (1909) 'Five Lectures on Psycho-Analysis', in *The Standard Edition of the Complete Psychological Works of Sigmund Freud*, vol. 11. London: Hogarth Press.

Gilligan, C. (1982) *In a Different Voice: psychological theory and woman's development*, Cambridge: Harvard University Press.

Gilligan, C.; Lyons, N. and Hanmer, T. (1990) *Making Connections*, Cambridge: Harvard University Press.

Gilligan, C., Rogers, A. and Tolman, D. (1991) *Women, Girls, & Psychotherapy*, Cambridge: Harvard University Press.

Howard, G. (1989) *A Tale of Two Stories: excursions into a narrative approach to psychology*, Notre Dame, IN: Academic Publications.

Huffington, C. and Brunning, H. (1994) *Internal Consultancy in the Public Sector: case studies*, London: Karnac Books.

Jameson, F. (1981) *The Political Unconscious: narrative as a socially symbolic act*, Ithaca, NY: Cornell University Press.

Jung, C.G. (1935) 'Principles of practical psychotherapy', in C.G. Jung's *Collected Works*, vol. 16. London: Routledge and Kegan Paul.

10

Mair, M. (1988) 'Psychology as Story Telling', *International Journal of Construct Psychology*, 1: 125-37.

McLeod, J. (1997) *Narrative and Psychotherapy*, London: Sage.

McNamee, S. and Gergen, K.J. (eds) (1992) *Therapy as Social Construction*, London: Sage.

Martin, F. and Knight, J. (1962) 'Joint Interviews as Part of Intake Procedure in a Child Psychiatric Clinic', *Journal of Child Psychology and Psychiatry*, 3: 17-26.

Minuchin, S. (1974) *Families and Family Therapy*, Boston: Harvard Press and London: Tavistock.

Parry, A. (1996) 'Story Enactments', *Context*, 28: 20-4.

Parry, A. and Doan, R.E. (1994) *Story Re-Visions: narrative therapy in the postmodern world*, New York: The Guilford Press.

Polkinghorne, D.E. (1988) *Narrative Knowing and the Human Sciences*, Albany: State University of New York Press.

Ricoeur, P. (1984-5) *Time and Narrative*, (in three volumes), Chicago: Chicago University Press.

Riessman, C.K. (1993) *Narrative Analysis*, London: Sage.

Riikonen, E. and Smith, G.M. (1997) *Re-imagining Therapy: living conversations and relational knowledge*, London: Sage.

Roberts, J. (1994) *Tales and Transformation: stories in families and family therapy*, New York: Norton.

Shotter, J. (1993) *Conversational Realities: constructing life through language*, London: Sage.

Sluzki, C.E. (1992) 'Transformations: a blueprint for narrative changes in therapy', *Family Process*, 30: 285-305.

Spence, D.P. (1982) *Narrative Truth and Historical Truth: meaning and interpretation in psychoanalysis*, New York: Norton.

Whiffen, R. and Byng-Hall, J. (eds) (1982) *Family Therapy Supervision: recent developments in practice*, London: Academic Press.

White, M. (1989) *Selected Papers*, Adelaide, Australia: Dulwich Centre Publications.

—— (1995) *Re-authoring Lives: interviews and essays*, Adelaide, Australia: Dulwich Centre Publications.

White, M. and Epston, D. (1991) *Narrative Means to Therapeutic Ends*, New York: W.W. Norton.

Zimmerman, J.L. and Dickerson, V.C. (1994) 'Using a Narrative Metaphor: implications for theory and clinical practice', *Family Process*, 33: 233-45.

11

# Part One

# Narrative

## Construing the Context

# 1

# The Other Side of the Story

## Listening for the Client's Experience of Therapy

### *David Campbell*

### Introduction

I have been a family researcher all of my life. As the second and last child born into my family I arrived to discover (or should I say invent) a ready-made family of mother, father and older brother, and I suppose I have been trying to make sense of how to 'fit in' ever since.

In many families the youngest child slots into a favoured role, but in my case, I was more interested in growing up and joining the others. I soon became interested in power and inequality and the struggle to get more power for myself without revealing my wish to destroy all my competitors. As I look back now on my childhood preoccupation with sports and teams, I see it as an opportunity to gain power in ways that are reasonably acceptable. I have always supported the 'underdog' to win a sporting competition because I can deeply identify with the struggle to overcome the odds.

As a family therapist, my most significant journey has been the one from structural family therapy to the Milan approach. Following training events with Minuchin, Aponte and Walters in the 1970s, I could see how effective these therapists were with troubled families; but they were also people holding and utilising considerable power; and, although I tried to master these new techniques, I couldn't help feeling this therapeutic style, unfortunately, just wasn't me. With the arrival of the Milan approach in the early 1980s with its emphasis on neutrality and an open, circular style of questioning, I felt this style allowed me to become powerful in more subtle ways which I was used to. Perhaps it allowed me to be powerful without openly demonstrating the exercise of power. And in the meantime, I feel I have now been able to develop a style which integrates different models and techniques because I am more interested, and more comfortable, exploring expressions of power and powerlessness in myself as well as the family as a basis of much of my work with families.

What does all this have to do with my approach to family research? The underlying assumption in my research is that the key to unlocking family problems lies within the stories families tell us, but families in therapy are 'underdogs', and as therapists in positions of power, we may not be able to hear the vital elements in the stories which lead to therapeutic change. The research is an attempt to give the 'underdogs' a stronger voice and ultimately encourage therapists to re-examine the way they listen and negotiate the use of power in the process of therapy.

This chapter is based on three years' work of a research team whose broad aim has been to understand the experience which families have when they take part in family therapy. The team has had a shifting membership during this time.[1] I have been the constant member of the team, and while my ideas have been influenced by discussions in the team, and I will refer to the projects of team members, I am presenting, here, my own thoughts which are based on my own interviews with families.[2]

Why this area of interest? Following the exciting and creative injection of family therapy techniques into the field from the early 1980s (see Hoffman, 1982; Penn 1983; Campbell et al. 1983 and Tomm, 1984, amongst many), I have more recently looked beyond the techniques of family therapy to the fundamental therapeutic process and specifically the developing relationship between therapist and clients (see Flaskas and Perlesz, 1996). I spend much of my time as a 'live' supervisor, and on the dark side of the one-way mirror there is plenty of time to think. I am more interested, today, to observe the way the therapist creates what I will call the 'therapeutic context' with families, and I frequently ask myself, what is the therapist doing (or not) to allow the family to trust enough to join the therapist in creating a therapeutic context?

There is more to this process than being a genuine and empathic person. I am interested in the process by which therapists become aware of the ongoing development of the therapeutic context and adjust their behaviour as a result. As a supervisor I aim to help therapists monitor the ongoing relationship between themselves and their clients. When I observe sessions I ask myself such questions as: Does the relationship, at this moment seem sufficiently therapeutic, i.e. is everyone in the room (both clients and therapists) safe and able to trust, yet also willing to be challenged to see things differently and to tolerate new feelings? Will therapists allow themselves to learn from clients and vice versa?

To develop greater awareness in this area therapists need to be more aware of clients' experiences of the therapeutic process. I am aware of often being absorbed by my own mental efforts to make some meaning out of what clients are saying. This self-absorption can then become a barrier between me and the clients, and I cease to be aware of the evolving relationship between me and them.

Perhaps more than anything, this chapter is about my attempt to think less about my own ideas and more about the client's. This is obviously a personal pursuit of my own, but I also find when therapists can do this the therapeutic context is established more quickly and it is maintained more assiduously throughout therapy. In the context of this book, this chapter is about the way therapists and clients create a narrative about their therapy together and how both clients and therapists can become more aware of this process.

## My Position as a Researcher

The traditional position of the researcher is to observe families and then categorise these observations. However, in the era of social construction we are challenged to take greater responsibility for what we observe; for the social discourses which influence how we observe; and for the process of consensual agreement which verifies our observations. Valuable discussions of the way social constructionism can be integrated with research methodology will be found in Burr, 1995; Burman and Parker, 1993; Hollway, 1989; and Steier, 1991. I will present my experience interviewing several families by clarifying my reasons for pursuing a particular method, the way I was affected by the feedback, and the reasons for changing to a new method.

I am interested in the problem of who is commenting on what families say? Are they to be taken at their word, or is it the place of a researcher to interpret what is said and give it a new meaning. And if this is deemed a helpful process, who is this researcher anyway? What are his or her credentials for doing this and how will he or she account for his or her own biases in making their interpretations?

I find that, as a struggling therapist, I would welcome some generalised research findings which I could apply to my own therapy, but I know they are also potential traps, for while research can unearth such 'truths', we still must be careful that the generalisation of such truths does not stop us from thinking, and from observing the evolving

17

therapeutic relationship. This chapter, then, has more to do with my attempts to raise my own awareness, by using a research methodology to understand more about the obstacles I encounter in listening to clients' experiences. I will share the problems designing this type of research project and I will share my own personal learning as a result of the project.

## Starting Out

I began the project by looking at the literature to learn what was known about families' experience. Reimers and Treacher, (1995) have produced a helpful guide into this area; nevertheless it is very difficult to summarise studies which have used different designs to contact diverse samples of users of family therapy. But there is some convergence of findings in studies trying to understand the consumer's experience. For example, one consistent finding (Woodward, 1978; Crane et al., 1986) is that many families feel therapy is not being carried out to their needs and expectations. Kuehl (1990) found users felt their direct questions were not met by therapists, and a frequent finding amongst many researchers is that family members want direct advice about what to do to ease their problems.

Levels of satisfaction with therapy vary from 50 to 85 per cent depending on which study is consulted. One major study by Piercy et al. (1986) stands out as the most positive. In addition to overall satisfaction, this team discovered high rates of satisfaction with technical aspects such as the team behind the screen, interruptions, video and phone-ins.

But the literature is replete with negative reactions to therapy which therapists must take seriously. For example, Richards (1995) set out to study the responses of working-class families to family therapy. Of 21 families interviewed in person, 19 were dissatisfied with therapy they had received. The major theme emerging from the data was the families sense on incomprehension. They did not understand what the workers were getting at, or felt the workers did not understand what their problems and needs were, or sometimes both. The purpose of the session did not seem to be understood by clients who consequently felt angry, frustrated or disorientated. The researchers also interviewed the workers in each case and found they were under no illusions about the outcomes of their work with the families, but they seemed to be unaware of how 'thoroughly disenchanted some of the clients were about their experience'.

This study suggests therapists may not be paying sufficient attention to whether their approach fits with their clients, and Richards concludes that differences of fit may be more pronounced with working-class families whose language and expectation of therapy are different from those of the therapist. I am not aware of any studies which look at therapy done with therapist and family each coming from a different culture, but I think we could all learn about the problem of fit by studying such a group of cases. Richard's views are echoed by Howe (1989) in Britain who studied 21 family therapy cases and concluded that systemic family therapy failed to understand the individual's subjective experiences, and fails to allow a genuine dialogue to take place between therapists and users. He felt therapists disempowered family members, but were themselves empowered by technique and theory and language which created a barrier for their clients. Howe's is one of several studies which report families found therapists 'robotic' and 'dehumanising' in some cases. Marshal et al. in 1989 set out to measure the degree satisfaction with Milan-style therapy found nearly half of the families contacted disliked the therapy they received. The strongest criticisms were reserved for the team behind the screen and long intervals between sessions.

## Home-Grown Findings

I now want to discuss briefly some of the findings which have emerged from our team before turning to the wider field. Rutherford found in child protection cases that the overwhelming fear that children would be taken from their families made it difficult to create a good working relationship with professionals. A central paradox for these families is: If people admit they need help with their children, will this be construed as evidence of inadequacy, which means they are one step nearer to having their children removed? Families came to the NSPCC Centre feeling blamed for being bad parents and expecting to be judged by the workers as to whether or not they were good enough. The intensity of this experience led to polarised feelings: either they were good or they were bad. Rutherford observed that this polarisation characterised their feelings about the workers, as if they were saying, 'It's not us, so it must be you.'

She concluded that there is a tendency for all child protection issues to be seen in terms of only one side of the question. For example, users views are either ignored completely as biased or inconsistent, or they are accepted at face value without sufficient attention to the context. In the press, workers are either gullible stooges or child snatchers. Parents are either abusers or victims. One of her conclusions is that the agency must address both sides of these issues and acknowledge the many layers of meaning which underlie the communication between the clients and workers in this field.

Richardson used a grounded theory approach to analyse the transcripts from her family interviews. In relation to the question, 'What was helpful about therapy?', five themes emerged consistently: 1) being able to talk to someone about their problem; 2) being able to express their feelings; 3) coming to terms with a problem or illness; 4) new realisations about the problem; and 5) changing their views of relationships. The first three of these would seem to be universal benefits of any type of 'talking cure', but the last two seem to confirm the benefits of a family therapy approach which places some emphasis on a kind of systemic understanding, and the significance of family relationships in maintaining family based problems.

Of the eight families she interviewed, two said family therapy was not helpful. All were asked to create a picture by describing the ingredients for a therapist who would be helpful for them, and again five themes emerged: 1) (most helpful) shows an interest in the family; 2) provides a focus for discussion; 3) asks everyone to speak; 4) asks questions about the past and future, and 5) asks surprising questions. We were surprised that the families responded with such specific ideas about what is helpful in therapy, not only in terms of the general atmosphere, but in terms of the therapist's technique. This may be the result of these families taking part in a type of therapy which emphasises certain techniques. The initial reading of this data suggests family members did respond in a particular way to the Milan approach, but Richardson will be looking further into this data for other possible explanations.

### Going Solo

My own research has become a two-phase project with two different methodologies. Within the framework of the researcher as a participant observer who is continuously modifying his or her view in response to feedback, the great challenge for research is not the *creation* of a research question but the *continuous reformulation* of the question as one's learning advances. In the first phase I chose to interview families in their homes using a semi-structured interview schedule 3 – 6 months following the termination of therapy.

I made a deliberate distinction between outcome and follow-up studies whose aim was to reflect back upon the outcome of therapy. Instead I aimed to explore:

a) what therapy experiences families wished to talk about;
b) how they expressed themselves on these topics; and
c) what questions seemed most helpful in stimulating these discussions.

I have not found any other studies which were framed in this way. Early on I found this unnerving because I could not find any guidelines from more experienced researchers, but this has also encouraged me to consider my own experiences more carefully and to look to the clients for any guidance I may need.

There is always a selection problem in studies such as these, because the families who elect to be interviewed are generally well-disposed to therapy. (Certainly the converse is true. I have several colleagues who have had difficulty engaging families who have dropped out of therapy in similar research projects.) However, I felt it was most important to get started and to complete some interviews which would allow me to review whether my method was supporting the research question. Therefore, I approached my colleagues and trainees in the Child and Family Department asking for names of families who had terminated therapy and who might be interested in participating in the study.

After some problems and cancellations I interviewed four families: Family A: two parents; Family B: one mother, two children; Family C: one mother, one child; Family D: two parents, two children. Each interview took place in the family's home, lasted approximately one hour, and was audio recorded with consent.

I designed a semi-structured interview which would enable families to comment on the more practical aspects of therapy as well as the process going on during the sessions. The number of questions was deliberately limited to allow me the opportunity to depart from the schedule to follow important themes raised by the families.

Following is the protocol used for my family interviews:

1. What did the family think about the technical aspects of the therapy sessions, e.g. the one-way mirror, the team, taking breaks, the length and gap between sessions?
2. What did they think of the therapist, e.g. style, gender, race?
3. What did they most want the therapist to appreciate or understand about their situation?

4.	How did the therapist respond to the issues presented by the family? Did he or she miss anything you wanted him or her to pick up?

5.	What did they think the therapist was interested in or wanted to convey to the family?

6.	What effect did the therapist's ideas have on them?

7.	Did their ideas change as a result of their work with the therapist? Did they feel the therapist changed his or her ideas as a result of the work?

8.	Were there any particular things you appreciated or things you did not like about the therapy?

9.	Would you want anything to have been different?

10.	Could you put into a few words what you think happened during your therapy at the Tavistock?

Some questions proved to be repetitive and some stimulated much discussion, others a cursory 'I don't know' but generally I felt satisfied that I had engaged these four families in discussion about therapy process.

I am going to present my findings as brief discussion around a single topic. I found in listening to the tapes that my thinking was pushed into my own reservoir of therapy experiences. I frequently turned the tape off to 'have my own thoughts', and therefore I want to present an amalgam of what these families said and what I brought to their responses from my own years on experience.

### The Difference Between Research and Therapy –
### Phase One

It quickly becomes clear when interviewing these families, that they seem, in different ways, to be expressing 'unfinished business' about therapy. This is particularly so when they are critical of the process or they are coping with further family problems. The dilemma for me was how to explore these feelings without overstepping the boundary and turning the interview into a therapy session. I tried to maintain the context of the research interview but this often meant holding back from delving into their feelings. I found this to be a serious limitation in this method of research, because without pursuing some of the things which are said, the researcher is left with a partial understanding. One solution to this may be to join the research interview more deliberately to therapy, which I have tried to do in phase two of this project.

## 1. The Other Side of the Story

### Reaction to the Apparatus of Therapy

My interviews confirm reports in the literature about families' displeasure with the video and the screen. I found that opinion ranged from 'putting up with' procedures to strong dislike of things which seemed 'intrusive', 'off-putting' or 'weird'. In my small sample adults were more tolerant of the procedures than the children, perhaps because they understood the therapists' needs for supervision.

I think many of us therapists underestimate the amount of distress caused by these procedures, and if we were more aware of it, we might well alter our procedures or at least discuss them with the family from a more sympathetic position.

### The Therapist as a Person

Only one of the families commented on the gender or race of the therapist (all therapists were white; three families were white, one non-white). A mother said she might have preferred to talk to a woman. But I was struck by the strength of feeling with which they all spoke about their therapists. Most of the adults (6) spoke very positively about their therapists independent of how much they felt helped by therapy. The children voiced more negative feelings but also delivered them with conviction.

I stopped to consider why this feedback was surprising to me and concluded that perhaps I, as a family therapist, focus my attention on the family patterns and the interaction between me and the family, perhaps to the exclusion of the family's developing relationship with me. Is this something which has been trained out of family therapists? Is it an area for potential therapeutic movement which has too long been ignored?

### What Do Families Value About Therapy?

I have collated the comments from my interviews and the work of my colleagues in our research team. They can be clustered under these headings and in order of frequency:

a. They want a place to come and talk where they will be listened to.
b. They want to be respected and appreciated for their lives and their struggles to cope.
c. They want an explanation for what is happening.

23

d.   They want specific advice about what they can do to improve their situation.

(a) and (b) represent similar values. It is surprising how frequently families stress the importance of being listened to and respected. This certainly seems to be a precursor to any therapeutic work. One representative response to the question, 'What would you most like your therapist to understand about your family?' was given by a father who said, 'What we were all about ... why life was so difficult ... half the time it was not about conveying things to him but gaining comfort from sharing with someone.' My own therapist's instincts would lead me to place more value on understanding family dynamics and the genesis of problems, but this comes further down the frequency list. Many families will describe what is important about therapy without mentioning understanding or insight. Yet some clearly do benefit from an explanation. The final point is about receiving advice, which some therapists are loathe to do. If a family comes to therapy wanting advice perhaps it behoves the therapist to find a way of giving advice without being trapped by the success or failure of advice. There must certainly be different ways of giving advice, some less likely to immediate failure than others. Cecchin (1994) makes the interesting point that denying a family the advice they are asking for can lead to a symmetrical stand off which stymies therapy.

### Who Attends Sessions?

Several families wanted to discuss the fact they had been asked to attend as a family when they had wanted different arrangements for attending sessions as therapy progressed. In two cases adults wanted to be seen without children; in another case, a teenager wanted to see someone separately. For different reasons, either the family did not present these requests to the therapist or the therapy team did not act on them when presented. This feedback has led me to question the extent to which family therapists persist in seeing whole families on the basis that we have theoretical frameworks and techniques which help us work in this setting, rather than negotiating the structure of treatment sessions with the families. Related to this theme is the rarely aired topic of the family model as a form of organisational hegemony in their own agencies.

## 1. The Other Side of the Story

### Do We Accept What Families Say?

One of the paradigm shifts being enacted in the systemic/family therapy field is the move from the therapist possessing a more 'truthful' understanding than the family to one in which the family's version of events is one of many 'truths' or 'knowledges' but one that prefigures a solution for family problems. This research project has forced me to address the new paradigm because I have been speaking to families as a researcher. This is a new position for me as a long-standing family therapist. I approach these interviews without formulating the 'truths' which I have often relied on as a therapist. And I am compelled during these interviews to accept what families say as a valid, 'knowledge' about what has happened in therapy. This process has had a big impact on me, not least to leave me more confused about taking families at their word.

What should a therapist do with their 'alternative' views? What about bringing new systemic awareness to light? Can families be helped by a therapist's advice based on work with other families? These are questions I have had to ask myself as a result of the project and I have come to the view that we can negotiate many different truths with families: ours, theirs; obvious, hidden; individual and social. But what is new and different about this for me, is bringing families into this process of negotiating amongst different realities as equal, active partners in the process. It becomes possible to say to families, 'Yes I take your point, but also from my perspective as a therapist working in this agency, I can also offer another point of view for us to consider ... what do you think about this?'

### Phase Two

As I became more interested in this process I also became more frustrated with my research interviews. The family members could not recall enough of the detail. I became more interested in understanding the process of how realities are negotiated and created in the session. I wanted to know how the things the therapist said affected what the family did and said next. I was being drawn toward the quagmire of process research which I had glimpsed years earlier (Campbell, 1984), but I was also determined to retain a method which was manageable on a small scale and also meaningful for family therapists.

I found that the families I spoke to could not recall the detail of the interaction I was increasingly interested in. As a result I decided to abandon the method of interviewing after the termination of therapy and design a method for interviewing families while therapy was going on. This was the beginning of phase two.

I was interested to find examples from a family therapy session of the therapist and family speaking directly or referring indirectly to the process of therapy. I decided to ignore discussions about the family problems, their background or the family's efforts to change their behaviour, but to isolate any segments of a session in which the family members were reflecting on the therapeutic process from a meta-position. That is, I distinguished verbal exchanges when the family were 'in' the therapy process from those exchanges when the family were 'outside' and observing themselves in the process. I expected to find examples of these exchanges in two areas of discussion:

1)  the family and therapist directly address their therapeutic relationship
2)  the family and therapist directly address what is happening in the therapy.

The arrangements for the 'live' research session began with a discussion with a therapist who was also a trainee member of a supervision group.[3] I met the group (3 trainees, one staff supervisor) to discuss the project and the therapist suggested she was seeing a family who might be interested. They were well engaged in therapy and had been coming for approximately one year, but they were also a family interested in therapy itself, so it seemed a good family to begin with.

The criteria I used for selecting a video tape was the recentness of the family therapy session, since I wanted to discuss therapy segments which would be fresh in the family's mind. The therapist suggested a tape of the previous session which turned out, because of a cancellation, to be about two months prior to my interview.

I invited the therapist to contribute her comments about this process, and she has reported the following about discussing the research with the family:

'When I first approached the family to ask if they would be willing to participate in the research their major reservation was that the session with David would replace one of their regular sessions with me, rather than be an additional session.

I had decided not to pressurise the family to agree to take part, but I did believe that it could therapeutically help our work together. I had been working with this family for nearly twelve months, and, although

26

there had been considerable movement and change over that time, I was beginning to feel a little 'stuck'. The family clearly wanted to appear 'helpful' to the Tavistock Clinic and, in the end, asked for my advice as to whether the research would help my work with them. I said that I thought it might, and they agreed.'

Once the family had discussed the research procedure and given their verbal permission for the research meeting, I reviewed the videotape and chose four segments which, in my judgement, fitted the criteria for discussion about the relationship to the therapist or the process of therapy itself. (One of the members of the research team suggested I might try to find a way to involve the family in selecting significant clips of their own therapy – an interesting idea for the future). I noted the place where these discussions appeared on the tape and prepared the tape to meet the family.

During the discussion with the therapy team it was also decided, for several reasons, to conduct the session with the therapist in the room and the observing team behind a one-way screen. Since the research meeting took place in the context of on-going family therapy, it was inevitable that the discussion would refer to thoughts and feelings about the therapy; and as such it seemed more clear and straightforward to have the therapy team present. Thus it was clear that the higher context was the therapy team and things which were said may be 'used' in the therapy, but there was also a lower order context of research in which the researcher, not a member of the therapy team, would create a separate, non-therapeutic relationship with the family leading to information for a different purpose.

The alternative procedure would be for me to interview the family independently from the therapist and team but then what would happen to aspects of the discussion which referred to the on-going therapy? The material, which might otherwise be helpful or informative for the family or team would be lost.

There are advantages and disadvantages for any procedure. As I saw it, the disadvantages of my approach were that the family may be inhibited from saying certain things in front of the therapist, and there may be confusion about whether the things said are used for research or therapy. On the other hand, interviewing a family in isolation about therapy which is ongoing takes the conversation out of context which may lead to wrong assumptions. Another advantage is the therapist was present to add a further voice to the discussion. And since one of the aims of this project is to explore the space between therapeutic and non-therapeutic conversations, I felt justified working in the presence of both the therapeutic (family therapy team) and non-therapeutic (the researcher) contexts.

The family consisted of two parents of European stock and three children. The eldest daughter was working and living independently; the second daughter lived at home but attended university, while the youngest, a son aged 13, lived at home and was referred with a problem of failure to attend school.

The family had been attending monthly sessions, most frequently attended by parents and son, for approximately one year . My interview followed a missed therapy session and a two-month gap since the previous session, and they could not remember some bits of the videotaped session which had happened two months earlier.

## Meeting the Family

The therapy for this family had been provided by a therapy team so they were used to having part of the therapy team behind a one-way screen. In the interview room, (which was the same room used for therapy sessions) the chairs were arranged for the family, the therapist and myself in a horseshoe around the video monitor where I would show the segments of the tape. All of this was being video recorded to enable me to analyse the relevant discussions. The therapist collected the family and introduced me to them.

## First Segment

Following a general discussion with the family about their experiences of the length and gap between sessions I presented my first segment of selected video tape, which was the first occasion therapy *per se* had been referred to in this session. Father was saying he had the impression that the Tavistock did not think things in the family were as bad as the family thought they were. I presented this segment and asked the family, 'What was the effect of thinking the Tavistock has a different view of you than you have of yourselves?'

> Father:     Not terribly good. It means their effectiveness is in question because they do not see how bad things are from our point of view.
>
> Paul (son):     … and you exaggerate things, papa, that's why we come here so they can see how you exaggerate.
>
> D.C.:     What's the effect on you of feeling the Tavistock doesn't

28

|            | understand something as you do ... do you feel discouraged ... or try to convince the therapist? |
|------------|------|
| Father:    | ... angry and frustrated. |
| Paul:      | I don't think I have such a different view from the way things are. I think my parents over-react. |
| D.C.:      | That's fine. The three of you may have different reactions to these tapes. |
| Father:    | Every month someone (at home) says, 'I'm going to tell them at the Tavistock what's really going on.' |
| Mother:    | I feel too much is left to us to find the value in what we are doing here. There is something underlying which is very important and must come to the surface. Paul (son) is so frightened of his school. This is something which needs close looking into. |

### Comment:

This conversation seems to be about how serious the problems are and who will take what problems seriously. Since the content of the problem is about Paul not attending school, Paul also seems to want to challenge his father's view of how serious things are, perhaps to minimise the focus on him as the problem.

Although the theme of seeing themselves differently seems to invite a conversation about therapy, it is also introduced by only one person, Father, and each person takes a different position on this theme. In fact it seems the son and mother respond with their own ideas which are only loosely connected to the theme raised by Father. For Paul, his theme is about establishing his parents tendency to exaggerate and for Mother, she believes underlying issues must be talked about.

From this I think one can conclude that conversations about therapy for this family are opportunities for people to establish their own, different versions of reality: 'What's really going on' and 'something underlying' and begin the process of negotiating who will accept which version. This process also creates alliances and coalitions, as, in Paul's case, when he criticises his father and then distances himself from both parents; it seems it is not what you think but 'who you agree with'.

### Second Segment

The second segment is an example of the therapist suggesting that, although the family did not acknowledge it, angry feelings expressed in relation to family members may also be meant for the therapist. I chose this section because it is an example of the therapist suggesting an idea that had not 'consciously' been expressed by the family. This highlights the difference between the therapist's knowledge and the family's knowledge and I wanted to know how the family experienced this.

> D.C.: In the tape somebody has been talking about being angry and Jane (therapist) says, 'I wonder if you may also be feeling angry at me.' What was your experience there of Jane bringing in the anger in a different way, although you had not brought that up yourself?
>
> Mother: I think we have gone beyond that stage ... when Jane said that ... one cannot be angry at Jane.
>
> D.C.: When she said that, did you feel it was impossible to follow that line of thinking or that she was wrong?
>
> Mother: I wouldn't go that far ... I didn't really remember what she meant.
>
> D.C.: So it was foreign to you ...
>
> Mother: Why should we be angry, I don't see any reason for it.
>
> Father: I didn't get the whole concept from the clip.

### Comment:

I want to begin with several technical points, one is that this extract may have been too brief for the family to place in context. This research method requires careful thought about the background as well as the specific content of each clip. Also, as I reread this transcript I became more aware of useful questions I could have asked to facilitate this discussion, such as, what it means to go 'beyond that stage', or 'what would happen if one got angry at Jane?' I am also aware of a lurking uncertainty about how much to let the clients tell their story uninterrupted and how much to engage in a full dialogue. There certainly seem to be technical issues which contributed to this clip presentation proffering less material for analysis.

The family's lack of response to this theme may substantiate the point made earlier that the therapist may not have been sufficiently aligned with the family's own story and when she introduced her own knowledge, it presented a new context which had not been negotiated with the family.

There are also issues of content to consider. Anger is a difficult emotion to live with and it was presented to the family as something they may not have been aware of, which could increase the difficulty of embracing this idea and exploring it in conversation. In relation to the previous clip about shielding the therapist from anger, this segment may, also have presented the family with a similar dilemma.

### Third Segment

The third segment was chosen because when I viewed the session as a whole, this seemed to encapsulate the central theme of the session: growing up and becoming independent. I wanted to learn something about how families experience a theme which (to an outside observer) is clearly being developed in different ways through therapeutic conversations throughout the session.

In the extract itself there is discussion about the therapist's reiteration of the idea that Paul is struggling to grow up and the parents should think more about their own lives while Paul was going through this. Following the segment I asked: 'What do you think about this type of discussion? Was it helpful ... was it to the point?'

|           |                                                                                                                                                                                                                                                                                                                             |
| --------- | --------------------------------------------------------------------------------------------------------------------------------------------------------------------------------------------------------------------------------------------------------------------------------------------------------------------------- |
| Father:   | It was to the point.                                                                                                                                                                                                                                                                                                         |
| Mother:   | I liked this conversation because we had to have more response from Paul and everything. I hoped Paul would gain from it. We don't sit at home and have these conversations.                                                                                                                                                   |
| D.C.:     | Paul, what effect did this theme have on you?                                                                                                                                                                                                                                                                                |
| Paul:     | I remember abstractly but not the detail ... I think ... I remember being annoyed getting my age wrong (Father had referred to Paul's age as one year younger than he is).                                                                                                                                                     |
| Father:   | One thing which stood out from this segment ... it's not feasible that problems are going to be solved in some miraculous way, but we should get on with our lives. We should look for improvements in our communication without hoping underlying problems are going to be completely solved.                                  |
| Mother:   | I thought *that* was the previous clip. I thought this was about ...                                                                                                                                                                                                                                                        |
| Father:   | (Interrupts) ... Paul's position in the family.                                                                                                                                                                                                                                                                              |
| Mother:   | Yes.                                                                                                                                                                                                                                                                                                                         |
| Paul:     | I think my mother thought that conversation had a pessimistic side to it ... that's what she said ... my parents should break away from me ... that they should start being more independent ... which upset me a bit because I think any problems I have are manageable. I can get rid of them. I think my mother read into it wrongly. |

### *Comment:*

At a moment like this a researcher who is also a family therapist can easily be drawn into drawing conclusions about family dynamics. For example there is confusion about whether to leave problems behind and move on. This leads to some misunderstanding between the parents, and Paul then reacts to his mother's upset. However I struggled to respond to this material as a researcher whose interest was in the family's experience of what was going on, so I asked a question about Paul feeling upset in the context of a therapy session. The confusions about this extract suggest this central theme is integral of family relationships and the family and therapist's ability to create new relationships. Perhaps it would be helpful for the therapist to give family members opportunities to understand the personal positions and feelings which lead to the misunderstandings in situations like this.

> D.C.: (To Paul) If you felt upset about something, what would you want the therapist to understand from that?
>
> Paul: I don't know ... perhaps ... if we could have explained more what we thought about it in the session ... because afterwards we all read different things into it.

### Comment:

This segment raises again the point that this family seem to talk in the session in a way they cannot do at home. Paul wanted more time to talk through the differences between family members. I wondered when hearing this, if therapists appreciate the difficulties of transferring knowledge from the session to the home and whether therapists give sufficient time in the session to allow each person to understand why there are the differences between family members. Could therapists check more frequently whether families have more to say on a subject and whether they clearly understand another's point of view?

> D.C.: (To Paul) If you were upset would you want her (the therapist) to back away and stop talking about that theme?
>
> Paul: No ...
>
> D.C.: ... or would you want her to stay with it even though it was uncomfortable?
>
> Mother: No, its better to stay with it. If we start talking about something, its better to finish. If something does upset me, its better to sort it out ... its part of the reason for coming here.

### Comment:

As therapists, we often ask ourselves how much to delve into painful feelings or traumatic events. In this segment both Paul and Mother confirmed it was better to stay with the difficult issues. It may be helpful for therapists, when appropriate, to discuss this issue with clients. I have frequently asked these questions and often get the reply, 'I don't know' but I understand that as neither a message to 'go ahead' nor to 'stop', and I am comfortable working with clients in this area of uncertainty. I also have come to believe that having such a discussion leads to a greater sense of shared responsibility for the risks which will need to be taken in the subsequent therapeutic work.

### Fourth Segment

The fourth and final segment was chosen because the family and therapist appear to be having a different kind of discussion. Instead of the family responding to the therapist's questions or comments, here, everyone in the room seems to be working together to find some answers. The therapist conveys a sense of 'not-knowing' (Anderson and Goolishian, 1992) which I did not observe at other times in the session. I speculated that this facet of their therapeutic relationship is conducive to discovering new understandings and I wanted to explore their experiences of this discussion.

On the tape, the family are discussing with the therapist what makes Paul unhappy, whether it was about school or other things. Following the tape, I asked the family:

D.C.: This is a part of the tape where *you* were doing a lot of the talking ... scratching your heads and trying to come up with your own ideas and Jane was not offering leading questions and offering interpretations. She was just asking: 'Well, what could it be?' I wondered what your experience of that was.

Mother: I don't expect anything. I don't come here with expectations. I respond to what I'm being asked and I, sort of ... deeply ... try to express why Paul is possibly unhappy.

D.C.: Yes, but on the tape you suggested, 'Maybe there was something about us having a cosy home life.' Jane did not suggest that. That came from you. These are some times in a session when a family produces their own ideas ...

Paul: Well, there are times when I get very stuck ... when Jane asks me something and I say, 'could you make that question more clear?' ... and I end up wondering what to say. I give an answer but maybe its not the right one for the question.

### *Comment:*

Both Mother and Paul comment on their relationship to the therapist and the process of being asked questions. It seems to have a powerful effect on them i.e. Mother has no prior expectations but responds to what she is asked while Paul 'gets stuck' and ends up wondering what to say, even though this is said in the context of a segment in which they are clearly exploring their own ideas. In this particular family the therapist seems to have a strong presence and this raises a question of how a therapist can use her influence to facilitate family members without burdening them with the thought that they have to say the right thing.

| | |
|---|---|
| D.C.: | But do you like the kind of space just to draw on your own ideas, or do you prefer it when she (the therapist) gives you her ideas? |
| Paul: | Its useful to have a time when you can have your own ideas ... it depends on the situation. I remember times when I would have done it one way and Jane did it the other way. |
| D.C.: | Mr S, do you have any comment on this last bit? |
| Father: | No, I think it is useful to develop our own ideas in parts of the session. |

## Comment:

Although I have introduced the distinction between 'therapist led' discussions and space to develop their own ideas, it appears to be a distinction Paul and Father recognise and value. Paul even seems to be aware of times the therapist created different contexts during their sessions.

When I planned this interview, I intended to bring the therapist into the conversation throughout, but I soon became aware that I would not be able to complete my four segments in the allotted time so I asked Jane for her comments at the end of the session while we were together with the family.

| | |
|---|---|
| Jane: | It's enormously helpful for our work to hear your (the family) views. This session represents one segment of work and we have been meeting for over a year and themes come in and out of other sessions which are similar to these. |
| D.C.: | Of all you've heard, what's been the most surprising or interesting to you? |
| Jane: | It was important for me to hear about Paul feeling hurt and upset about one aspect, and maybe I didn't pick that up. |

## 1. The Other Side of the Story

### Comment:

Jane's comments are a reminder that this interview has taken place in the context of therapy. She clearly suggests this session will contribute to future work and she picks up the hurt of one of the family members. This methodology lends itself to conducting a more comprehensive interview with the therapist and her team to assess whether the experience of hearing family members discuss their therapy does in fact affect the way the therapist thinks about the family or conducts her sessions in the future.

### The Therapist's View

In order to learn more about the effect of conducting a research interview during the course of family therapy, I wanted to know how the therapist thought her work with the family was affected. I asked her if she would like to add her comments and she has contributed the following:

> When I collected the family from the waiting room they all seemed tense and perhaps nervous, in a way I had not seen them before. When they met David for the first time in the therapy room they were reserved and rather 'tight-lipped'. Usually in our regular sessions they're very talkative, warm, friendly and emotional. It was as though they were being on their 'best behaviour'. As the therapist, I experienced feelings of responsibility, both towards the family (for putting them into this position), and towards David (for bringing him this polite but resistant family). This feeling of responsibility included my (silently) urging the family to relax and behave as they 'usually' did. At the same time I felt uncomfortable that they would feel they could not respond to David's questions about the therapy without appearing to be challenging or critical of me. They were too polite to do this, and may well have felt that there was too great a risk to our relationship, which would then affect our future work together. The session also created a dilemma for me, and I sensed, for the family, in respect to my role; was I there for them or for David? Who was David there for? Them? Me? Or himself?
>
> At the beginning of the first session after the research interview the family was a little reserved with me. I asked them if they would like to spend a few minutes talking about the session. They all immediately became animated. Mrs S said that it had been very powerful seeing herself on the video, as she had not realised how strong her accent was, and could not understand herself on the tape. Paul said that he had been shocked to see himself on the video. He said that he looked terrible and like 'a slob'. He had been embarrassed. Mr S spoke more cerebrally, asking if it had

35

been useful for the research project. They all wanted to know if it had helped me, and I told them that I thought it had probably helped all of us.

In the research session I did feel rather uncomfortable, possibly for two reasons: firstly, I had always been in charge of the sessions with this family and in this situation 'handed them over' to someone else; secondly, I was not totally conversant with the purpose of the research, and therefore was unclear as to my role within the session. However, it did afford me the opportunity to see how this family functions with a stranger in an unfamiliar situation. It would have been possible to observe this from behind the one-way screen, or even to watch a recording of the session. With respect to the question 'should the therapist be in the research session?' I feel that it may be interesting for the therapist, but less than helpful for the family and researcher. The family were, in this case, I believe, inhibited by my presence.

The most powerful therapeutic intervention, without doubt, was the family seeing themselves on video. This had a major effect on all of them, and there was a significant shift in our work together as a result.'

## The Researcher's View

My own view corroborates what the therapist has said; I felt the family were inhibited by the presence of the therapist, however if they wanted to protect Jane from negative criticism, they probably would have done so in any setting in which the research is associated with the therapy at the Tavistock Clinic. Nevertheless in terms of the aims of the research – to learn about the ways family members talk about therapy – these observations highlight the need for some clients to protect their therapists as they discuss the therapy.

At this point I would argue that researchers need to collaborate more closely with therapists (certainly more closely than I did with Jane) on a case by case basis, to design procedures which: 1) allow families to step back and observe and comment on the therapy they are a part of, and 2) allow the families and therapists to use these new insights to advance their therapeutic work together. Each researcher/therapist pair can decide which procedure and which role is best for the professionals and the family members.

But there is also a larger issue here. Should research into family therapy be done after the termination of therapy? In which case what does one do with new insights arising from the research? The family is gone, the new insights will presumably be applied in some way to future family work. But why cannot the family who participates in the research benefit from the new insights they have helped to generate? To address this question one has to re-examine the boundaries we traditionally create for therapy. A model of research which intervenes into an ongoing process is not new. Researchers at the Tavistock Institute created models of 'action research' years ago, but when applied to therapy it ceases to be called research and instead is labelled as some type of consultation or supervision. It is only important for purposes of academic communication whether the process is called consultation, supervision or research but what matters is that each researcher and therapist pair can engage a family in an effort to gain new understanding within a framework which is ethical and acceptable to all participants. And finally, a word of caution, that any negotiation about research with a family in therapy takes place in a context of unequal power with a potential for abuse of power, if the full meaning of the family-in-therapy is not comprehended by the researcher and therapist.

Steier (1991) argues from a social constructionist perspective that research is an intervention into a system 'in so far as the very questions we ask in trying to understand a group or culture create possibilities for change in that group' (p. 178). The current thinking about reflexivity in research suggests that the truth of an event does not lie within our observation but with the consensual agreement we can achieve within our own 'community of interpreters'. The emphasis shifts from perception to linguistic activity. I have found that a discussion by Mary Gergen (Gergen and Gergen, 1991) has helped me clarify some of my own experiences. She says, in a discussion about researching a concept like jealousy, 'an important step in a reflexively oriented inquiry into jealousy would be to formalise the understanding already contained in the common conventions for talking about jealousy' (p. 81). She goes on to develop a formulation for jealousy by elaborating 'common sense' ideas of jealousy which are already available to us within our cultural codes, and concludes, 'it is not empirical research that is required but a more concerted confrontation with the theory itself ' (p. 82).

For me, this implies that researchers must first explore the linguistic definitions and terms which they use to identify family behaviour. For example, in the S family, I could take more time to examine the cultural meanings influencing *my* definition and meaning of the 'anger', 'feeling upset' or 'getting stuck' which I observed in the family. The purpose of this is to become more aware of my own constructions which then frees me to listen and appreciate the family's constructions. Potentially, I think two things are possible: 1) the researcher makes a clear distinction between his constructions and those of the family and 2) by sensitising

37

oneself to the cultural influences upon our linguistic terms, we also become more aware of this process going on in the client family.

## Conclusion

Phase two of this project is still work in progress. Meeting this one family during family therapy work, and interviewing them about their recent experiences has brought me closer to understanding what it is like for families to take part in therapy. From my work with the transcript of one session, I am tentatively making these conclusions:

• Family members seemed to experience this session as an opportunity to talk together in ways they could not do at home. They made repeated references to life outside the session as though they go through a process of matching and fitting what happens in the session against their real life experiences.

• The session seemed to be an opportunity to say previously unsaid things to each other, as though the context sanctioned risk, and the chance to re-define one's own position and one's relationship to others.

• The family made strong ties to the therapist and it seemed very important to have the therapist's approval or at least acknowledgement that in their struggles, they were still acceptable to an outside authority.

• This work has made a big impact on my own work as a therapist and supervisor. I have become more interested in how we listen to clients; for example how we can hear alternative stories which are embedded in the things clients' tell us. I am also increasingly interested in discussing my own thinking and the process of therapy with clients; to involve them in my therapeutic dilemmas and options for developing the therapy in the future.

I plan to continue phase two of this project to gather more data about families experiences and what enables them to reflect upon and share those experiences and ultimately I would like to refer these thoughts back to the training and supervision of systemic therapists.

## Notes

1. During the first two years (1993-95) the team consisted of two M.Sc. students: Collette Richardson and Penny Rutherford and a Ph.D. student John Stancombe, whose research projects have been, respectively, *Families' experi-*

*ences of Milan techniques in family therapy, Families' experience of systemic work in child protection* and *The attribution of blame in the first session of family therapy.*

From October 1995 to July 1997 the team has consisted of M.Sc. students Keith Faull and Richard Middleton whose projects have investigated *The experience of men in family therapy and Families who terminate therapy prematurely after a few sessions;* and Ph.D. student Peter Griffiths studying family of origin influences which affect the way nurses function at work.

2. The organisation of this research team is described in more detail in Campbell, 1996.

3. I am grateful to the therapist, and her family (S family) for making this research interview possible.

### References

Anderson, H. and Goolishian (1992) 'The Client is the Expert: a not-knowing approach to therapy', in (McNamee, S. and Gergen, K. eds) *Therapy as Social Construction*, London: Sage.

Burman, E. and Parker, I. (eds) (1993) *Discourse Analytic Research: repertoires and readings of tests in action*, London: Routledge.

Burr, V. (1995) *An Introduction to Social Constructionism*, London: Routledge.

Campbell, D. (1996) 'Creating a Research Team to Understand Families' Experiences of Therapy', in *Old Ways, New Theories: traditional and contemporary family therapy connect in Africa*, 1: 159-66, Harare: Zimbabwe Institute of Systemic Therapy.

Campbell, D. and de Carteret, J. (1984) 'Guidelines for Clinicians Considering Family Therapy Research', in *Journal of Family Therapy*, 6.

Cecchin, G. (1992) *Irreverence*, London: Karnac Books.

Crane, R.; Griffin, W. and Hill, R. (1986) 'Influences of Therapist Skills on Client Perceptions of Marriage and Family Therapy Outcome: implications for supervision', in *Journal of Marital and Family Therapy*, 12: 91-6.

Flaskas, C. and Perlesz, A. (1996) *The Therapeutic Relationship in Systemic Therapy*, London: Karnac Books.

Gergen, K. and Gergen, M. (1991) 'Toward Reflexive Methodologies', in F. Steier (ed.) *Research and Reflexivity*, London: Sage.

Hollway, W. (1989) *Subjectivity and Method in Psychology*, London: Sage Publications.

Howe, D. (1989) *The Consumer's View of Family Therapy*, London: Gower.

Kuehl, B.; Newfield, N. and Joanning, H. (1990) 'A Client-Based Description of Family Therapy', in *Journal of Family Psychology*, 3: 310-21.

Marshal, M.; Feldman, R. and Sigal, J. (1989) 'The Unravelling of a Treatment Paradigm: a follow-up study of the Milan approach of family therapy', in *Family Process*, 28: 457-70.

Piercy, F.; Sprenkle, D. and Constantine, J. (1986) 'Family Members' Perceptions of Live Observation/Supervision: an exploratory study', in *Contemporary Family Therapy*, 8: 171-87.

Reimers, S. and Treacher, A. (1995) *Introducing User-Friendly Family Therapy*, London: Routledge.

Richards, B. (1995) British Psychological Society, Psychology Section, *Newsletter No 1*: 21-36.

Roy-Chowdury, S. (1994) Research Literature Review: *What Families Think of Family Therapy*, Tavistock MA course, (unpublished manuscript).

Steier, F. (1991) 'Reflexivity and Methodology: an ecological constructionism', in Steier, F. (ed.) *Research and Reflexivity*, London: Sage.

Woodward, C. et al. (1978) 'Aspects of consumer satisfaction with brief family therapy', in *Family Process*, 17: 399-407.

# 2

# What Narrative?

*Sebastian Kraemer*

*Therapists like talking about therapy, about their own kind and about other kinds. Whatever the task, human groups have to reinforce their identity by defining their own special ideas and skills and contrasting them with those of other groups. This tribal process is necessary in any enterprise which demands courage and skill and where there are in the end no right answers. Psychoanalysis and systems are the two tribes I know most about and the differences between them are compulsively interesting to those involved. But there are similarities too. The overriding effort to make sense of psychological or behavioural problems through observation and understanding is common to both practices, even if the techniques are different. Furthermore, there is inevitably a story to be unravelled in either of these kinds of therapy. The original work of psychoanalysis was to discover the nature of past events that had so disturbed the patient that she forgot them and developed psychological symptoms instead.[1] The debt owed to psychoanalysis by all subsequent psychotherapies is immense, but rarely acknowledged.*

## Introduction

Throughout its history family therapy has tended to disclaim any connection with psychoanalysis. Related to that is the frequent assertion that unlike the cold and unyielding analyst, the family therapist is much more equal and friendly. The origin of this stance lies at the beginning of family therapy, when it seemed necessary to overthrow the prevailing methods of psychiatry and psychoanalysis, as the Bolsheviks overthrew the Tzars. Existing authorities were simply ignored, as if they had never existed. Even psychology was removed and replaced with philosophy and engineering.

While it is true that the proper technique of psychoanalysis involves sitting behind the patient, out of sight, this does not have to render the relationship unfriendly. Analysts are famous for not answering questions, but there are reasons for that. Therapists should not become friends with their patients, but there must always be opportunities for closeness, often at an unexpected moment, which may lead to change. Recent writing in systemic therapy has emphasised the conversation that takes place between client and therapist. This is in contrast with the more hierarchical ('expert/dummy', Hoffman, 1985) interaction that is supposed to take place in psychoanalysis. The use of the word conversation to describe 'warmer' therapeutic encounters is also evident in work derived from analytic practice, such as Robert Hobson's (1985). It is a useful term for the process of therapy in that it shows that some kind of exchange is taking place. It is surely the essence of psychotherapy that each participant has a point of view and that one of the tasks is to share them, leading to new ideas about the patient's life. A problem becomes a story. Yet if I think about my own actual experience in clinical work, I do not find words like 'narrative' and 'conversation' cropping up very often. These are necessary shorthand terms for complex interpersonal processes. In day-to-day work with families most of us have also to make sense of much more intimate data, both from ourselves and our clients – movements, muscle tone, gestures, play, jokes, facial expressions, clothing and manner, even smell. Most therapists would probably accept this list, and could add more, but the language used to describe systemic work often filters out these bodily phenomena, so that only perceptions, thoughts and meanings are left. It is as if the therapy of the theories were really conducted over the phone.[2]

There is another use of the term conversation. The interaction between infant and mother (or other caregiver) has been described in this way (Stern, 1985; Trevarthen, 1984), yet it is clearly not one that could be reduced to verbal exchange (and therefore not suited to the telephone). This is the prototype of all intimate relationships, including psychoanalysis; an apparently helpless person, lying down, who may feel utterly dependent on the other. But what is missing from this account of it is any sense of the infant's agency, or indeed leadership. The infant is deeply dependent on the mother, yet she can do little for her child unless she is able to follow his (or her) cues. That is to say, if she is to look after him (or her) properly, she is also utterly dependent on the child. In the absence of attentiveness to the dependent being, no proper care can take place – it can only be neglectful, or worse.

The comparison of the therapeutic encounter with mother-baby interaction is a basic assumption of psychoanalysis, but one which has been censored during the evolution of family therapy. The principal reason for this was a possibly quite justifiable revolt against the patriarchal and linear attitude of psychoanalysis at the time, the 1950s, when family therapy was beginning in the USA, when transference interpretations seemed to be given to a horizontal patient as if they were injections of the truth. Yet transference is not something that was invented by psychoanalysts. They were the first to describe it in any detail, and made it an analytic tool that brings experience to life in the room. But it is a naturally occurring phenomenon. When you go into a shop, for example, you have certain expectations of service, which are carried over from previous encounters of asking something for yourself. Children at school from time to time call their teachers 'Mum'.

If we are to take the story seriously we must expect people in distress to have quite primitive assumptions about the kind of help we are going to offer them, alongside any more adult and reasonable requests they might make. The relationship to a helper will always involve these two elements – the 'agent' who has to ensure that some kind of co-operation with the therapist is possible, and the 'patient' who brings all sorts of assumptions, often unconscious, to the relationship. Therapy will be limited if either of these aspects is minimised. I think that psychoanalytic methods have risked neglecting the agent, while systemic therapies may have neglected the patient.

Part of my task here is to tell my own story, to describe my own efforts, almost twenty years ago, at integrating psychoanalytic and systems ideas. This was not my intention at the time. It was simply necessary to have tools with which to work as a child and adolescent psychiatrist, and these were closest to hand. Psychoanalysis came first. Working with individual children, in particular, it is impossible not to see how one is put into positions that come from the child's mind. Supervision of psychoanalytic work tends to focus as much on the therapist as on the patient, and there I found how much my own reactions could tell me about the process. Although it is easy to misuse the notion of countertransference,[3] there has to be some notion – whatever it is called – with which one can reflect on 'what is happening to me' in clinical work. But in order to do so it is necessary to have had some practice. This means having spent some time away from the therapy situation talking with someone else about 'how I felt' or 'how they made me feel'. This can be with a group behind a one-way screen but the safest place for it to happen is in one-to-one supervision. Yet much systemic training eschews individual meetings as they are not consistent with the open aims of the therapy.

Like a family itself, a group of colleagues is a more primitive organisation than an individual. This is an ethological, not a moral, statement. Humans are, like most (but not all) mammals, intensely social creatures and we have to accept the pressures both towards conformity and rivalry that surface in groups.[4] Far greater courage may be required to speak one's mind in the presence of peers. In spite of recent developments in systemic work with individuals, there is still a tendency in systems-based organisations to assume that group = good, individual = bad. Of course there can be good reasons for preferring group work, both in training and in therapy, but there may also be tribal pressure to conform to a collective method, without good reason. As long as the debt to psychoanalysis is not acknowledged it is likely that systemic therapy will remain at risk of acting out in this way. The principal source of resistance to one-to-one supervision may well be the similarity that it inevitably has to individual psychotherapy (Kraemer, 1992).

What is the nature of this resistance? Is there a suspicion that a family therapist would be so entranced by psychoanalysis that he or she could no longer work with systemic ideas?[5] I am often astonished to hear throwaway remarks about psychoanalysis made by systemic therapists which seem to have nothing to do with my understanding of it. Yet if you have no access to psychoanalytic thinking in practice, from case discussions with analytical colleagues, for example, or from your own therapy, it is harder to see what it is about, and easy to see only the sometimes awkward public face of its institutions, such as the Tavistock Clinic[6] and the Institute of Psychoanalysis. In spite of their best and most thoughtful efforts, these organisations have had considerable difficulty in showing to their critics that they have understood why the idea of analysis creates such terror. Transference is, after all, ubiquitous and there is a real and very primitive awe of its great power. The explicit criticisms of psychoanalysis are derived from this, in particular the quite proper anxiety about the possibility of abuse of that power.

Modern therapists have grown up with the ghastly revelations of sexual abuse, which we now know took place on a far greater scale than could have been believed in the past (one of the reasons, perhaps, why Freud changed his mind about the origins of hysteria). While psychoanalysis developed in spite of sexual abuse, the newer therapies have rightly sought to incorporate an understanding of all abuses of power into their methods. This has been the decisive shift in systems therapy during the 1980s, leaving behind many of the earlier innovators such as Salvador Minuchin and Jay Haley, and to some extent the Milan therapists too. By contrast the psychoanalytic organisations have until very recently seemed to be out of touch with social and historical abuses such as racism, sexism and homophobia. This is so in spite of many excellent publications on politics and psychoanalysis (e.g. Frosh 1991) and a successful series of conferences from the University of East London 'Psychoanalysis and the Public Sphere'. Such a difficulty is partly due to the nature of psychoanalysis itself. Important social changes in gender relationships do not necessarily impact on analytic ideas about early infant experience. However much fathers may increase their participation in child care, for example, it could be argued that for almost all infants the mother is still the primary psychological object, with whom the child wishes to have an exclusive relationship (Steiner, 1996). This basic pattern may be independent of culture, even if its expression varies. In some societies, and even within our own, there may be more than two parent figures, but the tensions between each relationship is still grist to the psychoanalytic mill. The Indian Psychoanalyst Sudhir Kakar argues that the Oedipal situation takes a very different form in an Indian setting, but it is still there[7] (Kakar, 1990).

But psychoanalysts *were* slow to acknowledge real external events in the lives of their patients:

> What is true is that psychoanalysis for a long time tended to close its eyes and ears to psychic trauma. This includes the abuse of power, for example by adults against children, as well as social terror and violence. The complaints of survivors who suffered persecution and were threatened with extermination were for too long attributed to neurotic mechanisms dating from childhood ... Ill-treatment of children, sexual abuse and incest were frequently overlooked. (Halberstadt-Freud, 1996, p. 988)

Yet, aside from that, there is also the dynamic that I am intent on exposing in this chapter, which is the amplification of real and necessary differences between psychoanalysis and systems therapy to create a split between them so that each denies the value of the others' work. It is likely that in the beginning of family therapy psychoanalysts were simply too horrified at the upstarts to take them seriously (Harold Searles, 1965, is an exception). The playful interventions of the Mental Research Institute in California for example must have seemed truly 'wild'. Later, the use of video and screens were regarded as unethical and intrusive, as they sometimes are. But they also created a new kind of openness between colleagues, and a guard against retrospective adornment of therapeutic bravado. While psychoanalysis has evolved greatly in the past forty years it has not acknowledged that any of this could have been due to the innovations of systemic therapy.[8]

Family therapists, meanwhile, have tended to see their own beginnings as a revolution rather than as any kind of development. (Amongst family therapists Carl Whitaker is an outstanding exception to this, and to almost all generalisations about family therapy). But by ignoring their roots, family therapists have written off the previous generation of therapists, with persecutory results. In particular I believe that there is a shared unconscious fantasy amongst systemic therapists of an autocratic and insensitive person who cannot understand anything about racism, sexism and homophobia, or indeed about modern families. This figure is the ghost of Sigmund Freud. A brief survey (in a specialist bookshop) of the lists of references in around a dozen texts in psychoanalysis and systems therapy showed no sign of mutual recognition. The vast majority of the texts cited by systems writers were published after 1956.

In that year, the centenary of Freud's birth, a brilliant quartet at Stanford University in California produced the first theoretical masterpiece of systems therapy – 'Towards a Theory of Schizophrenia' Bateson et al., 1956). This – the proposal of the double bind hypothesis – was a challenge not only to the prevailing practices of psychiatry, but also of psychoanalysis, which was far more influential in mainstream psychiatry than it is today. Bateson, Jackson, Haley and Weakland offered a radically different way of looking at the workings of minds in severe pain. They identified chronic misunderstandings in an intense relationship as a condition of thought disorder.[9] At first it seemed that the mother was being blamed for making the child schizophrenic, but later refinements of the double bind hypothesis (starting with Weakland, 1960) removed that, and also the focus on the dyad, thus becoming truly systemic.

New voices were being heard in many places. This was at a time of post war stirrings against imperial power in the Western world (decolonisation of the British and French empires, Suez, Hungary etc), the very beginnings of anti nuclear and antiracist protest, and the first expression of adolescent moods in theatre, literature and music.[10] In the mental health field in Britain the psychoanalyst John Bowlby found himself isolated as he began to introduce ethology to the study of childhood development (Holmes, 1996). He was also seeing families in therapy, which no one had done before (Bowlby, 1949). While Bowlby was undertaking a radical revision of psychoanalysis, the Palo Alto researchers overthrew it entirely. In fact they dispensed with psychology altogether, and in its place put a theory of communication based on the early mathematical work of Bertrand Russell and Alfred North White-head (and to a lesser extent on the theory of self governing systems derived originally from the science of engineering). This was a signifi-cant step which I believe has left family systems therapy without a developmental and psychological base. It is significant that much of the most original systems work was based on the Palo Alto studies and on the work of Gregory Bateson, who was an anthropologist with no claim to clinical competence at all.[11] (I once heard Salvador Minuchin de-scribe him as 'a miserable therapist', although others, including R.D. Laing, thought highly of his intuitive observations.)

While family therapy is only forty years old, psychoanalysis has reached its centenary. (*Studies on Hysteria*, by Josef Breuer and Sig-mund Freud, was published in 1895 [12]). Here we have the ingredients of a classical Oedipal contest[13] in which gratitude is stifled by anger and rivalry, and the fear of powerlessness is routinely projected by one into the other. Although, or perhaps because, many of the first family therapists had been trained as analysts there was a need to obliterate the record, but in so doing they replicated some of the patriarchal attitudes they had tried to escape from, until this was pointed out to them by the next generation, the first to be led by women therapists (Goldner, 1985). The fact is that none of us has the answers, but we must find, and hold, convictions sufficiently strong to keep us going in the heat of the clinical moment.

Psychotherapy, properly carried out, is potentially very demanding on all participants. Not much work can be done without some anxiety and some courage to deal with it. This is true of both therapists and patients, whatever kind of therapy they are doing. But the pressures on family therapists are of a different kind. Pure psychoanalytical tech-nique is limited in effectiveness in the presence of an active, restless group of people like a family in trouble. Family and systems therapists have had to devise new maps to guide them through the chaos. For example, Salvador Minuchin and his colleagues in the 1970s made a simple and enduring point about families: that children thrive when parents, or other caregivers, can collaborate in looking after them.[14] It is the unravelling of the nature of this process that has exercised systems therapists since those days, but, in spite of enormous economic and social changes, the emotional lives of children and parents continue much the same, especially when things are going wrong.

A particular application of the structural model is in dealing with families where the parents are separated and continue to fight over their children. Recently a colleague and I were asked to see a child who was said to be desperate about visiting her father. His mother sent us a tape recording of her screaming after a weekend with father. It was at once clear that the parents were in a poisonous and continuing dispute, involving lawyers, school teachers, family therapists and many more. With enormous difficulty we managed to get the parents together, without the child, and saw for ourselves how they could only argue. Yet there were tiny opportunities for compromise, and after 35 minutes I told them we had finished, that this was the best they could expect to achieve. I explained that they risked harming their child's emotional development if they continued to fight, and that she would gain nothing if one or other of them were to 'win'. With the parents' permission I put this in writing with a copy to the head teacher of the girl's school, whom mother had been particularly keen that I should contact. The child, whom I saw some months later on her own, seemed satisfied.

This is the kind of omnipotent case presentation that so infuriates psychoanalysts; and rightly, if it were to end there. During the brief session with the couple I found myself filled with magisterial power. There was very little opportunity for conversation or discussion. The parents were squabbling children and I responded by being a bossy parent. Had I not had a basic assumption about families in my mind this would quite possibly have been abusive therapy, in which I simply satisfied my own irritation at these people's mindless arguments. But I believe that if parents can reduce their disagreements, their children will benefit. This is a conviction that I could hold to during the session, which, together with the parents' demand for help, gave me the authority to do what I did.

A second conviction I maintain is that attachment within families can generate an immense capacity for loyal sacrifice. The so-called positive connotation is a way of accepting bad or mad behaviour by seeing it in terms of a desperate and usually hopeless desire to rescue or help another member of the family. Boszormenyi Nagy (1973) was the first to speak of 'invisible loyalties' and it is one of the basics of Milan therapy, as I understood it, to get past ones anger and side-taking in family therapy to reach a higher plane where deep love is floating, unseen and wasted. Reaching that stratosphere requires, again, a belief that it is there, and that getting there can change one's view of the family (Kraemer, 1994, see also Boscolo et al., 1987[15]). In 1972 Harold Searles (1975) spoke about the powerful urge in the infant to reverse roles and take care of a parent. In family therapy, where actions speak louder than words, it was necessary to exaggerate this tendency where it was evident. Some paradoxical interventions were in effect interpretations of unconscious fantasy turned into invitations to enact them. The commonest kind of parentification is between the identified patient and his or her mother. This is a 'marriage' that seems more powerful and interesting than the one between the parents themselves. It is a particular example of anxious attachment in which the child believes that mother would not survive without his or her devotions even, or especially, when they are expressed in destructive and apparently purposeless ways. Whatever it is called, this inflexible entanglement of child and parent is one of the conditions for the double bind and related psychopathology (e.g. Patrick et al., 1994; Leff and Vaughn, 1985).

The prevailing ethos of modern systems therapy is a plural one. We are open to the ideas and cultures of others and interested in, indeed compulsively curious about, how they get to be the way they are. This kind of openness is a wonderful tool, because it fosters a strategic neutrality which helps us not to side with factions in the family. Selvini Palazzoli and her colleagues (1978, the second masterpiece of systems therapy) understood and articulated this dynamic very well, but it was only later that the philosophy behind it was clarified – the view that our perceptions of other people, indeed of anything at all, are constructions powerfully determined by the physiological (particularly cerebral) and social contexts we find ourselves in.[16] But this is philosophy,[17] not psychology. The theory comes after the practice, in which therapists discovered that if they tried to change the patient, the patient tried to stay the same. We do not desire to be neutral for aesthetic reasons, but for strategic ones, because it permits progress in therapy.

The Milan therapists, rightly, made much of neutrality, and how one must be trained to achieve it – 'to see the system, to be interested in it, to appreciate this kind of system without wanting to change it' (Boscolo, 1987, p. 152). But it is not a new idea. Seventy five years ago Freud wrote of the analyst's obligation to have 'evenly suspended attention' in the presence of the patient, '... to avoid so far as is possible reflection and the construction of conscious expectations, not to try to fix anything that he heard particularly in his memory, and by these means to catch the drift of the patients unconscious with his own unconscious' (Freud, 1922). As far as I know no one in Western medicine and psychology had ever before suggested anything so radical. The conventional attitude of a healing practitioner was, and usually still is, to try very hard to work out what is wrong with the patient and to try equally hard to change it. Freud's instructions still read like a message from another culture, from the East rather than the West. The British psychoanalyst Wilfred Bion took up the theme with his dictum that the analyst should 'inhibit dwelling on memories and desires' (1970[18]). Later (1987) he spoke of the effort required to get to therapy, and advised analysts to be impressed by the very fact of the patient's attendance. As I see it there is a clear continuity between this approach and the developments of Milan systemic therapy. Gianfranco Cecchin's (1987) reflections on the mental state of systems therapists – 'an invitation to curiosity' – have become a classic in the family therapy literature. But neither neutrality nor curiosity can exist without a secure base of experience and conviction.

Of course Freud was a nineteenth-century man, and even Bion, though he died in 1985, could be regarded as a creature of a lost age. He had, after all, fought in the first world war. In contrast, modern systems therapists are proud of their acute consciousness of the influence of culture on judgement, but this does not mean that we are free from such influences. Indeed it may even become a restraint if you try to censor your observations for fear of being derogatory or prejudicial. What is curiosity? If you are curious about something you want to know more about it. Cecchin, demonstrating his approach in a conference discussion,[19] emphasised the urgency and compulsiveness of this state. Presenting work with a couple who are in a violent relationship, he asks them 'why do you do this to each other?' This seems to be just the sort of question that anyone might ask. How is this different from the similar-sounding comments made by the couple's friends and relatives? One important difference is that the therapist is actually struggling to be more interested in finding an answer than in stopping the offending behaviour. The usual reason for asking such a question is less out of curiosity and more a way of saying 'why do I have to be offended by the way the two of you treat each other?' which is not the same question at all.

Though neutrality is a goal to be aimed at, it is not achieved by ignoring one's prejudices. It is necessary to have some very ordinary emotions as a therapist, including rather innocent ones – as a small child might wonder about why people do what they do. Curiosity in a therapist requires an active exploration of ones own states of mind. Much of the material presented to us in clinical settings is really quite upsetting, sometimes disgusting. The activity of seeking to answer the simple question 'why?' must entail some kind of self-analysis. How else is it possible to know what to ask? One would not get very far, in Cecchin's case, if one had not oneself been in a potentially violent situation with a loved person.

## 2. What Narrative?

In general, although it is possible to ask quite penetrating questions about the circumstances of any event, there will come a moment when some kind of developmental hypothesis is required. In the past I understood systemic therapy to be 'the end of blaming' because it was the end of linear causality. In truth, however, we do want to know how people come to be the way they are, and why they go on doing what they do, not to blame them but to make sense of the problem. If we are to generate hypotheses in clinical work, we need a theory, or theories, about human psychology to begin with. A philosophical theory of beliefs and perceptions is not sufficient.[20]

> The view that the world is a product of our own cultural definitions or is, or can be, constructed largely in accordance with our wills, represents a critique of the idea of nature and of inherent constraint. The idea that psychotherapy is a process of constructing meaningful "narratives", rather than of discovering or recognising psychic realities, is an extension of this way of thinking. (Rustin, 1996)

Our effectiveness as therapists depends ultimately on the fact that we are suffering humans too, with the advantage that we have been thinking about suffering and have a language is which to talk about it. None of this is novel or surprising, yet I see little evidence in systemic literature that therapists are willing to say where their questions come from.[21] Of course they come from our own minds, but these are minds that have been practising for years to think, and talk, about love and hate, about mental and physical pain, grief and gratitude, dreams, desire, anxiety, anger, resentment, powerlessness, guilt and shame, masochism, sadism and revenge, envy, dishonesty and betrayal, and so on.

\*

One important question about the development of psychotherapy is to define precisely where the revolutions have occurred – where are the punctuations? Clearly Freud's innovations, although they were introduced over several decades, ushered in an entirely new way of thinking about clinical problems. Likewise, for our story, the quartet of Bateson, Haley, Weakland and Jackson uprooted prevailing wisdom, both in psychiatry and in psychoanalysis. But since then there have been many radical changes in family and systems therapy, each one capturing the minds of eager therapists wishing to learn new ways of solving old problems. This development has been far more unsettled than that of

51

psychoanalysis, which is by nature more conservative and respectful of its past. Because of its origins in the (apparent) overthrow of the preceding order, family systems therapy carries within it a script of change and continuous renovation (rather like modern jazz[22]), as if that were part of its task. This creates a sort of restlessness that might confuse interested outsiders such as potential trainees, health and social services managers, and the authorities who have to accredit therapy qualifications, but it also opens the door to new social and intellectual trends.

Since the first and second generations of family therapists (1950s – 1970s) the most important changes in society have been brought about by women, whose collective voice has been taken seriously as a group for the first time in history.[23] In terms of its social effects, however limited they may still be, this is arguably more important than the impact of Freud,[24] in that the whole of the Western world is now just beginning to face the fact that women are equal to men, and in some unexpected areas, clearly better. The fact that this is continually challenged does not diminish the change – it can no longer be dismissed as it was in the even quite recent past. It could therefore be argued that the innovations in therapy, by women or by men, which have come out of a feminist understanding must themselves be the most revolutionary (e.g. Perelberg and Miller, 1990; Burck and Daniel, 1995; Burck and Speed, 1995, to name only some of the British contributions). For the first time it is possible to see just how invisible are our assumptions about what is 'ordinary' or 'normal'. 'We' by definition are normal – white, male, heterosexual, (physician, too) – and the problem belongs to 'them', who are not.[25] This is startlingly evident in thinking about racism, for example, in which the idea of a 'black identity' is much discussed, but no-one sees the need to ask what a white identity is (Lennox Thomas, 1996), but it applies as much to assumptions about women, men and children; assumptions about sex, power and privacy.

But feminism is not therapy, nor was it ever intended to be. It is a powerful political and philosophical force which will not now be stopped. Therapy, on the other hand, while it inevitably draws social concepts into its talk and thinking, is essentially a psychological enterprise. Social and psychological discourses must overlap, but they must also have their own exclusive areas. What feminism has done is extend the area of overlap between the personal and the social, and thus, rightly, introduce uncertainty at the boundary between them. But it has not removed the boundary. Social thinking, particularly about power and its abuses, must influence the theories and practice of therapy, but it cannot replace them. Nor is therapy a social intervention, except in a trivial sense. 'I am relatively pessimistic about the capacity of therapy "to eliminate the dominance of male assumptions".' (Perelberg, 1990) 'Even the best therapy cannot bring about radical social change' (Luepnitz, 1988, p. 315).

If therapy were only a social activity then we would all do it very differently! The fact is that we depend upon people coming to us, one by one, or family by family, for help. This is a necessary condition of therapy and our only chance of being effective. You cannot offer therapy to people who do not ask for it.[26] The task is set by the request for help and is defined by the naming of the problem. If that turns out only to be a social one no therapy is possible, nor is it ethical to attempt it. It is interesting how clearly and intuitively people understand this. They do not come to us to change the injustices of the political world. I have very rarely, if ever, encountered a clinical case that did not have personal pain close to its leading edge. And this pain is powerfully determined by the intimate spirals that entwine members of families to one another, both past and present and, indeed, the inevitable injustices of such relationships. All this takes place in a social context (including one that seeks to protect dependent individuals from abuse) but it is not a social process. Even when it seems friendly, it is not a task that real friends can properly perform. While personal relationships can be profoundly therapeutic, that is a side-effect, not a end in itself.

The moments of transformation that we seek in therapy may require the therapist to take considerable risks, which would not be ethical without a firm base in good practice and good theory. Besides sympathy and understanding, bullying and seduction are also ingredients in a strong interpersonal relationship, whether social or therapeutic. An explicit commitment to avoid these undesirables is necessary in any therapy training, but it is not on its own sufficient to prevent it. The double bind describes a pathological pattern of relating but it does not, and was not intended to, explore how it develops. We are all capable of acting on perverse logic without realising it, and psychoanalysis has in general been better at elucidating the origins of unconscious self deceptions. To make mental life bearable it is necessary to keep some things in mind, and others out.

The final conviction I have about therapy is that there is always a story to tell about attachments and origins. Two people, a man and a woman, create a third, and a new chapter of the story begins. The earlier chapters are of course the stories from the previous generation, and they exert a powerful influence on what comes next. The triangles of family relationships are the stuff of psychotherapy, from the Oedipus complex to circular questioning, and beyond. Whatever form the family takes – lone parent, adoptive, step, extended – it will be made up of interlinking triangular relationships, even when these are not evident to outsiders. This is common knowledge amongst the child and adolescent mental health professions (to which all the contributors of this book belong), but it is also implicit in the observation that one of the primary functions of ordinary conversations is to talk about 'third parties', that is, to gossip (Dunbar, 1996). Dunbar argues that, while apes cement social relationships by grooming, humans, who live in larger groupings (and have not enough body hair), use gossip for the same purpose. In our conversations we are almost always busy with observations about others, but it is the original triangle, so elegantly described in a much-quoted paragraph by Ronald Britton, that we are all born into:

> If the link between the parents perceived in love and hate can be tolerated in the child's mind it provides him with a prototype for an object relationship of a third kind in which he is a witness and not a participant. A third position then comes into existence from which object relationships can be observed. Given this, we can also envisage being observed. This provides us with a capacity for seeing ourselves in interaction with others and for entertaining another point of view whilst retaining our own, for reflecting on ourselves whilst being ourselves.
>
> 1989, p. 87

The theories that explore this process most fully are psychoanalysis and its derivatives, especially family therapy and attachment theory. It is interesting that the originator of attachment theory, John Bowlby, who is not regarded as a clinical pioneer, was the first in Britain to write about family intervention. It may be due to him that family therapy has become most established within child and adolescent mental health in Britain. It is natural, too, that attachment theory, which contains elements of psychoanalysis and systems theory, should offer itself as the 'centre ground' in the dispute I am describing. While the theory has little to say about therapeutic strategy it does provide a good basis for a developmental psychology. The essential notion is one of protection. Infants are indeed profoundly dependent on their caregivers for the integrity and development of both mental and physical processes. The protection given to the child by secure attachments is less from external danger, such as predators, and more from internal ones, such as excessive arousal, anxiety, mistrust and hostility. Bowlby's collaborator Mary Ainsworth coined the term 'secure base' to describe the function provided by the caregiver. Once mobility is achieved, the child is able to explore the world around, but quickly seeks to return to base as soon as danger is perceived, or when he is tired or in pain.

This is well known and accepted by most clinicians in child mental health, yet it does have implications for therapy (Byng-Hall, 1995). The crucial assertion of attachment theory is that the 'dependency' of an infant is not passive. When things go well both child and caregiver are together in a 'dance', the child's expressions, noises, movements, changes of colour and so on are all taken in and understood by the caregiver, helping the infant to make sense of his or her states of mind and body. This 'making sense' must be the basis of narrative competence. If it is accepted that patterns of relating, to self and others, have their origins in early experience then that will inevitably influence the kinds of clinical hypotheses we make and the questions we ask. It is interesting that, in spite of the revolutionary tone of their seminal paper, Bateson and his colleagues wrote '... we are taking sound motion pictures of mothers and disturbed, presumably preschizophrenic, children. Our hope is that these operations will provide a clearly evident record of the continuing, repetitive double binding which we hypothesise *goes on steadily from infantile beginnings* in the family of individuals who become schizophrenic' (1956, p. 195, italics added). One limitation of attachment theory so far is that it has been more useful in unravelling the qualities of two-person relationships. 'Give me time' said Bowlby in his eighties, but it will be up to others to take this research forward.

The impressive results of systematic studies on secure and insecure attachment cannot now be ignored by anyone in the field,[27] in particular the remarkable findings of continuity across generations. It is as if the stories of early love and hate are embedded in the mind and carried forward through life. The mechanism of this 'transference' of attachment patterns is evidently partly a mental one, although attachment is also a biological process (Hofer, 1996). These studies may be seen as validating clinical wisdom, confirmation of what we already knew. Styles of relating to others, particularly in intimate relationships, are likely to be replicated but, importantly, not in every case. Perhaps the most interesting findings are that even amongst those who have been abused and neglected in childhood, a proportion are able to provide a coherent narrative of their pain and trauma, and are therefore more likely to benefit from therapy (Holmes, 1997; Main, 1995). This gives us hope that a capacity for narrative is immensely resilient in the human mind.

The fact that non-clinical research on attachment turns out to support clinical experience does add greater authority to our work (Goldberg et al. 1995). At no time since the beginning of psychoanalysis has it, or any psychotherapy related to it, had a secure scientific or political base. The most powerful authorities in science, medicine and mental health are not generally friendly to therapy, because 'there is no evidence that it works' (even though there is: Hazelrigg et al., 1987; Holmes, 1994). The polarisation between therapies that I am describing is even more evident between psychotherapists as a whole and their detractors. From Mars, or even from the offices of any national newspaper, the differences between systems therapy and psychoanalysis are virtually undetectable. Our arguments can be ascribed to 'the narcissism of minor differences' (to use Freud's apt phrase[28]) but they are, like sectarian religious or tribal ones, necessary anthropological processes. These are disputes not only about therapy but about human nature itself. The more open-minded and plural our work, the more we need to scrutinise the base from which we explore.

As therapists we have our own stories, too, and probably more than our fair share of anxieties and insecurities. The path to becoming a psychotherapist is bound to be a search for meaning in our own work, if not our own lives. This is as it should be, but there is always the risk that, rather than providing us with a secure base for clinical exploration, our convictions themselves become objects of anxious attachment (see Holmes, 1997).

In the end the tale is a moral one. Moments of change in therapy depend on making connections, primarily between experience and thought, but the quality that makes the difference is authenticity. This is not a philosophical category about the correspondence between a story and historical events, but an aesthetic sense of rightness that (almost) everyone can recognise. It is what makes the difference between good and bad drama, novels, poems and so on. Whatever else it involves, our craft is a dramatic and literary one, with all the possibilities and pitfalls that that entails. The greatest crime that the therapist, or the client, can commit is lying. We do not have to have a theory of 'truth' to accept that dishonesty undermines therapy. The quality of contact between therapist and client is, as every research study invariably concludes, the strongest predictor of effectiveness. Reviewing my clinical failures I think that lack of honesty or courage, on my part or on the clients', is a common factor.

My purpose in this chapter is not to propose an integration of psychoanalytic and systems techniques but to encourage the putting together of the fractured story of therapy. No doubt it was necessary to make the break in the 1950s and 1960s. The gravitational pull of the prevailing theories was just too strong to allow for radical change. But now that the revolution is over an appreciation of the past is necessary, and evolution can take its place.

*I am grateful to Jeremy Holmes, Peter Loader, Anne McFadyen and Justin Schlicht for helpful comments*

## Notes

1. 'Hysterics suffer mainly from reminiscences.' (Breuer and Freud, 1895)

2. One of the most useful 'techniques' I have is to tell people what I see: 'just look at the expression on your/his/her face!' I call it a technique because I don't talk like that when I am not working, though it is useful in team meetings as well. This is simply a way of bringing nonverbal data into the conversation, but I find that a teasing but affectionate style can break the ice.

3. The term 'countertransference' can be used to sanitise some of these reactions, as if one were not really responsible for them at all. Perhaps perceived dishonesty of this kind was one of the things that drove family therapists away from psychoanalysis. My father William Kraemer wrote several papers on this subject (e.g. Kraemer, 1957). After he died in 1982 I found amongst his papers a letter from the Palo Alto Medical Clinic, dated July 1957: 'Dear Dr Kraemer, May I congratulate you on your interestingly written and provocatively honest paper "Transference and Countertransference". I would indeed appreciate a copy ... Don D. Jackson MD.' At least one founding father of systems therapy was reading analytic literature.

4. We know this from the work of two icons of therapy, but from opposite sides of the fence, Gregory Bateson and his contemporary Wilfred Bion. Bateson: 'severe pain and maladjustment can be induced by putting a mammal in the wrong regarding its rules for making sense of an important relationship with another mammal' (Bateson, 1973, p. 248). On the other hand, anyone who has attended a group relations events will recognise Bion's descriptions of 'basic assumptions' which are highlighted by the method of self study which is the primary task of such conferences (Bion, 1961).

5. It does make a difference, as Bebe Speed admits (1996).

6. The irony that this book comes from the Tavistock Clinic is not lost on me. The clinic is, however, best known around the world for its work in applying psychoanalysis in the public sector. I have noted how over the past twenty years systemic ideas, after an initial period of downright hostility, have been treated with bemused indifference by the majority of the psychoanalytic staff. Child psychotherapists have worked in close proximity to their systems therapy colleagues, and, although they do not cite the literature, have clearly taken on many of the insights of systems thinking.

7. He also points out how analytic practice needs to be modified for a

different culture: 'the actively didactic stance of the Indian analyst, as he engages in a lively interaction with the patient, fits more with the model of the guru-disciple than the doctor-patient relationship' (Kakar, 1990, p. 431).

8. This observation, and indeed the principal theme of the chapter, is also discussed by Anne McFadyen (1997) in a paper written at around the same time, but which I did not see until this was completed. See also Roberts (1996).

9. You can hear the psychoanalyst saying 'We knew that all along'; to which the reply must be 'Well, you didn't behave as if you did.'

10. The first Campaign for Nuclear Disarmament march took place in 1956. Also in that year Martin Luther King made his first speech; *Look Back in Anger* by John Osborne was first performed, and Elvis Presley's *Blue Suede Shoes* took over from *Davy Crockett* and *The Yellow Rose of Texas*. I often wondered if Jay Haley was related to Bill.

11. Besides neglecting clinical precedent Bateson also failed to mention his philosophical sources, such as Plato, Leibniz, Frege, and William James (Luepnitz, 1988). Luepnitz also makes the point that systems therapists have neglected their past: 'Not to acknowledge our origins in Freud's work is to deprive ourselves of the richness of his thought, to risk repeating his errors, and to accelerate the process of social amnesia, which leads us to overvalue the contemporary and to treat everything else and quaint and disposable' (p. 170). She suggests that one reason for this is the poor translations of Freud's text into English, which lost much of the liveliness of the original German.

The systemic therapists Anita Morawetz and Gillian Walker also caution against throwing out the baby with the bath water: 'it seems important that in our haste to move away from the linear model of psychoanalysis we should not also throw out one of its most important contributions – the idea of the replication or transference of patterns of interaction' (Morawetz and Walker, 1984, p. 76). They go on to quote Gregory Bateson's later views on transference as 'a general phenomenon in human relations' (Bateson, 1979, p. 14).

12. In the year that X-rays were discovered, and the motion picture camera and radio telegraphy were invented.

13. Anne McFadyen asks 'if it is Oedipal, who is *the mother*?' I used to say that family therapy was the offspring of psychoanalysis and behaviourism, and that may be so, but behaviourism is not much of a mother. I suppose that the mother in this triangle could be the object relations psychoanalysts who were, by definition, more interested in patterns of relationship rather than in individual pathology.

14. One of the disappointing facts about Minuchin is that he did not appear to develop any further. Perhaps he did not need to but I found his later writing (*Family Healing*, 1994) to be devoid of humility and of references to other therapists, as if all he could say was what a wonderful therapist he is, which is indeed true. Likewise, Jay Haley's brilliantly simple formulations, worked out with Salvador Minuchin, were reframings of the classical Oedipal triangle (1976) but he has never acknowledged that nor stopped attacking psychoanalysis.

**15.** 'While this is often taken to be similar to the strategy of positive reframing ... actually it is much closer to a restructuring of the therapist's consciousness.' (Boscolo et al., 1987, p. 7)

**16.** This is a modern version of Plato's statement that we never see reality, only its derivatives, thrown like shadows on the walls of the cave. The difference is that Plato believed that his élite corps of philosophers could face the other way and see reality directly.

**17.** De Shazer clearly takes this position. He says: 'The two alternatives [are] ... Freud's idea that "whatever is going on is a mask for what's really going on." And Wittgenstein's idea that "It's just a matter of we can't decipher it", which is different' (Hoyt, 1996, p. 73). Hoyt jokes 'I'm expecting to read a psychoanalytic article soon called "Postmodernism as a Defense against Reality" ' (1996, p. 76). What is funny about that?

**18.** 'It is important that the analyst should avoid mental activity, memory and desire, which is as harmful to his mental fitness as some forms of physical activity are to physical fitness'. (Bion, 1970, p. 9)

**19.** *Families at Risk European Conference*, London 1992.

**20.** Some of the claims made by new therapies are startlingly naive, whatever the merits of the method. For narrative therapists to claim that they 'do not pathologise patients like others therapies' is a case in point (see Dickerson and Zimmerman, 1996 and Freedman and Combs, 1996). 'Would you rather work with "that borderline" or "the woman who is so angry about the way patriarchal paternalistic staff members are treating her"?' (p. 24). As if there were no other options . There is a potentially dangerous evangelism around the innovators of narrative therapy, as noted by Bruggen and Byng-Hall (1996).

**21.** An honourable exception is a brave text on some of the topics raised in this chapter, *The Therapeutic Relationship in Systemic Therapy*, edited by Carmel Flaskas and Amaryll Perlesz (1996), and Flaskas' later piece in the Journal of Family Therapy (1997). Cognitive behavioural therapy, which has the powerful backing of systematic research in its favour, has also come to recognise the centrality of the therapeutic relationship (Blackburn and Twaddle, 1996).

**22.** The similarities between systems therapy and jazz are amusing. In the 1970s and 80s the master therapists would travel the world doing demonstration interviews in front of large audiences. It was as if Sonny Rollins had come to town and we would go to hear him play.

**23.** This is a linear view of the matter, in that men must also have changed in order to listen in a new way, but the truths of politics are not systemic in any case. Force of one kind or another, such as humiliation and mockery, sometimes has to be used to make social change.

**24.** Psychoanalysis has of course had an enormous intellectual impact, far beyond the confines of the helping professions. The literary critic Frank Kermode writes: 'Interpreters usually belong to an institution, such as a guild as heralds, toastmasters, thieves, and merchants have been known to form; and as members they enjoy certain privileges and suffer certain constraints. Perhaps the most important of these are the right to affirm, and the obligations to accept, the superiority of latent over manifest sense. It is a preference of great antiquity, though we recognise it as modern when we see it in its Freudian form ...' (Kermode, 1979, p. 2). Political rivalry for the right to interpret the world is not confined to therapists, and whatever writers may think of the practice of psychoanalysis, Kermode shows just how awesome Freud has become in literary terms. It is hard to ignore genius, even when it is politically outdated.

25. 'The therapy room is like a room lined with mirrors ...' (Hare-Mustin, 1994)

26. Although one can use therapy skills to support people who are told they 'have to' have therapy.

27. Attachment is a universal process in higher mammals but its manifestations vary greatly, even amongst different human cultures (Parvez Rashid, 1996). We have to be careful not to mistake the surface phenomena for the deep processes.

28. '... it is precisely communities with adjoining territories, and related to each other in other ways as well, who are engaged in constant feuds and in ridiculing each other ...' (Freud, 1930, p. 114)

## References

Bateson, G.; Jackson, D.; Haley, J. and Weakland, J. (1956) 'Towards a Theory of Schizophrenia', *Behavioral Science*, 1(4), reprinted in: G. Bateson, *Steps to an Ecology of Mind*, St Albans: Paladin, p. 195, (1973).

Bateson, G. (1979) *Mind and Nature: A Necessary Unity*, London: Wildwood House, p. 14.

Bion, W. (1961) *Experiences in Groups*, London: Tavistock.

—— (1970) *Attention and Interpretation*, London: Tavistock, p. 42.

—— (1987) *Clinical Seminars, Brasilia and São Paulo, and Four Papers*, Abingdon: Fleetwood Press.

Blackburn, I. and Twaddle, V. (1996) *Cognitive Therapy in Action*, London: Souvenir Press, ch. 1.

Boscolo, L.; Cecchin, G.; Hoffman, L. and Penn, P. (1987) *Milan Systemic Family Therapy: conversations in theory and practice*, New York: Basic Books.

Boszormenyi-Nagy, I. and Spark, G. (1973) *Invisible Loyalties: reciprocity in intergenerational family therapy*, Hagerstown, Maryland, Harper & Row.

Bowlby, J. (1949) 'The Study and Reduction of Group Tensions in the Family', *Human Relations*, 2: 123-28, reprinted in: (eds) E. Trist & H. Murray, *The Social Engagement of Social Science: a Tavistock anthology, Vol 1: the Socio-Psychological Perspective*, Philadelphia, University of Pennsylvania Press, 291-8, (1990).

Breuer, J. and Freud, S. (1895) *Studien über Hysterie*, Leipzig/Vienna: Deuticke, p. 7.

Britton, R. (1989) 'The Missing link; parental sexuality in the Oedipus Complex', in: (ed.) J. Steiner, *The Oedipus Complex Today: clinical implications*, London: Karnac.

Bruggen, P. and Byng-Hall, J. (1996) letter to the Editor, *Context*, 29: 32-3.

Burck, C. and Daniel, G. (1994) *Gender and Family Therapy*, London: Karnac.

Burck, C. and Speed, B. (eds) (1995) *Gender, Power and Relationships: new developments*, London: Routledge.

Byng-Hall, J. (1996) *Rewriting Family Scripts*, New York: The Guilford Press.

Cecchin, G. (1987) 'Hypothesizing, Circularity, Neutrality Revisited: an invitation to curiosity', *Family Process*, 26: 405-13.

Dickerson, V. and Zimmerman, J. (1996) 'Myth, Misconception and a Word or Two About Politics', *Journal of Systemic Therapies*, Special Issue on Narrative, 15 (1) 79-88.

Dunbar, R. (1996) *Grooming, Gossip and the Evolution of Language*, London: Faber & Faber.

Flaskas, C. and Perlesz, A. (1996) *The Therapeutic Relationship in Systemic Therapy*, London: Karnac.

Flaskas, C. (1997) 'Reclaiming the Idea of Truth: some thoughts on theory in response to practice', *Journal of Family Therapy*, 19 (1), 1-20.

Freedman, J. and Combs, G. (1996) *Narrative Therapy: the social construction of preferred realities*, New York: W.W.Norton.

Freud, S. (1922) 'Two Encyclopaedia Articles, (A) Psycho-Analysis', in *The Standard Edition of the Complete Psychological Works of Sigmund Freud*, (trans. J. Strachey), vol XVIII, London: The Hogarth Press, (1955), p. 239.

Freud, S. (1930) 'Civilization and its Discontents', in *The Standard Edition of the Complete Psychological Works of Sigmund Freud*, (trans. J. Strachey), vol XXI, London: The Hogarth Press, (1961), p. 114.

Frosh, S. (1991) *Identity Crisis: Modernity, Psychoanalysis and the Self*, London: Macmillan.

Goldberg, S.; Muir, R. and Kerr, J. (eds) (1995) *Attachment Theory: social, developmental and clinical perspectives*, Hillsdale NJ: The Analytic Press.

Goldner, V. (1985) 'Feminism and family therapy', *Family Process*, 24: 31-45.

Halberstadt-Freud, H.C. (1996) 'Studies on Hysteria, One Hundred Years On: a Century of Psychoanalysis', *International Journal of Psycho-Analysis*, 77, 983-96.

Haley, J. (1976) *Problem-Solving Therapy*, San Francisco: Jossey-Bass.

Hare-Mustin, R. (1994) 'Discourses in a Mirrored Room: a postmodern analysis of therapy', *Family Process*, 33, 19-35, p. 22.

Hazelrigg, M.D.; Cooper, H.M. and Borduin, C.M. (1987) 'Evaluating the Effectiveness of Family Therapies: an integrative review and analysis', *Psychological Bulletin*, 101(3), 428-42.

Hobson, R.F. (1985) *Forms of Feeling*, London: Tavistock.

Hofer, (1995) 'Hidden Regulators: implications for a new understanding of attachment, separation, and loss', in: (eds) S. Goldberg, R. Muir and J. Kerr *Attachment Theory: Social, Developmental and Clinical Perspectives*, Hillside NJ: The Analytic Press.

Hoffman, L. (1985) 'Beyond Power and Control: Towards a "Second Order" Family Systems Therapy', *Family Systems Medicine*, 3 (4) 381-96.

Holmes, J. (1994) 'Psychotherapy – a luxury the NHS cannot afford?', *British Medical Journal*, 309, 1070-2.

— (1996) 'Attachment Theory: A Secure Base for Policy?', in: (eds) S.Kraemer & J.Roberts *The Politics of Attachment*, London: Free Association Books.

—— (1997) 'The Fortress and the Drawbridge: Defensive and creative uses of narrative in psychotherapy – an attachment perspective', in: (eds) G. Roberts and J.Holmes *Narrative in Psychiatry and Psychotherapy*, Oxford University Press.

Hoyt, M. (1996) 'Solution Building and Language Games: A Conversation with Steve de Shazer', in: (ed.) M.F. Hoyt *Constructive Therapies* Vol. 2, New York: The Guilford Press.

Kakar, S. (1990) 'Stories from Indian Psychoanalysis: context and text', in: (eds) J.W. Stigler, R.A. Shweder & G. Herdt *Cultural Psychology: Essays on Comparative Human Development*, Cambridge: Cambridge University Press.

Kermode, F. (1979) *The Genesis of Secrecy: on the interpretation of narrative*, Cambridge, Mass: Harvard University Press, p. 2.

Kraemer, S. (1992) 'Creating a Space to Supervise: opportunity or persecution?', *Tavistock Gazette*, 34.

—— (1994) 'The Promise of Family Therapy', *British Journal of Psychotherapy*, 11, 32-45.

Kraemer, W.P. (1957) 'Transference and countertransference', *British Journal of Medical Psychology*, 30 (2), 63-74.

Leff, J. and Vaughn, C. (1985) *Expressed Emotion in Families: Its Significance for Mental Illness*, New York: Guilford Press.

Luepnitz, D. (1988) *The Family Interpreted*, New York: Basic Books, ch. 11.

Main, M. (1995) 'Discourse, Prediction, and Recent Studies in Attachment: Implications for Psychoanalysis', in: (eds) T. Shapiro & R.N. Emde, *Research in Psychoanalysis: Process, Development, Outcome*, Madison CT: International Universities Press.

McFadyen, A. (1997) 'Rapprochement in Sight?: postmodern family therapy and psychoanalysis', *Journal of Family Therapy*.

Minuchin, S. (1994) *Family Healing*, New York: The Free Press.

Morawetz, A. and Walker, G. (1984) *Brief Therapy with Single-Parent Families*, New York: Brunner/Mazel.

Parvez Rashid, S. (1996) 'Attachment Reviewed Through a Cultural Lens', in: (ed.) D. Howe, *Attachment and Loss in Child and Family Social Work*, Aldershot, England: Avebury, 59-81.

Patrick, M.; Hobson, R.P.; Castle, D.; Howard, R. and Maughan, B. (1994) 'Personality disorder and mental representation of early social experience', *Development and Psychopathology*, 6: 375-88.

Perelberg, R.J. (1990) 'Equality, asymmetry, and diversity: on conceptualizations of gender', in: (eds) R.J. Perelberg & A.C. Miller, *Gender and Power in Families*, London: Routledge, p. 46.

Perelberg, R.J. and Miller, A.C. *Gender and Power in Families*, London: Routledge.

Roberts, J. (1996) 'Perceptions of the significant other of the effects of psychodynamic psychotherapy: Implications for thinking about psychodynamic and systemic approaches', *British Journal of Psychiatry*, 168: 87-93.

Rustin, M. (1996) 'Attachment in Context', in: (eds) S. Kraemer & J. Roberts, *The Politics of Attachment*, London: Free Association Books, p. 223.

## 2. What Narrative?

Searles, H.F. (1959) 'The effort to drive the other person crazy – an element in the aetiology and psychotherapy of schizophrenia', in: *Collected Papers on Schizophrenia and Related Subjects*, London: The Hogarth Press and the Institute of Psycho-Analysis, (1965), 254-83.

—— (1975) 'The patient as therapist to his analyst', in: *Countertransference and Related Subjects: selected papers*, New York: International Universities Press, (1979), 380-459.

Selvini Palazzoli, M.; Boscolo, L.; Cecchin, G. and Prata, G. (1978) *Paradox and Counterparadox: a new model in the therapy of the family in schizophrenic transaction*, New York: Jason Aronson.

Speed, S. (1996) 'You cannot not relate', in: (eds) C. Flaskas & A. Perlesz, *The Therapeutic Relationship in Systemic Therapy*, London: Karnac, 108-22.

Steiner, J. (1996) 'The Aim of Psychoanalysis in Theory and in Practice', *International Journal of Psycho-Analysis*, 77, 1073-83.

Stern, D. (1985) *The Interpersonal World of the Infant*, New York: Basic Books.

Thomas, L. (1996) 'Black Self-Hatred and the Proxy Self: obstacles in the psychological development of the African and Asian child', *Tavistock Clinic Scientific Meeting*, 9 December.

Trevarthen, C. (1984) 'Emotions in Infancy: regulators of contacts and relationships with persons', in: (eds) K. Scherer & P. Ekman, *Approaches to Emotion*, Hillsdale NJ: Erlbaum.

Weakland, J. (1960) 'The "double-bind" hypothesis of schizophrenia and three-party interaction', in: (eds) C. Sluzki & D. Ransom, *Double Bind: the foundation of the communicational approach to the family*, New York: Grune & Stratton, (1970), 23-37.

## 3

# Language and Narrative

## Learning from Bilingualism

### *Charlotte Burck*

Learn a new language and get a new soul
Czech proverb

### Narrative

As narrative has become a significant metaphor in the systemic therapy field, attention has focused on how people construct and live their identities. The central tenet of narrative theory is that the self is constructed – is storied through interaction with others, and that in this process language produces meaning and does not just reflect experience. A vivid illustration of an extreme form of this construction of self is provided by Oliver Sacks in his description of one of his patients who had lost his memory. This man confabulated frenziedly, continually creating a world and 'self' from the evidence before him, to replace what was constantly being forgotten and lost – he 'literally ma[d]e himself (and his world) up every moment' (1985, p. 105). Most of us, in ordinary circumstances, find ways to keep at least some threads of continuity running through our accounts, and to maintain a sense that we are the same person throughout.

Many family therapists, those in this book included, would now describe their work as placing an emphasis on the stories that people tell about themselves and on ways in which different stories can be developed. White and Epston (1990) have probably become the most well known proponents of the narrative approaches. Central to this work is the idea that the stories we develop about ourselves in interaction with others will not encompass all our experiences (Bruner, 1986), that other stories would also 'fit' and indeed would be more liberating and helpful. Memory is not seen as recovering and remembering the 'facts' but

64

considered a process of storying and re-storying. Social constructionists proposed a notion of a fluidity of narratives of self and also brought into question the essentialist construct of a 'core self' of psychological, psychoanalytic and popular traditions (Henriques et al., 1984; Benjamin 1990; Fisher, 1996).

Currently theorists propose that selfhood is 'produced' rather than discovered. This has been theorised at two levels: that of personal relationship – the way our stories of self are developed in interaction with those with whom we are in relationship (Stern 1985) and that of societal discourse – the way our subjectivity is 'dynamic and multiple, always positioned in relation to particular discourses and practices and produced by these' (Henriques et al., 1984, p. 3). Over the last decade considerable attention has been paid to the identification of dominant societal discourses – the social organisation of talk, and what this talk enables to be experienced, acknowledged or ignored (Potter and Wetherell 1987, Hollway 1989). Identities cannot be picked up and lived at will. The cultural stories available and the way we are positioned in the dominant discourses will powerfully shape the personal stories we develop in interaction with those around us. Goldner (1991) includes a quote by De Lauretis on the effect of being positioned as object in discourse 'the paradox of a being that is at once captive and absent in discourse, constantly spoken of, but itself inaudible or inexpressible, displayed as spectacle and still unrepresented or unrepresentable, invisible, yet constituted as the object of vision: a being whose existence and specificity are simultaneously denied, negated and controlled' (De Lauretis, 1990, p. 115). At the same time as highlighting these processes, there has been a search for alternative discourses, ways to subvert and challenge dominant discourse. As Burr (1995), amongst others, suggests, 'the process of constructing and negotiating our own identities will often be conflict ridden as we struggle to claim or resist images available through discourse'. In conjunction with this process, the idea of multiple subjectivities, multiple narratives of self has been further developed (see Bhavnani and Phoenix, 1994, in relation to racism).

There are moments in life when we encounter a description or idea which suddenly illuminates aspects of our experience which we had previously ignored or merely lived without reflection. That sense of a new connection which shifts a frame, that flash of new recognition is what good narrative therapy is all about and can sometimes be observed in the middle of a therapeutic conversation. On encountering the concept of 'multiple subjectivities', I had just such an experience, finding a new description which gave form and validation to my own experiences of having lived in three different cultures. This brought home how crucial it may be to find a context in which one's contradictory and multiple experiences can be validated.

In this chapter I explore issues of language and narrative through the experience of bilinguals which have been neglected within the family therapy and systemic fields. After considering the wider context, I will discuss some of the research literature and highlight some of the important issues. I draw on the experiences of bilingual persons I have interviewed as well as those portrayed in literature, and also make reference to personal experiences which inform my thinking as author and researcher. Finally I discuss implications for clinical work and highlight some crucial issues for the future.

### Language and Therapy

Given the centrality of language to the way we make sense of ourselves and to the therapeutic project, the family therapy field was relatively slow to examine the process of how meanings are made and changed through language. The larger questions of how we develop language at all and the relationship between language and thought have spawned considerable research and debate but cannot really be tackled here (see Pinker, 1994, for a clear, entertaining and interesting account of one view of language development).

In the research work Stephen Frosh and I have carried out, we have concentrated on studying the language used in therapy. We have attempted to apply the methodology of discourse analysis to study the process of change in family therapy. Using this kind of analysis, in which language is considered constitutive, we have been able to identify central themes in therapeutic discussions and the ways in which conversations about these themes changed over the course of therapy (Frosh et al., 1996; Burck et al., 1996; Burck et al., forthcoming). These initial explorations suggest that it is possible to identify significant changes in the ways family members discuss themselves and their situations throughout their therapy sessions; that individuals moved to tolerate and draw on more and various discourses in their talk. This ability to move between discourses rather than being aligned with one seems linked to a more complex experience of selfhood, an appreciation of others' perspectives and an increased flexibility in relationships. These changes may also be linked to Heilbrun's (1988) argument that what is important is 'the ability to take one's place in whatever discourse is essential to action and the right to have one's part matter'.

### 3. Language and Narrative

This is not, however, to suggest that all meanings can be changed through language; there are always other constraints on meaning-making. Identities are not only produced through language, they are also embedded in power and status relations which constrain options. Just as language has real effects, material conditions and societal structures significantly shape personal meanings and it is crucial to keep this in our framework.

### Bilingualism

While the constitutive aspect of language received relatively little attention until recently within family therapy, an area even less considered within the field has been the impact of living life in two different languages. This is connected with the relative slowness of the field to address issues of cultural diversity and racism. De Zulueta (1990) is one of the few who has written specifically about bilingualism in relation to family therapy. Others have concentrated on the issues of working cross-languages and with interpreters, and the importance of offering therapy in the family's first language if all family members are not fluent in their second language (Dwivedi, 1996; Lau, 1984, 1991; Raval, 1996). Difficulties of the therapist becoming aligned with the person most in favour of adapting to the dominant culture and of children unhelpfully being used as interpreters have been raised. Of particular note are Raval's (1996) and De Zulueta's (1990) findings that many professionals felt less effective working with an interpreter; whereas, although families would chose it over struggling with an unfamiliar language, they would have preferred a professional who spoke their language.

Grosjean (1982) has suggested that over half the world's population are bilingual (having the ability to use two languages alternately), although there are few reliable statistics which are gathered about this. This would mean that bilingualism is more usual than monolingualism, although this idea cannot be said to be very evident in much of the writing in the Western context, which tended to view bilingualism very much in terms of a deficit model, at least until the 1980s.

A wider context to a study of bilingualism is Pinker's (1994) argument that 90 per cent of the estimated 3600-5400 languages in the world today are threatened with extinction in the next century. The forces towards language extinction he lists include genocide, forced assimilation, and bombardment by the electronic media (with the Internet now probably playing a central part). Others have also passionately derided the effect of English becoming the most common spoken language throughout the world, conveying with it a national hegemony mainly from the USA, and contributing to a more general loss of diversity. Here in the British context, the position of English as a dominant world language contributes to an undervaluing of both speaking and acquiring other languages.

A more personal context to exploring issues of bilingualism is my own experience of growing up in a Dutch family who moved when I was young to live in an English/French bilingual community in the province of Quebec, Canada. Interestingly, I had ignored much of this aspect of my personal experience working as an English-speaking family therapist in Britain.

### Research on Bilingualism

Research into bilingualism seems to have concentrated on its acquisition, language 'choice' and its effects.

Some research questions have concerned developmental and neurological aspects of second language acquisition. Language researchers debate the effect of age on acquiring language with Pinker (1994) proposing that children's brains are specifically structured to acquire language because this is functional and that we lose this ability as we grow older. Grosjean (1982) on the other hand, has argued that it is perceived necessity which is the most pertinent factor to becoming bilingual although he agrees accent can be affected by learning the language later.

The developmental sequence for a young child exposed to two languages in becoming bilingual has been described by Grosjean (1982). At first a child will speak as if they have one language system which contains words from both languages, choice being dictated by ease of use. They then move to using two languages, while using only one grammar system. The next stage is a move to using two grammar systems, with each language being relationship dependent, so that particular persons are associated with a particular language. At this point children can become upset if adults challenge their language choice. Later the languages become less relationship dependent, and the child will also move to become a translator between languages. Throughout this process the dominance of one language can effect the way in which the other is learned. There will also be variations in whether children and adults keep their languages separate speaking different languages to different people, switch back and forth between languages within a relationship, or conduct relationships in which one person speaks one language and one the other.

Another area of research in bilingualism concerns language 'choice', examining how bilinguals choose which language to speak with whom, as well as when they switch between languages or code-switch – use phrases or words from one within another. An important factor in language choice, as one might imagine, is that of relationship, with certain relationships being conducted in certain languages (Grosjean, 1982). Language use has also been found to relate to the function of the interaction (Grosjean, 1982), as a communication about process, for example to signify belonging, to exclude or include others, to signal status or to make a political statement. Code-switching too, can be used as a communicative strategy, to assert group membership, to claim identity, to make cultural connections or just to play. On the other hand, the context or content of the discourse may determine language use, so that one might speak about one's employment or education in the language used at work or school or use untranslated technical terms. (It has been found that people tend to do mathematics throughout their lives in the language in which they first learned this.) Many of these studies neglect issues of power and colonisation, situations of little choice, which are crucial to language use and individuals positioning within language.

Much research into bilingualism has been preoccupied with neurological and organic questions of whether a bilingual person's brain is structured differently from that of a monolingual. Here the research is somewhat equivocal, with some studies suggesting that there is more right brain involvement in bilingual speakers, particularly if they learned the language after age 11 (Grosjean, 1982; De Zulueta, 1990, 1995). Current findings suggest that there are certain areas of the brain which deal with both languages, and others which are involved with only one of them (Pinker, 1994).

In this area, interesting studies have been reported of aphasics – those with disturbances of speech and language caused by brain damage. A range of different patterns of language recovery have been described which suggest a multifactorial and complex picture of bilingualism. In one review, about half of the aphasics were found to have similar rates of recovery for similarly impaired languages, but the other half have different rates, including one-quarter who never regained one of the languages (Grosjean, 1982). Factors such as which language was first learned, and affective components were found to have an effect on recovery. Grosjean gives a fascinating account of a case of Minkowski's

69

(1928) of a trilingual person whose mother tongue was Swiss German, spoke formal German at school and for business, and had learned French from his father and first fell in love in French. When he became aphasic because of a stroke, he recovered his French first although neither his wife nor his children understood this; he then began to speak German, and lastly four months later, Swiss German, the language he spoke with his family. Six months after the injury, he still spoke French best, when suddenly during the Christmas vacation he became fluent in Swiss German and started to lose his French. This kind of case in which the inquiry focused on neurological aspects raises very interesting questions about the subjective experiences and relationship issues of the bilingual persons involved.

## *Effect of Bilingualism*

Other researchers have studied the effects of bilingualism with contradictory findings. Some research found an earlier and greater awareness of the arbitrariness of language in children (Saunders, 1981; Ben-Zeev, 1977; Grosjean, 1982). Adult bilinguals too have been reported to have a greater awareness of the relativity of things (Vildomec 1971 in Grosjean 1982).

As children begin to differentiate between two different systems of language and language rules they learn, as adults do, that some concepts are untranslatable from one language to another and that different distinctions are drawn within different languages. The well-known story to illustrate this point, about the many words in the Inuit language for snow, has been debunked as a myth by Pinker (1994). There are however, many other illustrations. Dwivedi (1996) highlights the richness of Asian languages in describing feelings and in the use of mind-body idioms, which are often translated incorrectly as somatisation in English with its Western approaches to mind-body splitting. The complexity of language available to describe relationships in Asian languages encodes distinctions made in relationships not possible in English (Dwivedi, 1996). Sacks (1989) discusses the differences between sign languages which can represent experiences and concepts in four dimensions simultaneously in a multi-levelled way, and spoken languages which can only represent experience as linear, sequential and temporal. Solberg (1996) discusses how she prefers to use the literal Norwegian translation 'child families' to the English term 'families with children' which she dislikes because it embeds a notion of adults having children as possessions. Such examples of different concepts indicate that there are different assumptions and world views embedded within language.

This idea that different languages encompass different world views makes it understandable that bilingual persons report that they have very different experiences in different languages. Ervin (1964) found that bilinguals tell different stories in each language when asked to relate what they see on TAT cards (Grosjean, 1982). She found a shift in values and sex-roles in individuals depending on which language they used. Grosjean's (1982) research subjects also describe a 'change of personality' on changing language. These kinds of differences were also described by Haugen (1956), Di Pietro (1977), Mkilifi (1978), Gallagher (1968) and Ervin-Tripp (1968, 1973) (all referred to by Grosjean, 1982). and intimate an overlap between bilingualism and biculturalism. Languages can thus be viewed not only as being constitutive of meaning but also as contexts within which we position ourselves and are positioned.

The idea of different positionings within different languages connects with the recent theorisation about multiple subjectivities. Mama (1995) discusses this in relation to her study of black women in Britain, where issues of racism are crucial. Her view is that 'black people living in Britain often develop the skill of moving in and out of their various subject positions with great alacrity in the course of their social relationships and interactions with a diverse array of groups in their personal, political and working lives'. When she discussed this with some of her research subjects, they struggled to describe this experience, using words like 'schizophrenic' and 'many personalities' which were not satisfactory because of their pathological or deterministic and unitary connotations. Crucial to the acknowledging and reporting of these experiences will be language and a context which supports them, which is why the concepts of 'multiple subjectivities' and 'multiple narratives' can have such a validating effect. Ang-Lygate (1996) however, has argued that dominant representation attempts to reduce such multilayered subjectivities/identities to the simplified concept of 'other' and that this needs to be resisted for complexity and contradiction to be acknowledged and valued.

And there are many diversities of experience and narratives among bilingual individuals and families in Britain which are important to elaborate – individuals are positioned differently depending on 'race', culture, religious affiliation, gender and class. Experience of racism, differential valuing of languages and cultures, politicisation, as well as the dissimilar ways in which individuals interpret cultural themes in their relationships and lives (Krause 1995) all contribute to major differences of experience.

## Colonisation and Hierarchies of Language

Historically, negative ideas were propounded about the effect of bilingualism, probably linked to colonisation and the push to acculturation (meaning, of course, the taking on of the dominant culture/language) which went alongside the marginalisation and exclusion of those seen as different. For example, Adler (1977) stated: 'Often bilinguals have split minds ... all the particularities which language conveys, historical, geographical, cultural, are re-embodied in the bilingual twice: he (sic) is neither here nor there; he is a marginal man (sic)'. In describing the bilingual child, he goes on to say 'his standards are split, he becomes more inarticulate than one would expect of one who can express himself in two languages, his emotions are more instinctive, in short, bilingualism can lead to a split personality and at worst to schizophrenia'. (in Grosjean 1982). Some of these ideas are still prevalent today, with some professionals still giving families advice not to speak their first language to their children at the first sign of language difficulty.

The wider context powerfully affects the ways languages can be owned or reclaimed. Hooks (1989) argues that people are often trapped 'in a cultural context that defines freedom solely in terms of learning the oppressor's language'. Asad (1986) writing about anthropology warns that the inequality of languages in the world, with English being a 'strong' language, leads to other languages being submitted to forcible transformation in the translation process rather than taking part in a two-way process. He is also concerned about the effect of Western languages producing and deploying 'desired knowledge' more readily than others. These power relationships also affect personal experience of language use.

## Personal Relationship to Language

Bilingual persons who haven't learned both languages at the same time, often make reference to a special relationship to their first language (I do not want to use the term 'mother tongue' here, with its traditional assumption of parenting arrangements, although most writers continue to use it). Many people refer to the importance of their first language to express emotional truths and in which to be intimate.

'I do not believe in bilingualness in poetry' says Paul Celan, a poet,

## 3. Language and Narrative

'only in one's mother tongue can one express one's own truth. In a foreign language the poet lies' (in Felman and Laub 1992). A Polish-English bilingual who grew up in a Polish family in Britain said when speaking about this: 'I cannot lie in Polish. It is much easier to dissemble in English'.

John Berger (1996) vividly conveys this emotional relationship in the context of migration:

Migrant Words

In a pocket of earth
I buried all the accents
of my mother tongue

there they lie
like needles of pine
assembled by ants

one day the stumbling cry
of another wanderer
may set them alight

then warm and comforted
he will hear all night
the truth as lullaby

These descriptions imply a notion of 'emotional honesty' as well as emotional attachment to one's first language, some idea of 'being at home' in it. Several research studies have found that bilinguals will switch languages to connote intimacy – in Paraguay, for example, when individuals start courting they do so in Spanish, but when they become more intimate Guarani is used more and more (Grosjean, 1982). Literature also provides examples of this kind: 'He sang her a Gaelic lullaby which made him cry because, if such a thing was possible, he loved her more in his mother tongue' (MacDonald, 1996).

These descriptions raise important questions for individuals' experiences as well as for their relationships. Does the use of one's first language access aspects of oneself connected with earlier experiences of attachment which aid the expression of intimacy? How does one's first language help one 'perform intimacy'? What is the effect on one's sense of self as well as on a relationship if one is learning to be intimate in a second language? When can one's second language help one learn to be intimate? These questions may be influenced by the current fluency of the individual in each of their languages, as this may change over time.

## Language and Identities

The writer, Eva Hoffman (1989) vividly described her experiences of the link between language and identity. As a Polish girl of 13 moving to live in Canada she struggled with whether to write her diary in Polish or English. 'Polish is becoming a dead language, the language of the untranslatable past ... I finally choose English. If I'm to write about the present, I have to write in the language of the present, even if it's not the language of the self ... I write, in my public language in order to update what might have been my other self. The diary is about me and not about me at all' (1989, p. 121).

She has this to say about the experiences of self she discovers and brings forth in her second language: 'Refracted through the double distance of English and writing, this self – my English self – becomes oddly objective, more than anything, it perceives. It exists more easily in the abstract sphere of thoughts and observations than in the world. For a while, this impersonal self, this cultural negative capability, becomes the truest thing about me. When I write, I have a real existence that is proper to the activity of writing – an existence that takes place midway between me and the sphere of artifice, art, pure language. This language is beginning to invent another me. However I discover something odd. It seems that when I write (or, for that matter, think) in English, I am unable to use the word "I". I do not go as far as the schizophrenic 'she', but I am driven, as by a compulsion, to the double, the Siamese-twin "you".' (p. 121), bilinguals may hold considerable contradictions in their experiences.

Hoffman draws distinctions such as public/private abstract/in the world, observing/experiencing and objective/subjective between her English and Polish identities. Her experience suggest important differences in her construction of selves including a 'written self '.

Languages have embed cultures with very different constructions of self, for example, a more relational and communal sense of self in Asian societies and the autonomous individual self in Western societies (Dwivedi ,1996; Tamura and Lau, 1992), bilinguals may hold considerable contradictions in their experiences.

Individual identities may also be profoundly influenced by the relationship to a language. A woman of Sicilian origin born in Britain, whose parents spoke Albanian in the family, reported that she never felt 'at home' in any of the languages she learned – Albanian, Italian, English, because she always felt positioned as outsider. Now married to a French man with whom she speaks English in England and French when in France she says she feels best speaking French. For her it is the most neutral language, a language she could make her own. This fourth language opened up space for her to construct a different identity and discover a different sense of belonging.

My own experience of presenting my professional work for the first time in Holland, the country of my birth, was also an interesting and powerful experience. Deciding to make my introduction in Dutch, the language I use almost entirely for family relationships, I suddenly became overwhelmed by emotion as I began to speak; indeed, the chair of the session looked at me rather anxiously. Crossing over identities, or possible merging two was a very physical and emotional experience and made me wonder about the power and implications of this kind of experience.

## Different Relationship to Language and Thought?

Because bilingual persons are not located just within one language system, it is possible for them to become observers to each of their language systems, an extremely difficult task for the monolingual immersed within one. I would argue that the bilingual's ability to develop an alternative view engenders a stance from which bilinguals recognise and experience Wittgenstein's famous phrase: 'the limits of my language are the limits of my world'. Bilinguals are 'ironists' in Rorty's (1989) sense of this word, who recognise that their thinking is contingent on their language and who have ongoing radical doubts about their 'final vocabulary' (because they always have another one). Indeed, Hoffman (1989) described it like this: 'because I have learned the relativity of cultural meanings on my skin I can never take one set of meanings as final' (1989, p. 275). Bilingual persons vividly live the experience of knowing that the 'use of *these* words get in the way of our use of *those* other words?' (Rorty, 1989).

Rorty has argued that a sense of contingency creates freedom and a potential for speaking differently, which he considers crucial to change. Bilinguals' sense of contingency may explain some research findings that bilingual children showed greater cognitive flexibility, greater creativity, and more divergent thought than their monolingual counterparts (Ben-Zeev, 1977; Lambert, 1977; Saunders, 1982). Simon (1996) describes this freedom: 'I prefer writers who don't always seem to be in linguistic command, or who allow the bones of other languages to jut through the skin of their own words – writers who struggle to open that gash between languages through which revelation comes', and says how much she enjoys 'bad/ incomplete' translations which 'open cracks in the usually solid facade of linguistic knowledge, suggesting larger and more troubling thoughts'.

These philosophical diversions are not, I hope, mere reversals of previous negative connotations of bilinguals but point to important aspects of bilinguals' experiences which would benefit from further unpacking.

## Implications for Therapy

The neglect of the subjective experiences and narratives of bilingual persons in much of the research is paralleled by the lack of attention paid to bilingual experiences in the therapy literature. Some of the research already discussed points to issues and areas which would benefit from explicit attention when individuals and families come for therapeutic help. These include bilinguals' different experiences in different languages, the effect of conducting relationships in different languages, issues of finding a liberational voice, and the living of multiple identities. It seems pertinent, possibly even crucial, for therapists to take responsibility for ensuring that these dimensions be considered in the process of working with families to find creative ways to help resolve their difficulties.

### Language and Relationships

Because children brought up bilingually often conduct different relationships in different languages this can have important effects on how their relationships are experienced. One research participant described how he had been brought up bilingually with a Spanish speaking mother and French-speaking father in a Spanish context. When young he felt close to his father when he spoke French and felt distant from and even devalued his mother's Spanish. When speaking Spanish he felt close to his mother and had a very different relationship with her. In this kind of situation important information for the family which could contribute to developing different ways to converse and relate may be missed if they come for therapy in one language.

Families at times present issues directly connected to language use and relationships. For example, a family came for help because its bilingualism had become a battleground between the parents. The mother in the family spoke to the children in Turkish which the

English-speaking father did not speak very well. The father complained about being left out and the mother struggled with the dilemma of wanting to mother in her first language and ensure that her children became fluent Turkish speakers, and of dealing with her partner's complaints and 'his refusal to learn her language' (her view)/'his inability to learn languages' (his view). Because the father drew on two dominant discourses: the lack of necessity and valuing of learning other languages embedded in beliefs about not being 'good at languages', and that of mothers keeping fathers peripheral, the therapist needed to unpack these wider contextual issues in the session in order to develop some different perspectives.

Some migrant and refugee families who come for therapeutic help struggle with another aspect of bilingualism as their children learn English more easily than parents. Adolescents often use this second language to develop aspects of themselves apart from their families which may highlight their parents' fears of bad influences and cultural corruption. The process of family change taking place in two distinct languages can often highlight and heighten the tensions involved in these transitions, but particularly so if the languages/cultures are viewed as mutually exclusive by the dominant culture and by the family. The idea of multiple subjectivities may facilitate positioning in both cultures.

Adult bilinguals have used language to draw boundaries between themselves and their family. Joseph Conrad's first language was Polish. He became fluent in French, but chose to write in his third language, English, although he never felt confident in speaking it. It has been hypothesised that his refusal to write in Polish was his way of separating himself from his father and his culture (Grosjean, 1982). Casement (1982) similarly, has argued that Samuel Beckett, whose first language was English, wrote in French to distance himself from his mother whom he experienced as suffocating and only after her death was he able to translate his works into his 'mother's tongue'. Beckett himself said that, as there were things he didn't like about himself, French had the right 'weakening effect'. His translations back to English really became new creations demonstrating more complexity in his writing. This use of a second language to construct new narratives not accessible in the first opens possibilities for its use in the therapeutic process.

One powerful effect for myself of becoming a mother in a different language from the one in which my parents had brought me up was that I have never had the experience of repeating their phrases – something many parents report despairingly. Here a change of language helpfully disrupted some family patterns I would not have wanted to repeat.

## Language and Trauma

A female research participant described how following a horrendous childhood, she came to England and was able to become a successful professional, challenging her family's belief that she was unable to learn. After establishing herself, she went through a period of 'being out of sync' with herself having a difficult time for some years. She began to realise the need to link her English identity/experiences and those of her first language. In this process she reported her feeling of joy when she was able to learn a poem in her first language for the first time. She had been able to use a second language and culture in helpful ways to distance herself from difficult emotional experiences, to grow and develop in ways which felt impossible within the constraints of her first language and her family and then use these experiences to transform her narratives of self and relationships in her first language.

Not everyone will want to use a second language in this way. Paul Celan, the poet, felt very strongly that he must write in German following his survival of the Holocaust because he felt he needed 'to reclaim and repossess the language of the murderers of his parents', therefore, 'the language in which the testimony *must* be given' (Felman and Laub, 1992, p. 28).

The giving of testimony bridges the private and public for a very particular purpose. Others will make other choices. Anita Lasker (1996) the cellist, another Holocaust survivor, who married a German musician reported that she found it impossible to speak German to her children. Her wish to protect her children from her past experiences may have seemed more possible if she did not speak to them in the language in which the atrocities had taken place. Or perhaps, she just could not imagine that the language of atrocity could become the language of nurture.

In these situations using another language can be seen as a way to protect oneself from trauma in order to allow other narratives to be developed, while others attempt to challenge atrocity by re-claiming language. It will also be important to explore different gendered experiences and meanings of language use.

## Exploring the Use of Multiple Narratives

Various clinical examples have been reported about patients who are psychotic in one language and 'appear' sane in the other. Adler (1977) described a person suffering from schizophrenia who heard voices in

78

only one language, and when asked in the other language about these, denied having heard them (Grosjean, 1982). De Zulueta (1995) discussed an English speaking young man suffering from manic-depression with hallucinations and thought disorder, who had learned Spanish at school and was able to speak to her coherently in Spanish as well as comment, 'Isn't it strange but when I speak to you in Spanish my mind is quite clear and when I talk to you in English I become all confused'. She reports other examples in the literature of this kind and relates this to neurological findings in which different areas of the brain are involved in second language learning. Hughes (1981) also discussed findings of bilingual patients suffering from major functional disorders having experiences of hearing voices in only one language, or hearing aggressive or unpleasant voices in their second language and positive protective ones in their first.

Although these writers suggest that psychotic patients only *appear* less psychotic in their second language, it is possible that they *are* less psychotic in their second language which could be usefully explored therapeutically. Recent work by Halliwell and Gainza (personal communication) in which they have explored with groups of adolescents different aspects of the voices they were hearing, such as which gender they were and how that related to their content, has had beneficial effects on these adolescents' relationships to their voices as well as on their relationships with others. This very creative work could be helpfully developed to include explorations around language.

## The Use of Different Languages in Therapy

There is considerable evidence as well as strong feeling that it is important to be able to offer therapy in an individual or family's first language. It may also be helpful to offer bilingual or multilingual persons the opportunity to explore issues in all their languages. A few multilingual therapists have described how language switches during therapy can be examined as important process (Krapf, 1955; Mehler et al., 1990). Thomas (1995) discussed the therapy of a Zairean man who had escaped from political persecution who asked for a therapist able to speak French. He spoke French throughout the first interview, but by the third session had changed to English. Thomas presented various hypotheses about this man's language choices, including that English could be used to distance himself from emotional trauma, and that French might be experienced as the coloniser's language with whom the therapist could be seen to be identified. Including the individuals'

79

different experiences of and in their different languages in the therapy would enable these kinds of hypotheses to be explored; although bilingual therapists may not often be available.

The paying of explicit attention to language can help expand the therapeutic repertoire for families and therapists, in unpacking the meaning of different languages for narrative and for relationships.

A French family who had been living in England for a few years came for help concerning their daughter. Following some work which focused on the daughter's difficulties, the parents presented their own differences as a source of concern for the family. The therapist began to explore the way the family talked together to resolve issues. The parents reported that neither came from a family where emotional issues were discussed. When the therapist began to ask more explicitly about the effect of talking in French or English, the parents said it would have been impossible for them to come to therapy in France/in French. Somehow coming to therapy in English helped them to bypass their family rules about not speaking about problems. This discovery led to a more explicit thinking about the meaning of different languages and how this might be used differently by the family members. It was decided that, as the parents often had great difficulty talking about any of the issues important to them at home (which was much less obvious in the session with the therapist) it might be useful for them to conduct some discussions at home in English. This explicit 'playing with language' in the process of therapeutic change was a fruitful way for the family to disrupt and transform some of the more problematic patterns of communication which had developed between them.

Many issues need further addressing in therapeutic work with individuals and families where there are cross-language, as well as cross-cultural communications. Many of these complexities concern issues of racism and the ways in which British society has construed both the idea of a core self and an excluding English identity. The lack of value placed on languages in Britain constitutes only one aspect of this process, but has a powerful effect. Dwivedi quotes a study in which it was found that 65 per cent of patients in the Health Service who required an interpreter were not offered one (Leisten and Richardson, 1994, in Dwivedi, 1996). If and when interpreters are available, writers have drawn attention to the importance of exploring the acceptability of the interpreter to the family in relation to differences of class, gender and culture prior to the beginning of therapeutic work. They have argued strongly for an expanded role in which interpreters are able to offer cultural consultation to the therapeutic process (De Zulueta,

1990; Dwivedi, 1996; Raval, 1996). This change requires a commitment on the part of therapists to develop their relationships with interpreters and to unpack issues of cultural and linguistic translation with them and the families with which they work. Indeed, interpreters who by definition are bilingual, will also be managing their different narratives and subjectivities in these sessions.

Issues for therapists who are bilingual and bicultural are also important to address explicitly, particularly in relation to training. Some professionals have highlighted how their training excluded and disqualified their cultural experiences and knowledges (Patel, 1997) instead of inviting an interaction and interconnection which might enable the 'language' and 'narratives' of therapy to be affected and even transformed.

The unpacking of a therapist's experience of conducting therapy in their second language may also be helpful in relation to issues of joining, manoeuvrability within language, and translation issues. At times therapy in a second language can enable helpful interactions not otherwise possible. A Belgian therapist described a thought-provoking experience of working in English. She had been struck that she had no difficulties in working with a working-class white English father whom her other English-speaking colleagues found very difficult. She began to realise that the father's frequent swearing was detoxified for her because it was in English. This allowed her to be curious and accepting of him rather than threatened like the other staff. She also became aware that her own struggle for words in English allowed her to get alongside this man who himself was struggling for words to express his feelings, and thereby enabled a collaborative relationship to develop between her and the family. (Squires, personal communication.)

The complexities of using different languages and their influence on narratives and relationships invite therapists as well as trainers to unpack these issues further.

## Conclusion

In this chapter I have argued for the importance for bilinguals of having their experiences in and of their different languages explored and taken into account. This is particularly the case in Britain where despite the tenacity of bilinguals over centuries (e.g. the Welsh), little value is given to languages and a deficit model of bilingualism which was prevalent until recently still has adherents. This is only the beginning of an exploration of considerable complexity and diversity, but some important issues have already emerged from the literature reviewed, from interviews with bilingual individuals and from families who have come for therapeutic help.

Most importantly, the concepts of multiple subjectivities and multiple narratives seem crucial to validate. And because bilingual families' experiences will be very diverse, depending on differences of 'race', culture and class, their different positionalities are important to explore. The ability to unpack diversity and value these complexities while at the same time resisting and subverting dominant discourse and practices present considerable challenges both within therapy and outside it.

The most useful therapy for bilingual families and individuals may be with a bilingual therapist whose languages match theirs, or a therapist who speaks their first or most fluent language. However, issues of language may also be attended to by monolingual therapists or in work with interpreters. The different narratives developed both outside and within the therapy can be validated as complexity 'natural' for the bilingual individual, and contradictions, the crossing over or merging of narratives may be explored. Similar to findings about therapeutic change within one language (Frosh et al., 1996), the enabling of the ability to be positioned in both languages with agency may be crucial.

Bilinguals' experience pose important questions which would benefit from continuing examination. It will be important to investigate further the effects of developing multiple perspectives through different languages. The influence of societal and personal valuing or discrediting of languages is also pertinent to bilinguals' narratives and useful to pursue. It seems crucial to explore gender difference in the context of bilingualism as this has been neglected in this chapter as it has in much of the other literature on bilingualism (Tonkin, 1994). The relationship between the experiencing and living of multiplicity and the concept of coherence recently privileged in research findings on attachment (George et al., 1996) is also germane.

The ongoing research of bilinguals' subjective experiences and narratives should provide further ideas about working with bilingual families and those who speak languages different from the dominant one. It may also prove to be a useful context for exploring more general questions about identities, the constitutive nature of language and discourse use.

It certainly seems timely and critical for all of us to learn more about multiple identities and narratives, how these can be successfully lived and how as therapists we can contribute to contexts which sustain and support them.

## References

Ang-Lygate, M. (1996) 'Waking From a Dream of Chinese Shadows' in S. Wilkinson & C. Kitzinger (eds) *Representing the Other*, London: Sage Publications.

Asad, T. (1986) 'The Concept of Cultural Translation', in J. Clifford & G.E. Marcus (eds) *Writing Culture: the poetics and politics of ethnography*, Berkeley: University of California Press.

Benjamin, J. (1990) *The Bonds of Love: psychoanalysis, feminism and the problem of domination*, London: Virago.

Ben-Zeev, S. (1977) 'The Influence of Bilingualism on Cognitive Strategy and Cognitive Development', *Child Development*, 48: 1009-18.

Berger, J. (1996) *Pages of the Wound*, Bloomsbury: Circle Press.

Bhavnani, K. and Phoenix, A. (eds) (1994) 'Shifting Identities Shifting Racisms: an introduction', *Shifting Identities Shifting Racisms*, London: Sage.

Bruner, J. (1986) *Actual Minds, Possible Worlds*, Cambridge MA: Harvard University Press.

Burck, C. and Daniel, G. (1995) 'Gender and Subjectivity', in *Gender and Family Therapy*, London: Karnac.

Burck, C.; Hildebrand, J. and Mann, J. (1996) 'Women's Tales: systemic groupwork with mothers post-separation', *Journal of Family Therapy*, Vol 18 no 2: 163-82.

Burck, C.; Frosh, S.; Strickland-Clark, L. and Morgan, K. (forthcoming) 'The Process of Enabling Change: a study of therapist interventions in family therapy'.

Burr, V. (1995 ) *An Introduction to Social Constructionism*.

Casement, P. (1982) 'Samuel Beckett's Relationship to His Mother Tongue', *International Review of Psychoanalysis*, 9: 35-44.

Castillo, J.C. (1970) 'The Influence of Language Upon Symptomatology in Foreign-born Patients', *American Journal of Psychiatry*, 127: 160-2.

de Zulueta, F. (1990) 'Bilingualism and Family Therapy', *Journal of Family Therapy*, 12: 255-65.

— (1995) 'Bilingualism, Culture and Identity', *Group Analysis*, Vol 28: 179-90.

Dwivedi, K. (1996) 'Race and the Child's Perspective', in R. Davie, G. Upton & V. Varma (eds) *The Voice of the Child: a handbook for professionals*, London: Falmer Press.

Ervin, S. (1964) 'Language and TAT Content in Bilinguals', *Journal of Abnormal and Social Psychology*, 68: 500-7.

Ervin-Tripp, S. (1968) 'An Analysis of the Interaction of Language, Topic and Listener', in *Readings in the Sociology of Language*, ed. J. Fishman, The Hague: Mouton.

— (1973) 'Identification and Bilingualism', in *Language Acquisition and Communication Choice*, ed. A. Dil Stanford: Stanford University Press.

Felman, S. and Laub, D. (1992) *Testimony: crisis of witnessing in literature, psychoanalysis and history*, Routledge.

Fisher, J. (1996) 'The Domain of the Self ', Scientific Lecture, Tavistock Clinic.

Frosh, S.; Burck, C.; Strickland-Clark, L. and Morgan, K. (1996) 'Engaging with Change: a process study of family therapy', *Journal of Family Therapy*, Vol 18 No 2: 141-62.

George, C., Kaplan, N. and Main M. (1996). *Adult Attachment Interview.* Unpublished manuscript. Dept. of Psychology. University of California Berkeley (3rd edition).

Goldner, V. (1991) 'Sex, Power and Gender', in Thelma Jean Goodrich (ed.) *Women and Power: perspectives for family therapy*, New York: W.W. Norton & Co.

Grosjean, F. (1982) *Life with Two Languages*, Cambridge, Mass: Harvard University Press.

Heilbrun, C.G. (1988) *Writing a Woman's Life*, New York: Ballantine Books.

Henriques, J.; Hollway, W.; Urwin, C.; Venn, C. and Walkerdine, V. (1984) *Changing the Subject: psychology, social regulation and subjectivity*, London: Methuen.

Hoffman, E. (1989) *Lost in Translation: life in a new language*, Minerva.

Hollway, W. (1989) *Subjectivity and Method in Psychology*, London: Sage.

Hooks, B. (1989) *Talking Back: thinking feminist, thinking black*, London: Sheba Feminist Publishers.

Hornby, P.A. (ed.) (1977) *Bilingualism: psychological, social and educational implications*, London: Academic Press.

Hughes, G.W. (1981) 'Neuropsychiatric Aspects of Bilingualism: a brief review', *British Journal of Psychiatry*, 139: 25-8.

Krapf, E.E. (1955) 'The Choice of Language in Polyglot Psychoanalysis', *Psychoanalytic Quarterly*, 24: 343-57.

Krause, I. (1995) 'Personhood, Culture and Family Therapy', *Journal of Family Therapy*, Vol 17 No 4: 363-82.

Lambert, W. (1977) 'Culture and Language as Factors in Learning and Education', in *Current Themes in Linguistics: bilingualism, experimental linguistics and language typologies*, ed. F. Eckman, Washington D.C.: Hemisphere Publishing.

Lasker, A. (1996) Desert Island Discs, BBC Radio 4.

Lau, A. (1984) 'Tanscultural Issues in Family Therapy', *Journal of Family Therapy*, 6: 91-112.

—— (1991) Book review of D.W. Sue & D. Sue, 'Counselling the Culturally Different: theory and practice', *Journal of Family Therapy*, Vol 13. No. 4: 429-31.

MacDonald, A. (1996) *Fall On Your Knees*, Canada: Alfred A Knopf.

McNamee, S. and Gergen, K.J. (eds) (1992) *Therapy as Social Construction*, London: Sage.

Mama, A. (1995) *Beyond the Masks. Race, Gender and Subjectivity*, London: Routledge.

Mehler, J.A.; Argentieri, S. and Canestri, J. (1990) 'The Babel of the Unconscious', *International Journal of Psychoanalysis*, 71: 569-82.

Patel, N. (1997) 'Spirituality, Complementary Approaches and Therapy', paper presented at Working with Families in a Multi Ethnic Society: Confronting Racism and Taking Account of Culture II. London.

## 3. Language and Narrative

Pinker, S. (1994) *The Language Instinct*, Penguin.

Potter, J. and Wetherell, M. (1987) *Discourse and Social Psychology*, London: Sage.

Raval, H. (1996) 'A Systemic Perspective on Working with Interpreters', *Journal of Child Psychology and Psychiatry*, Vol 1.

Rorty, R. (1989) *Contingency, Irony and Solidarity*, Cambridge University Press.

Sacks, O. (1989) *Seeing Voices*, Picador.

—— (1985) *The Man Who Mistook His Wife for a Hat*, Picador.

Saunders, G. (1982) *Bilingual Children: Guidance for the Family*, Multilingual Matters Ltd.

Simon, S. (1996) 'Some Border Incidents', *Brick. A literary journal*, No. 55: 22-4.

Solberg, A. (1996) 'The Challenge in Child Research: from "being" to "doing" ', in J. Brannen & M. O'Brien (eds) *Children in Families. Research and Policy*, London: Falmer Press.

Spalding, E. (1996) 'A Conversation with Janice Kulyk Keefer', *Brick. A literary journal*, No 55: 31-8.

Stern, D. (1985) *The Interpersonal World of the Infant*, New York: Basic Books.

Tamura, T. and Lau, A. (1992) 'Connectedness versus Separations: applicability of family therapy to Japanese families', *Family Process*, 31. 4: 319-40.

Thomas, L. (1995) 'Psychotherapy in the Context of Race and Culture: an inter-cultural therapeutic approach', in S. Fernando (ed.) *Mental Health in a Multi-ethnic Society. A Multi-disciplinary Handbook*, London: Routledge.

Tonkin, E. (1994) 'Engendering Language Difference', in P. Burton, K. Kushari Dyson, and S. Ardener (eds) *Bilingual Women: Anthropological Approaches to Second Language Use*. Oxford/Procidence: Berg.

White, M. and Epston, D. (1990) *Narrative Means to Therapeutic Ends*, New York: Norton.

4

# Postmodern Narratives

## or Muddles in the Mind

### Stephen Frosh

### Reading the Reality of Postmodern Texts
### (or, 'Reading' the 'Reality' of 'Postmodern' 'Texts')

You are about to begin reading Stephen Frosh's latest article, *Postmodern Narratives, or Muddles in the Mind*. Relax. Concentrate. Dispel every other thought. Let the world around you fade. Best to close the door; the TV is always on in the next room. Tell the others right away, 'No, I don't want to watch TV!' Raise your voice – they won't hear you otherwise – 'I'm reading! I don't want to be disturbed!' Maybe they haven't heard you, with all that racket; speak louder, yell: 'I'm beginning to read Stephen Frosh's new article!' Or if you prefer, don't say anything; just hope they'll leave you alone.

This is, of course, a parody of the opening of Italo Calvino's (1981) novel, *If On a Winter's Night a Traveller*. When I say, 'of course', of course, I am suggesting that this is a novel known to all. Because I am suggesting this, readers are likely to feel they should know it, so I can claim it as an authoritative voice, something with credentials and credibility. My 'of course' is equivalent to a statement that this is an important and well-known text, to be taken seriously as a cultural expression, and hence useable as a reference. 'Of course' my opening is a parody of the opening of *If On a Winter's Night a Traveller*, how could anyone not know that? By the way, when I use the term 'parody', I mean it is an almost exact copy. I suppose, however, that given that this article is about postmodernism, I ought really to say that I have written a pastiche. In Jameson's (1984) terms:

> Pastiche is, like parody, the imitation of a peculiar mask, speech in a dead language: but it is a neutral practice of such mimicry, without any of the parody's ulterior motives, amputated of the satiric impulse, devoid of

86

laughter and of any conviction that alongside the abnormal tongue you have momentarily borrowed, some healthy linguistic normality still exists. (p. 65)

Under postmodernism, parody gives way to pastiche, because there is no actuality to the original, no moral force behind it. To parody something, it has to have value; the parody is an attempt to unsettle and undermine it. In postmodern times, however, nothing is original nor of special value, so there is nothing to parody. All stories are of equal value, so if I distort or appropriate Calvino's words, I am simply producing an alternative text.

Additionally, when I write 'opening', as in 'the opening of *If On a Winter's Night a Traveller*', I could almost say 'closed' or 'before-you-get-to-the-opening'. In the Picador edition of *If On a Winter's Night a Traveller*, the passage I have copied appears on the cover, as well as at the start of Chapter 1. To save the trouble of actually opening the book – a tiresome trouble under contemporary social conditions in which narrative is broken up into miniature fragments and concentration for more than a moment is a sign of bourgeois élitism – I will just reproduce the cover.

You are about to begin reading Italo Calvino's latest novel, *If On a Winter's Night a Traveller*. Relax. Concentrate. Dispel every other thought. Let the world around you fade. Best to close the door; the TV is always on in the next room. Tell the others right away, 'No, I don't want to watch TV!' Raise your voice – they won't hear you otherwise – 'I'm reading! I don't want to be disturbed!' Maybe they haven't heard you, with all that racket; speak louder, yell: 'I'm beginning to read Italo Calvino's new novel!' Or if you prefer, don't say anything; just hope they'll leave you alone.

Find the most comfortable position: seated, stretched out, curled up, or lying flat. Flat on your back, on your side, on your stomach. In an easy chair, on the sofa, in the rocker, the desk chair, on the hassock. In the hammock, if you have a hammock. On the top of your bed, of course, or in the bed. You can even stand on your hands, head down, in the yoga position. With the book upside down, naturally.

Of course, the ideal position for reading is something you can never find. In the old days they used to read standing up, at a lectern. People were accustomed to standing on their feet, without moving. They rested like that when they were tired of horseback riding. Nobody ever thought of reading on ...

That's where the cover stops. To find out more, you have, I'm afraid, to open the book.[1] By the way, the cover is not an exact copy of the opening page of the book: the word 'traveller' is spelt differently on the cover from on the inside, where it has lost an 'l'. Is this parody or pastiche? According to many postmodernists, desire inheres in the letter, so the absence or presence of an 'l' might make all the difference. It is, after all, all that differentiates male from female, or so they say ...[2]

On the face of it, *If On a Winter's Night a Traveller* is a quintessentially postmodern novel, made up of a series of beginnings which continually go over the same ground from different perspectives, offering different readings or accounts rather than developing a story through time. It appears to parallel (and as postmodernism is primarily concerned with appearance this is sufficient to mean it does *actually* parallel) the systemic interest in overlapping stories, some of them dominant (strong stories), some of them subjugated (weak stories from one perspective, but – joyful prospect of always reading things again! – subversive stories from another). Lyotard (1979, p. 81), postmodernist guru, writes, 'I define *postmodern* as incredulity towards metanarratives' (p. xxiv). So long as nothing seamless is postulated, we have a postmodern text.

Calvino's book is about the pleasures and frustrations of reading; it is, therefore, a text about texts and our relationships to texts.[3] In fact, at first glance anyway, it is a book about the necessary fragmentation of texts – the absence not just of a metanarrative, but of anything that might be complete enough to be a narrative at all. As the protagonist in the novel, the Reader (and indeed the other protagonist, the Other Reader as well) tries to read Italo Calvino's new novel, he discovers that he cannot do so, because he only has a fragmentary version of it. Searching for the true version, all he comes up with are several other texts, each one a beginning of a totally different story, each one left hanging as the text disappears. A fine metaphor, not a million miles away from the experience of doing family therapy, or perhaps it is a parody or a pastiche: searching for the true text we find only fragments, yet (here we are talking about desire), it is precisely this lack of closure, this failure to come to a conclusion, that keeps the game in motion. Each little extract is so stimulating, it makes you want to read more; as we never get to the end, we are left in this unconsummated yet excited state, searching still more for that obscure little object of .... This, no doubt, is one of the appeals of 'virtual reality' as well as the therapy game: nothing, in 'reality', is ever consummated.

But being a postmodern novel, or perhaps *not* being a postmodern novel, *If On a Winter's Night a Traveller* is a more tricky entity. It only *seems* to be about the pleasures of reading and the delicate stimulation caused by the interchangeability of texts. *In fact*, that is, *in truth*, it is about the relationship between the male Reader and the female *Other Reader*. Why does the Reader pursue the texts? Not just for their own sake, but for the sake of communicating with the Other Reader, of linking with her. Precisely in order to have another kind of consummation, a more significant one. Fortunately, there is a happy ending to the book, at least in a bourgeois nineteenth century sense (love! at last). But what of Calvino's reading of sexual bliss? In a world constituted only by stories (and created in this instance within the covers of a book, just as we therapists create our little worlds within the time and space boundaries of our sessions, artificially walled as they are), what can constitute the fulfilment of desire? Only another mode of reading, presumably. Part of the playfulness of Calvino and the difficulty of answering the *extremely important* question of whether he is postmodern or not (purity before truth, please!), is that it is not quite clear whether these imagined characters have more to them than their existence as signifiers on the page. Here is the crucial erotic passage, on page 125.

> Today each of you is the object of the other's reading, each reads in the other the unwritten story. Tomorrow, Reader and Other Reader, if you are together, if you lie down in the same bed like a settled couple, each will turn on the lamp at the side of the bed and sink into his or her book; two parallel readings will accompany the approach of sleep; first you, then you, will turn out the light; returning from separated universes, you will find each other fleetingly in the darkness, where all separations are erased, before divergent dreams draw you again, one to one side, and one to the other. But do not wax ironic on this prospect of conjugal harmony: what happier image of a couple could you set against it?

Calvino seems to imply that something about love, something about caring relationships, fixes the meaning of a text; reading in parallel is possible because from time to time we are 'in a network of lines that intersect' (to quote the title of one of his unfinished stories; another, very different, is called, 'In a network of lines that enlace'). Of course, the problem with this modernist rendition of an apparently postmodern novel – the critique that goes, 'but underneath the textual play there is sexual play, that is, there is something else being signified' – is that it all takes place in a novel, within the covers of a book. And we have already found out what the cover holds: it holds the first page of the book. Is there no escape from this totalising linguistic dystopia? Put bluntly, in our context, does postmodern therapy have anything to do with the real?

### Postposterous Family Therapy

As a reminder that the narrative revolution is well and truly in place in family therapy, here are some of my favourite straw texts. The first is from one of the most-cited articles in the family therapy literature, by Hoffman (1990, p. 11).

> The therapeutic interview is a performative text, as the postmodernist jargon has it. This text will take its shape according to the emergent qualities of the conversations that have inspired it, and will hopefully create an emancipatory dialogue rather than reinforce the oppressive or monolithic one that so often comes in the door .... In therapy, we listen to a story and then we collaborate with the persons we are seeing to invent other stories or other meanings for the stories that are told.

In a similar vein, Parry (1991, p. 41) claims that, through its opposition to any notion of a transcendent Other and through its deconstructionist elements, the 'post-modern sensibility offers a propitious context for the transition to a narrative paradigm for family therapy'. Narrative is a good thing, in this argument, because of its democratising tendency: rather than knowing the 'truth' of the other person/client, the therapist knows only how to help others tell a more creative story about their life. This includes the therapist knowing how to share her or his ideas as alternative stories instead of as expert knowledge. For Parry,

> The post-modern treatment of a story as simply a story, hence something endlessly inventive, offers the narrative therapist a tool for enabling clients to shake off constraining beliefs so that they can live their stories henceforth as they choose. Their stories need no longer live them. (pp. 42-3)

What is liberating about such a linguistic approach is that it enables people ('they', it seems) to choose the stories they wish to live by. Let us leave aside the epistemological problems associated with the ludicrous use of the notion of 'choice' here (a: if we are only narrative fictions, how do we stand outside this state to 'choose' anything? b: who is so unconstrained by social forces that they 'can live their stories henceforth as they choose'?) and go straight for its vision of postmodernism. We all know, it seems, that postmodernism, at least as reflected in therapeutic practice, is a business of democratic and deconstructionist linguistic playfulness, freeing clients from their ideological (modernist) belief in real reality, and enabling them to find other stories to move

90

them on. A family wants help because it is experiencing difficulties. The problem? Too strong a belief in reality, a kind of failure to see the joke. The solution? Help family members appreciate that they can liberate themselves by articulating alternatives, widening their field of perception, allowing subjugated narratives to be expressed. Polymorphous linguistic perversity is the recipe: a therapy of garrulousness in which the act of talking is more important than what is said. Text, text and more text: submerging the story line brought by the family in all the possible alternative stories which might have been written about them (Calvino's endlessly intersecting and enlacing lines, beginning and beginning and beginning). Emancipatory dialogues, endless invention, emergent conversations: internet therapy is on its way, and fast, the chatter of storylines everywhere, all at once. As Calvino says, do not wax on ironically; no longer just therapy, but just talk.

Even without its epistemological vacuousness, this vision of postmodern therapy misses most of the interesting advances produced by postmodernism itself. The discovery here is not that reality is constituted in language – a fact known to everyone, or at least to all the old, high-culture modernists from whom the non-élitist, instantly accessible postmodernists distance themselves so avidly. In the specific context of therapy, for example, it can hardly be anywhere else (though the plethora of expressive body-oriented 'alternative' therapies spawned in postmodern times is an interesting counterbalance to the view that life is a conversation; there, it often seems to be more like a massage). Rather, the important discovery of postmodernism is that it might be impossible to put into words the things which matter; that all this endless talk does not really liberate, because it misses the point. This is why narratives are interchangeable: not because everything is the same, but because language is self-referential, caught in a closed symbolic circuit. As Freud knew, it only hints at what is there.

I certainly do not mean to deny the importance either of language or of fragmentation in the contemporary world, which I would also not hesitate to describe as 'postmodern'. But where systems therapy is in a muddle is in its identification of postmodernism with linguistic relativism – and with a specific view of this relativism that grants it emancipatory (hence 'therapeutic') qualities. Parry writes that the 'postmodern treatment of a story as simply a story, hence something endlessly inventive, offers the narrative therapist a tool for enabling clients to shake off constraining beliefs', but in fact it does nothing of the sort, it simply reveals how inadequate all our story-making must be. If a story is just a story, than that is all it is; it does not emancipate or enable anyone to do anything. At best it entertains, and even then the let-down afterwards can be profound. If one reads this as a postmodernist insight, which it is, then the lesson of postmodernism for family therapy is pretty much the opposite of what it is usually taken to be. Playing games with stories becomes a diversion, an ideological obfuscation; it may even represent a betrayal of people's search for something real. Take as an illustration of the issues here, Lyotard's (1979) definition of postmodernism.

> The Postmodern is that which, in the modern, puts forward the unpresentable in presentation itself; that which denies itself the solace of good forms, the consensus of a taste which would make it possible to share the nostalgia for the unattainable; that which searches for new presentations, not in order to enjoy them but in order to impart a stronger sense of the unpresentable. (p. 81)

What is this 'really' about, if I may use such a locution? It seems to me to be saying that postmodernism, by focusing on the act of presentation whilst also removing the props of aesthetic coherence which underlie the modernist sensibility, directly evokes the 'unpresentable', that aspect of human experience which cannot be reduced to symbolic form, whether 'co-constructed' or not. The 'solace of good forms' and of 'nostalgia' are denied, as postmodernism makes all symbolic narratives equivalent; but the effect of this is precisely to draw attention to the limitations of all narratives, their inability to get anywhere near the real. Postmodernism imparts 'a stronger sense of the unpresentable', it does not do away with it. Instead, it evokes the tantalising horror and excitement of that which stands outside language or (to use a related metaphor very dear to postmodernists, fascinated as they are by images) that which lurks at the edge of vision, caught as a glimpse in the corner of the mirror, but never there when you look directly for it. 'In moments of social crisis (wars, plagues),' writes Zizek (1991, p. 29), 'unusual celestial phenomena (comets, eclipses, etc.) are read as prophetic signs.' When the chips are down, when, for example, death stalks the streets in a country dissolving into civil war, that which is not symbolisable comes into its own.

I would say that this is close to the experience of many of our clients: they know what it is like to live in a postmodern world characterised by dislocation, identity loss, narcissism and arbitrary violence. The postmodernist perception is not that 'everything is only linguistic/metaphorical/symbolic', but rather that behind the symbolic register lies something quite devastating, known technically as well as commonsensically as the 'real'. Unfortunately, perhaps, this real breaks through rather too often, not (to borrow another phrase from Zizek, 1991, p. 143), as a 'sublime, charismatic apparition' but as a 'disgusting reject': unarticulated passions that produce only pain. To state this as openly as possible: postmodernism is not built on the argument that language is everything, that true emancipation occurs through story-telling. Instead, postmodernism demonstrates the insufficiency of language, the way in which all this narrativising is a defence against something else, something less easily pronounceable, but more powerfully disruptive. In extolling narrative too enthusiastically, family therapy mistakes the symptom for the cure.

### Do You Mean to Say that There is Something Real Here After All?

I want to try to be as clear as possible about my point of view here:

1. The 'postmodern' is best understood as a term given to the current state of modernity, identifiable particularly with the information revolution but with its roots in the abandonment of projects for rational perfecting of the human condition – an abandonment which has occurred at an escalating pace throughout this century. Some of the seeds of this perception can be found in Freud, despite his identification with the modernist project, for although early psychoanalysis took as an aim the colonising of the irrational by the rational, it also gave voice to irrationality – to the slippery workings of the unconscious. Reason could never fully dominate the world, because the use of reason itself has unconscious determinants. (We may think we just want to master nature, but actually we are attacking the mother's body ...) But mainly it is the escalating pace of global technological change that has forced on us all the fragmenting processes that send so many of us scurrying for roots. We are part of grand networks everywhere, but we are invisible ciphers too, in every one of them.

2. 'Postmodernism' is an artistic and philosophical movement expressing a number of linked views on this state of modernity. In particular, it offers a critique of rationalist assumptions and a set of procedures for recognising the limitations of the rationalist world view. Spelt out, as in the work of Hebdige (1988), the critique embodies a number of linked 'negations', particularly opposition to grand theories of origin or meaning, or indeed to generalisations of all kinds (except this generalisation ...).

3. Partly because modernism stays within the perspective of rationalism, despite its difficulties, postmodernism claims that modernism is self-deceiving and ideological in a simple sense: it offers a view of the world which is systematically distorted. This view is constituted by the claim that pure reason can exist. Although the hegemony of reason does have some democratising tendencies compared, for example, with domination by virtue of birth or wealth, the consequences of modernism's view are to privilege certain élites, identified particularly with white, western male culture. This is a product of modernism's colonising tendency and its imperialist claim for the predominance of certain modes of subjectivity, and of its denigration of complex, emotionally driven ways of perception and being.

4. Postmodernism, through its playful refusal to take any particular world view as true, has revealed the presence of irrational structures at the heart of the rationalist enterprise. This calls into question the epistemological standing of modernist claims and also offers a political programme in which assumptions concerning truth and virtue – loosely identifiable with patriarchy and racism in modernist thought – are deconstructed. As all reason is infiltrated by irrational components, rationality itself cannot stand as the moral guarantor for claims of domination. In performing this useful service, however, postmodernism runs the risk of promoting not just democratisation but also anarchism, not to say nihilism, if one takes it to imply that there are *no* grounds for making value decisions.

5. Postmodernism has also revealed what lies behind modernism's symptom structure, its attempt to find the 'truth' in the activities of reason. Once this is recognised as merely a symptom, an illusion or imaginary structure, one has to confront the terror of something unsymbolisable at the heart of human experience. No amount of words can remove this unsymbolisable real; they can only evoke its presence.

6. Psychotherapy, including family therapy, does well to heed postmodernism's critique of rationalism. But it goes nowhere if all it learns from postmodernism is that people's lives can be construed in narrative form, a completely banal discovery in any case. *Of course* lives are narratives; some kind of story can be told about anything. Actually, postmodernism reveals the limits of all narrative and debunks the idea that simply replacing one story with another will move people anywhere at all. It is precisely part of postmodernism's point that all stories are interchange-

able – that for every discarded narrative there are 'plenty more fish in the sea'.

7. Faced with this, there is only one way forward for psychotherapeutic practice. Whilst recognising the impossibility of ever confronting the real directly, we must struggle for constantly renewed versions of it. This is rather like the claims of 'critical realism', but without the optimism. Telling more interesting stories is not therapy, it is just story-telling. As therapists, we are required to pay attention to what the therapeutic encounter evokes, what is being asked for, what demand is being made. This does not mean that we neglect language, nor does it remove the important insights concerning the productivity of language, its performative status: of course talking and symbolising produces meanings, how else can anything work? But language only has importance because it connects people and people, people and things.

I am arguing here against the idea that narrative can, of itself, constitute therapy. In doing so, I am taking seriously the claims of postmodernism to have revealed more than just that there are many ways of looking at something and that they do not always make a whole. I think postmodernism genuinely demonstrates the presence of 'the unpresentable in presentation itself ', drawing attention to the not-quite-there, the movement-in-the-corner-of-the-mirror, the thing-we-wish-to-say-which-will-not-find-itself-in-words. What is the nature of this thing? The early family therapists, when they did not have their heads in a basin of cybernetics, knew the answer just as well as other therapists have always known: the real has its locus in relationships, in what happens intersubjectively, which is to say, between you and I. While we prattle away in therapy, externalising this and reframing that, reflecting the one and narrativising the other, something either does or does not happen; a person feels heard or recognised, ignored or misunderstood. This does not necessarily mean that anything new can be named; it just means that something transformative has occurred because a bunch of people have tried to understand one another. The meaning here, the truth or new narrative, is a simple yet profound one: a gift has been given, a caring act has occurred, one person has found a way to connect with what is real, upsetting or exciting in another.

Many people, myself included, will feel deeply uncomfortable about the romantic nature of this vision of therapy. Does anyone still believe that it is possible for a therapist to offer something personal in therapy, to use her or his imaginative capacity to lend a thinking presence to the other? It is much more fun, and much less embarrassing, to think of our work as a process of telling stories. Amongst other benefits, we can use our verbal skills to keep from forming too close a relationship with our clients, and we can protect ourselves from criticism and hurt. I think I might try this game; it is less tiring than taking risks with the real.

In a supervision group which I am currently running, some inexperienced but immensely talented young psychologists are working with a family which is trying to recover from the murder of the father by an acquaintance. The mother, eighteen months after the event, remains in a state of anxiety and shock, diagnosable by current criteria as 'post-traumatic stress disorder'. The three children do what they can to live a normal life, with school, friends, and arguments at home. They miss their father deeply, but in many ways they miss more the mother they used, or would wish, to have. Everyone – therapists, supervisor, mother, children – understands a lot of what is going on in the same terms. The mother is devastated by her loss and is in a bind which runs as follows: if she makes progress and starts to rebuild her life, she is betraying her dead husband by not grieving sufficiently; if she does not make progress she is betraying him by not looking after herself and the children properly. So she is stuck and the children are too. What is the nature of the therapeutic task here?

It is not too difficult to cast the work in narrative terms, as the therapists identify the bind and sympathetically attempt to articulate an alternative in which the mother can see herself moving on whilst still treasuring the memory of her husband. The children, faced with the fear that their mother will disintegrate, can be helped to understand her predicament in terms of grieving, to identify with it and yet also to see the very many ways in which she supports their developmental impulses. This is all correct and indeed helpful as a way of construing the aims and methods of the therapy. But what it fails to convey is the *experience* of working with this family. Whether from behind the screen or in the room, there is a palpable sense that the family is putting out feelers to discover whether anyone can stay in contact with them while they explain and relive the events surrounding the murder and while they 'irrationally' find a place for it as a foundation stone for the rest of their lives. The therapists do not just feel drained; they feel like something is entering into them from afar, an otherness which is full of pain, but which also has its own recognisable, strange strength. Behind the one-way screen, there is no generating of new narratives; there is instead a silent and respectful witnessing, completely compelling, of the therapists in the room – young, remember, and inexperienced – as they try to find a way to be linked with the family without becoming submerged in grief. What, to ask it again, is the nature of the therapeutic task here? It is for the family to discover that their experience can be witnessed and respected, that they can be recognised and are not isolated, that it is possible to be touched by this vicious piece of the 'real' and come back without going mad.

There is no magic in this just because it is not reducible to something linguistic. The communications are approximate and rely on words plus some gross and easily observable nonverbal signs (tears, for one). But to the extent that narrative operates here, it is as a carrier of something else, not as an end in itself. It allows the family to feel in contact with – contacted by, one might say – the therapeutic team. In particular, it flags up the continuing attempt to maintain meaning, to understand. My claim is that the success of this piece of work depends not on the therapists' ability to generate new stories, but on their capacity to stay with the family's experience of the real; and it is only to the extent that narrative supports this capacity that it has any value at all. Imagination, in the sense of an ability to think oneself into the emotional position of another, might be a more useful term. If I am to link with you, it is likely to be through words, but the words are not transparent, they do not say only what they say. Postmodernists mostly know this, as their interest in otherness, strangeness and exile poignantly attests.

### Consummation

Let me finish by coming back to *If On a Winter's Night a Traveller*. The Reader and Other Reader find each other in the end, are man and wife in bed together. But consummation has to wait until the Reader finishes his book. This book, of course, is *If On a Winter's Night a Traveller*. The reality of the lovers' contact can only happen outside the book, when the covers are closed. If we think postmodernism means that we can happily immerse ourselves in the sea of stories and do nothing else, we may miss what it is about. Postmodernism, as a way of understanding the world, makes a vital contribution to thinking about personal meanings and transformation. In its assault on modernism it makes problematic some of the foundational assumptions of the dominant social and political order, in particular the notion that it is even theoretically possible to know the truth. Postmodernism is not congruent with authoritarianism and fascism, even though its apparent relativity over values has led some critics to suggest that it has no political stance of its own, and that this absence coupled with the playfulness of much postmodernist work smacks of cynicism and anti-humanist despair. If one looks at serious articulations of the postmodernist viewpoint, in Lyotard, Baudrillard, Hebdige, Jameson and Zizek, for instance, then the political critique does not seem sustainable. These postmodernists are all too aware of the dangers of the fascist and authoritarian state (and state of mind) and see their assault on metanarratives, teleology and interpretation as strategies to oppose this.

The best modernists, Freud amongst them, always saw reality as complex and organised their perceptions of it in line with this complexity – faced with ambiguity, they struggled with the difficulty of living in doubt. Postmodernism adds to this an appreciation of the ambiguous dynamics of the process of making sense itself – of how the activity of story-telling reflects confusion, emotional investment and desire, and cannot be reduced to rationality, including the implied rationality of freedom of choice. When postmodernism limits itself to leaving this appreciation spinning in the air, so that one story is allowed to replace another without rhyme or reason, without debate over values and power, then it is possible that it will turn into something cynical and nihilistic. The claim that everything is the same shifts quickly into the feeling that nothing matters. My argument in this chapter has been that a nihilistic stance like this, which we are too prone to leave ourselves open to with the 'narrative turn' in therapy, is based on a reading of postmodernist texts which neglects their most significant insight: that many stories can be told about something not because they are all equivalent, but because of the intrinsic insufficiency of language. The real is too slippery, it stands outside the symbolic system; we guess at it all the time, missing it in the dark. In the therapeutic arena, it also misses the main point of what therapy offers when it works: a method of interpersonal recognition, a sign of not being alone.

When all is said and said, the family leaves the room, goes home, lives its life. The family members talk, perhaps, about what has happened. 'Did you understand what they were going on about?' they ask each other. 'Haven't a clue', says the father. 'Don't know,' says the adolescent. 'Huh?' asks the five year old. 'Well, I thought they were on my side', says the mother, 'But now I can't remember what they said.' Then they decide that (a) therapy is a waste of time and nothing has changed; and/or (b) they can't stand each other any longer and can't see any way forward except to separate; or (c) even though they don't understand much of the point of the therapy, at least it was a chance to talk about things, and (d) they feel a bit better understood and a bit hopeful about the future. They do not say, 'We have shaken off

constraining beliefs and can live our stories henceforth as we choose.'
It seems to me unlikely that anyone ever would.

## Notes

1. The first version of this chapter was given as a lecture to family therapy students. They seemed shocked that I should stand at a lectern and read a paper to them, rather than just sit comfortably and talk. Standing seemed to suggest to them that I was making claims to expert status, which of course is very different from what I was really doing.

2. See Gallop's (1985, pp. 137-140) beautiful discussion of the difference (vive?) between 'le' and 'la' phallus. Admittedly, it is not the 'l' which changes here, but that which modifies the 'l'. Still, what is a curving or erect line between friends?

3. Steiner (1995, p. 442) claims, 'Crucially, a person is not a text.' Clearly, he is wrong.

## References

Calvino, I. (1981) *If On a Winter's Night a Traveller*, London: Picador.

Gallop, J. (1985) *Reading Lacan*, Ithaca: Cornell University Press.

Hebdige, D. (1988) *Hiding in the Light*, London: Routledge.

Hoffman, L. (1990) 'Constructing Realities: an art of lenses', *Family Process*, 29: 1-12.

Jameson, F. (1984) 'Postmodernism, or the Cultural Logic of Late Capitalism', *New Left Review*, 146: 53-93.

Lyotard, J-F. (1979) *The Postmodern Condition*, Manchester: Manchester University Press, (1984).

Parry, A. (1991) 'A Universe of Stories', *Family Process*, 30: 37-54.

Steiner, R. (1995) 'Hermeneutics or Hermes-mess?', *International Journal of Psycho-analysis*, 76: 435-46.

Zizek, S. (1991) *Looking Awry*, Cambridge, Mass: MIT Press.

# Part Two

# Narrative

## Applications

# Toward a Coherent Story About Illness and Loss

*John Byng-Hall*

### My Personal Story

I was brought up on an isolated farm in the Rift Valley in Kenya. My nuclear family was very close, yet very distant from everyone else. I was suddenly thrust into the distance myself at the age of seven by being sent to boarding school. When I was older I could begin to tell a coherent story about that experience. It was not that my family wanted to get rid of me, but because schools were a day's drive away and it was either boarding school or no school. Some of my worst memories were of being sick at school.

When I left home at the age of 18 to go to University in England I became sick on the liner while it was passing through the Suez Canal. It was not until the ship was in mid Mediterranean that polio was diagnosed. I was paralysed from the waist down. Feeling awful and frightened, I can vividly remember one of the nurses looking very scared of me and running to the door. From then on she monitored my breathing by watching from the door. Would it spread upwards to affect my breathing? I was taken off the boat at Brindisi in Southern Italy. No one spoke English.

Luckily my friend Peter who was also going to University stayed with me. He saved my sanity, and even now it gives me a warm glow whenever I think of him. Apart from the pain and dreadful medical care one of my enduring memories was of staying awake for most of the five weeks I was there, watching the door of the ward and looking at my watch every five minutes. I puzzled about that for many years until I was reading Bowlby and discovered that separated sick children spend most of their time searching for their parents in a very similar way. I had been waiting for my parents to come. They never did. They told me in a letter that they had put all their efforts and money into arranging for me to be flown to England. I accepted that version until I was in analysis fifteen years later and started to work out what it had meant emotionally. Eventually I got up enough courage to ask my parents why they had not come. They told me that they had booked tickets on the first available plane to Italy when my father suddenly went down with a high temperature. He was isolated in hospital because he was suspected of having polio as well, which he might well have had but luckily without the paralysis. My poor mother was absolutely distraught about who to be with. They did not send messages about my father's illness, or tell me later, because it might have upset me! When my father finally started to get better the Italian hospital made the wrong diagnosis of polyneuritis, which my parents discovered was not infectious and had a good prognosis with full recovery expected, so the urgency went out of their coming to see me. I learned the hard way what not telling the full story can do. It can remove the coherence of the story leaving dreadful implications to fill the gap. I also discovered that I could hide these implications from myself for many years. But at what cost.

Once in hospital in England my sister aged 19 stayed many hours by my bedside. I learned what a hand held and a loving smile can do, and that other members of the family can take the place of parents. When I was well enough to use a wheel chair I spent hours going round the wards of the long-stay orthopaedic hospital talking to those on respirators trying to comfort them and talk about their experiences. I became a self-taught psychotherapist, and identified with the doctors.

It is no surprise then that I became a doctor interested in: (1) working with attachments in families (Byng-Hall, 1990, 1995a, 1995b); (2) 'too close/too far' family systems (Byng-Hall, 1980); (3) how to help families with seriously ill or disabled members (Byng-Hall, 1995a, 1996, in press a). (4) the nature of family myths (Byng-Hall, 1973), stories (Byng-Hall, 1979) and legends (Byng-Hall, 1982), family scripts (Byng-Hall, 1995a), and how to help families to talk to each other, all elements of what has become known as the narrative aspect of family therapy. How these narrative ideas evolved and are interrelated are discussed in Byng-Hall (in press b).

## Introduction

This chapter will discuss some work done in a research group on the impact of serious illness on the family. The group includes my colleagues Barbara Dale (1996) and Jenny Altschuler (1996) (see Chapter 6), together with MSc and PhD students. For my part I used attachment theory and research data as a base from which to explore this issue of illness. The aspect that I explored was how the security of family attachments may hinder or help in care of seriously ill or disabled members. Illness is one of the phenomena that elicits attachment behaviour, which involves the ill person seeking care from other members of the family, which if attachments are secure elicits appropriate caregiving. When attachments are insecure the illness may sometimes either fail to evoke adequate caregiving, or, in contrast, looking after the ill person may become all consuming, providing the justification for maintaining a close bond rather than merely providing care during the illness. It may then be difficult for the ill person to get better, and for both caretaker and ill person to relinquish this closeness. This phenomenon was demonstrated by Pianta et al. (1996), in which psychogenic pain prolonged caregiving well after the cause of the pain disappeared. In this chapter I focus on ill children rather than ill parents.

Mary Main and her associates (Main et al., 1985) started a series of investigations that have shown that the coherence of narrative of parents about attachments as illustrated in their descriptions of their childhoods, predicts that they are more likely to have secure attachments to their children. This is clinically relevant as securely attached children are likely to function better and have fewer problems than insecurely attached children. A consistent finding is that the type of incoherent narrative can predict the analogous type of insecure attachment the child has to that parent. This provides a unique research link between mental representation of interaction and the matching observable interaction patterns.

The majority of parents who have had very traumatic childhoods have incoherent narrative styles, and have insecurely attached children. One particularly important finding, however, is that some adults who, despite having had very traumatic childhoods about which they can nevertheless tell coherent stories, are likely to have securely attached children. One important therapeutic implication of this finding is that it may be helpful, perhaps even transforming, to help the family to tell a more coherent story about its painful experiences, including its illnesses.

I do not see myself as a narrative therapist. This term is in my view a mistake in logical typing; all talking therapies are narrative therapies. I see my understanding of narrative, and how it can enhance my work as being an integral part of my practice of family therapy. Context is crucial in narrative. A story is told in the context of listening. The way a family story is heard and responded to moulds the story itself. A family discussion provides a context in which everyone is both narrator and listener. A family therapist joins this process. By listening for what can be linked together into a coherent whole the therapist can play a part in eliciting a more coherent story about the family's predicaments. The therapist can also help the family to create a more coherent co-constructed version of what happens by being a narrator to how he or she perceives the family interacting. To do this, however, the therapist needs ideas about what constitutes coherent and incoherent narrative. Attachment research provides research data on the nature of narrative.

## Attachments and Security

### Coherence of Narrative

The concept of coherence has two central components (Main 1991, p. 144). Firstly internal consistency in which elements of the narrative do not contradict each other. Secondly whether or not it is plausible – does the story fit with what is likely to happen in real life? In the Adult Attachment Interview (AAI) (Main and Goldwyn, 1985-96) the individual is asked about his or her childhood attachments. At first the interviewee is asked for five adjectives describing each parent, and then he or she is asked to describe an episode that illustrates each adjective. This may reveal an internal inconsistency, for instance a parent may be described as caring whereas the episode illustrates neglect. Enquiries about a time that the interviewee had been ill or in distress may reveal further inconsistencies. Coherence in the capacity to portray continuity over time is elicited by asking how what happened in childhood might have contributed to the interviewee's current personality.

The transcripts of the interview are rated as coherent if it is internally consistent and plausible, and the rater feels satisfied that the picture conveyed was close to what the interviewee had experienced (see Main 1991 for a good discussion of rating of coherence). In other words the rater felt he or she could empathise fairly accurately with the narrator through his or her story. To achieve this the story should convey appropriate emotions to fit the episodes described and include the narrator's own behaviour to help explain why parents responded as they did. Fonagy et al. (1991) devised an additional scale in the AAI. for rating the interviewee's capacity to gauge people's motives for doing what they do, which was called Self Reflective Function (SRF) scale. This indicates a coherent awareness of their own and other's thoughts and feelings, and the complex relationship between mental states and interpersonal behaviour. The SRF scale, as in the Coherency scale,

106

predicted that the interviewee who scored highly would have a securely attached child. All this suggests that understanding motives enables one to tell a meaningful story about relationships, which helps one to tune into and understand children's attachment cues, such as crying or clinging, and to respond appropriately. To extend the concept of coherence and self reflective function to family relationships the concept of capacity for interactional awareness has been proposed (Byng-Hall, 1995a, p. 39). Interactional awareness enables the individual to understand what the currently unfolding scenario means to those involved, and why everyone including him or herself responds as they do in that situation. This is a clinical concept and has yet to be researched. The core capacity is to be able to take an observer or metaposition in relationship to the processes that others and oneself are involved; this allows a coherent story to be told about what is happening.

When coherence is rated highly the rater is also likely to feel that the story conveys one consistent model of relationships (Main, 1991). An individual is, however, likely to acquire many mental representations of relationships stemming from many experiences of relating, or observing others relating to each other. He or she must then have a way of assessing whether any two representations are incompatible with one another. One way of doing this is to use metacognitive monitoring (Main 1991) which is thinking about thinking. Children can develop this capacity between 3 and 6 years old. After that they can step back and ponder their own thoughts and assess whether one set of ideas would exclude another. In this way they can dismiss some ideas while integrating others into a more comprehensive but consistent model of what happens in relationships. To do this they are also likely to need a parent who already has a consistent and coherent view about relationships. The research data on intergenerational pattern fits this idea as securely attached children who have had coherent parents are more likely to be able tell a coherent story about their own earlier childhood (Slade and Cohen, 1996).

### *Incoherent Narrative: multiple models, misinterpretations and metacognitive monitoring*

Mary Main (1991) discusses how incoherent narrative could be based on multiple models for the same situation that are contradictory to each other, an idea first introduced by Bowlby (1973). Bowlby discussed how children that are told one thing but observe something very different are prone to develop incompatible models. He discusses a study (Cain and Fast, 1972) in which very disturbed children had witnessed the suicide of a parent but were told something quite contrary, for instance one child found a parent hanging but was told that the parent had died in a car accident. In this way discrepancies can occur between semantic memory which holds beliefs built up from what a child has been told, and episodic memory which is based on memory of events. Main (1991) argues that young children who have not developed a capacity for metacognitions are prone to maintain multiple contradictory models of the same situation, as they cannot discount incompatible models. Meta-cognitive monitoring is also more difficult if the information is distorted. Many defensive or self-deceiving processes that parents use are compartmentalising processes which act to separate feeling, attention, perception and memory, which inherently limits metacognitive monitoring (Main 1991, p. 146). Not surprisingly insecurely attached children who may have parents that use such defensive mechanisms have lower metacognitive capacity than securely attached children. A further common distortion is when parents tell contradictory stories about the situation. This is especially common when parents are in the process of breaking up or have separated and divorced. The effects of this on the child's story of his or her parent's divorce is explored further by Gorell Barnes and Dowling in Chapter 9.

Some events can be can also be interpreted in contradictory ways by a child. This can happen when different behavioural systems include similar behaviours whose functions and motivations are very different. A classical example of this would be a parent who becomes angry on coming home at night after hearing about some misdemeanour. This might be experienced as uncaring and a sign of rejection from within the attachment/caregiving system, while from within the authority system the same anger can be framed as caring as it can lead to appropriate discipline. If the parent is also in a muddle about his or her own motives for the anger, the child is even more likely to develop contradictory models. Medical and nursing care can also be readily misinterpreted. Is an operation an assault or a caring act? Is an injection a way of hurting or curing?

### A Classical Relationship Dilemma: get close or keep a suitable distance?

A securely attached child has the freedom to move to and fro; close to the parent at one moment, exploring autonomously the next. This is made possible by the shared knowledge that the parent loves the child and the child feels loveable, and he or she can then rely on the parent to be available if needed, for instance when ill the child's attachment behaviour is activated and so seeks proximity to the parent who can be relied upon to respond by looking after the child. Insecure attachments do not have this certainty about either love, or availability. In this situation two main strategies are available to the child. The first is to stay close and cling on to avoid being abandoned; attachment behaviour thus becomes permanently activated. Second is to keep a distance to avoid the pain of being rejected when wanting comfort; attachment behaviour then becomes permanently deactivated. The price is to forfeit either autonomy, or adequate care. Although each strategy may be successful in the short term, clinging drives the parent to want to escape, and distancing does indeed, in time, distance; thus each strategy can create further insecurity. This is the dilemma in insecure attachments, the choice appears to be between clinging or distancing, but either way the relationship becomes more insecure.

A more acute dilemma is created when the parent is the source of danger, for instance as an abuser. The danger activates attachment behaviour as the child is programmed to go to the parent for protection, but the child also wants to escape from the parent. There is no adequate strategy to deal with this approach/avoidance conflict. Freezing so as to avoid either moving toward or away can be one consequence. Both autonomy and care are sacrificed.

Many families have both distancing and clinging strategies within the family's relationships. When this happens in a dyadic relationship, say between the parents, it creates a pursuer/distancer escalations, in which the pursuer feels too far away and clings, while the distancer feels too close and tries to escape even more, provoking even more clinging, and so on, in what can be called a 'too close/too far' family system (Byng-Hall, 1980). There then appears to the children to be two incompatible models operating for distance within their parent's relationship, but one which is experienced and reported on as totally different, and often as wrong, by each parent: 'He deserts me', 'She traps me'. This is a potential source of incoherent narrative within a family.

The main hypothesis in this chapter is that a coherent story can nevertheless be told if family members can understand that everyone has a need to be able to move away at times to be autonomous, as well as to be able to get together to be intimate. It can then be appreciated that each parent's move can be seen as intended to achieve one or other of these necessary states, but because each focuses on one strategy they block each other. It becomes possible to understand how and why one pursues and the other distances by exploring what actually happens in various scenarios. Children can also start to see why each parent comes to blame the other for what went wrong. Eventually they come to appreciate that the two models are not incompatible, they are complementary; if put together they can work.

### Family Narrative Styles in Illness

Family narratives have been classified along lines similar to AAI categories from clinical perspectives (Byng-Hall, 1995a p. 139, Byng-Hall, in press, b). These classifications can also be focused on narrative styles when discussing illness in the following way:

### *Incoherent/Dismissive Style:*
### *'If you don't care you won't be upset'*

Parents who are categorised as Dismissive on the AAI are likely to have children who are categorised Insecure/Avoidant on the Strange Situation (SS) (Ainsworth et al., 1978), which is a laboratory procedure in which infants are exposed to brief separations from a parent which reveals the nature of their attachment. The parent dismisses attachments as being unimportant and defensively excludes information that is hurtful to remember. These parents are likely to have been rejected by their parents when they had been upset and wanted comfort as children, and so when their own children are upset and make demands on them they push the child away to avoid the painful reminder of what happened to them. The defensive exclusion leads to inability to recall large parts of their childhood. They idealise their own parents but then give accounts of lack of care during illnesses. One person described her mother as being wonderful, but later how she had broken her arm but had not been able to tell her mother about it for three days. By failing to see the discrepancy between the nice belief and the hurtful memory 'dismissive' individuals are saved from facing some very uncomfortable conclusions. Interaction between parent and child becomes detached and emotionally cool. This is adaptive within this particular relationship as the child learns that emotional demands often lead to rejection, but this can be maladaptive when ill and closeness is needed.

Family stories told about illnesses are dismissive of emotional issues, and often focus on the bald facts of the illness, or are in praise of suffering in silence. Narrators often idealise their own or their parent's nursing care, but descriptions of nursing may not bear this out.

## 5. Toward a Coherent Story About Illness and Loss

### Incoherent/Preoccupied Style:
#### ghosts of illnesses past

Parents who are categorised Preoccupied on the AAI are likely to have children who are Insecure/Ambivalent in the SS. These parents spend much time being preoccupied with the past. In contrast to dismissive parents, they focus on past painful memories, often dwelling angrily on the perceived injustices. Their children learn that if they work hard enough at getting attention, say by being demanding, the parent may suddenly come back into the present and be temporarily warm and loving. This of course reinforces the demanding and clinging behaviour. Children keep an eye on the parent's whereabouts and current motivation; is he or she available, or lost to the past? Another strategy is to parent the parent as a way of making oneself indispensable. These families have an enmeshed style of relating in which there are intrusive attempts to find out what is in other people's minds, and lengthy imposition of one's own preoccupations on others. Illness provides a justification to remain permanently close.

The family stories are often preoccupied with the rights and wrongs of what happened in various illnesses which are often described in rambling detail. It is as if the teller has disappeared into the past which lives on, and ghosts of ancestors flit across the stage. Current members may find themselves cast in past nursing or patient roles and expected to make up for old injustices; but are often destined, nevertheless, to repeat the disappointment.

### Contradictory Stories:
#### 'You pamper!', 'But you neglect!'

Enmeshed as well as distant relationships exist within the family. A passionate dispute can arise between contrasting approaches to illness. One parent may protect him or herself by remaining detached and encouraging the independence of the ill child, while the other focuses on pain and suffering and the need to comfort and protect. Protagonists of each approach try to persuade the other to change what appears to be a catastrophic course of action. Parental relationships are often 'too close/too far' which leads to pursuing/distancing escalations. A sick child may well become the parents' distance regulator (Byng-Hall, 1980). Each parent's caregiving is activated, which brings them together in a non-intimate way that does not threaten anxieties about becoming too close. The symptom may then be maintained as a solution to the frightening too close/too far distance conflict.

This is the group of families that can be helped to see that each strategy is not merely the antithesis of the other, but represents differing strategies for achieving a sense of security. It may then be possible to see that each approach has complementary aspects which put together makes for some potentially good team work; caring for while encouraging appropriate autonomy of the ill child. This may also encourage parents to value each other's contribution and not to drift into an all too common situation in which the most 'distant' parent leaves home, while the 'close' parent becomes bound night and day to the sick child, satisfying both the parent's and the child's need for an attachment, but making it difficult for the sick child to become independent.

### Unresolved Mourning or Trauma

An important group of insecure attachments include parents who are either abusing, or categorised Incoherent/Unresolved on the AAI, They are likely to have children that are categorised as Insecure Disorganised/Disorientated on the SS.

This is probably the most important group clinically as they are more likely to develop problems than either of the other two insecure groups. The approach/avoidance conflict generated by abusing parents has been mentioned above. Those parents who are categorised as Unresolved are coherent until discussing an important attachment figure who has died, or a particular trauma is mentioned. The account then becomes incoherent and disjointed, e.g. speaking as if the person is still alive. Main and Hesse (1990) suggest that the child's attachment behaviour triggers dissociated memories that are disturbing to the parent, who are then perceived as frightened and/or frightening to the child, thus also creating approach/avoidance conflicts.

Pianta, Marvin, Britner and Borowitz (1996) explored the narrative of 91 parents of children with either epilepsy or cerebral palsy. When the parents were asked to discuss how they responded to the diagnosis that had been given between 2-50 months previously, half of them showed that they had resolved the trauma while the other half showed signs of unresolved narrative. Those who had resolved issues had faced the realities of what had happened, and the implications of the diagnosis and prognosis; and what it meant to them personally, balancing the negative consequences with some ideas about finding strength in responding to the crisis. These parents had mostly used a 'thinking' approach to working it out, while a smaller proportion had successfully used a 'feeling', or 'action' led approach.

Parents who were Unresolved seemed 'stuck in the past', often immersed in continuing mourning, sometimes challenging the diagnosis or being unrealistic, for instance, thinking that the condition would pass with age. Subcategories of Unresolved narrative included: being (1) emotionally overwhelmed with sadness and pain, experiencing continual crisis, and enlisting the interviewer's sympathy; (2) depressed, resigned and feeling hopeless about the future and about being able to cope; (3) angrily preoccupied, enlisting sympathy for their anger (similar to Preoccupied on AAI); (4) neutralising, no report or negative emotion related to diagnosis; could recall details of diagnosis but no recall of emotion felt (similar to Dismissive on AAI); (5) distorted and unbalanced in expectations of future, (6) confused and rambling, loosing train of thought, oscillating between polarised positions. ([5] and [6] are common findings in Unresolved category in AAI). It is obviously not possible to characterise the narrative style of the whole group. In brief these parents showed signs of failing to grieve the loss of a healthy future for their child and showed characteristics of incoherent narrative. These unresolved patterns were not related to severity or chronicity of symptoms suggesting it was related to preexisting styles of handling loss.

### Therapeutic Implications

#### *Overall Aim of Family Therapy*

In my practice the goal of family therapy is to provide a temporary secure therapeutic base for the family, so that they then can explore ways in which they can increase the security of their own base. They can then go on solving problems after therapy (Byng-Hall, 1995b) and feel secure enough to explore uncomfortable ideas. Therapy focuses on the many factors in the family that undermine the security felt in the family (Byng-Hall 1995a, p. 106). These include among other things: lack of availability of parents, either physically or emotionally; or parental conflicts that are so threatening that it takes precedence over caring for children or breakdown of parental authority. Techniques for increasing the coherence of the story are discussed in Byng-Hall (in press b). Exploring contrasting styles of narrative and how to link them into a coherent story will now be explored through a case study.

### Case Study : a struggle against illness and loss

Pierre, aged 7, was referred with the following story. His mother Marie, aged 34, had come to London from Toulouse in France 10 years before. She had been depressed during her pregnancy with Pierre and had taken an overdose because her husband had gone off with another woman. When Pierre was 3, Henrie, aged 41, also from Toulouse, joined the family and Angelique was born a year later. Angelique died in a cot death when she was six months old. The family was very distressed and Pierre started to go off his food and complain of head aches. Eventually a rare brain tumour was diagnosed which was removed when Pierre was 5. Radiotherapy followed and the prognosis is uncertain as it is such a rare tumour. He then developed post-operative epilepsy, and was sexually abused by a teenager when on holiday. Pierre was hyperactive and demanding and Marie was reaching the end of her tether, afraid that she might hurt him when he drove her to distraction.

### First Session: *differing narrative styles emerge*

Pierre was a live wire, roaming round the room, voluble and amusing. He took centre stage and no one including myself could finish a sentence. He waded in with a description of how his mother had been abandoned by his father, and then how he had been abused by the teenager. When I asked what they wanted from me Pierre immediately said 'Try to get us back together again as a happy family ... no rows, less shouting ... just be happy'. When asked the same question stepfather said 'I am not sure ...' Pierre interrupts rudely, 'What's the point of coming here if you don't even know what you want!' Henrie replies 'of course I want a happy family, but we all have to do our own little bit'. Mother said 'I want to learn to control my anger and frustration because I seem to direct it at Pierre'.

Pierre's operation scar went from ear to ear over the top of his head, and his hair was missing from this area because of the radiotherapy. I asked to see the scar. I do this with children with localised illnesses or deforming features as this enables the child to experience me trying to empathise with what it must have been like for them, and also to show that I can accept any disfigurement. Pierre came and knelt down and I ran my fingers the length of the huge scar, muttering sympathetically. We exchanged smiles and I feel a surge of warmth for him. He says, 'Can I look at your walking stick, John?' and picked it up and hobbled round the room. I had explored what it was like to be him, and he explored what it might be like to be me.

Pierre then turned the stick into a weapon and described how someone was nasty to him in the post office and made a prodding motion with the stick at an imaginary man. As he walked round the room I said, 'A lot of people have done some ...' Pierre interrupted, 'nasty things, abusive things'. As he came full circle back to me, he pointed the stick at me and made the same prodding motion. I said, 'Even those who have helped you have done some nasty things to you ... with those operations' Pierre nods, and gave me (a doctor) back my stick.

This set the scene for some work over several sessions on how to manage his confusion about medical procedures and injections which he experienced as both attacks and attempts to help. His parents also have to give him injections of growth hormone every day. I started this work by asking him about the operations, and he gave me graphic accounts of what happened, with additional elaborations by the parents. Marie tells me about the distress; Henrie described the gory details of the operation with a little laugh.

Eventually Pierre settled down and concentrated on a book over quite a long period. It was notable that Angelique's death was not mentioned until near the end of the session, when Marie said, 'I think the shock of Pierre's sister dying caused Pierre's tumour ... I really believe that happened'. During this conversation Henrie was helping Pierre to find a page in his book. I asked Pierre, 'Do you remember your sister?' He looked up momentarily, 'Yes ... but I just want to look at my book'. He has had enough.

My experience of this session is of one disaster after another being discussed, mostly by Pierre, although his parents let him do this. Just as one was out in the open another was raised. It seemed that this was one way of not dwelling on anything painful for long enough to get overwhelmingly upset. Mother desperately wanted every topic to be raised, perhaps adding to Pierre's pressure of talk. Stepfather encouraged slowing down and avoiding issues. Pierre showed his capacity for both approaches; recalling many painful events but avoiding talking about his dead sister.

### Parents Polarise in Their Styles of Facing Loss

In the third session I saw the parents on their own. Marie told me she had been reading Dorothy Judd's book about working with a dying child (Judd, 1989). Marie said, 'It gave me courage to ask Richard if he was frightened of dying. She (Judd) was counselling this boy who could not say anything to his parents because they denied that he was going to die. I wanted Pierre to be able to talk to us.' I asked whether it had been helpful and she told me it had been. I asked Henrie, 'Did you read the book?' He smiled and said 'I don't read things that are likely to upset me', and laughed. Marie reminded him about how he had turned off a television programme about a child dying. Father commented 'It brought tears to my eyes. I thought: I don't want to watch this. Its no good seeing all the suffering they went through ... imagining what they went through'. I commented 'So you did not want to be taken through it.' He continued, 'I can switch myself off to other people's pain, because it does not concern us. We have got enough to think about in our situation.' I commented 'You limit the amount of pain you experience by not getting into how other people go through painful experiences'. He agrees. I say to mother 'You go in the opposite direction', she replies 'Exactly. I have to watch that sort of thing. I know it will upset me.' I ask whether they discuss it afterwards and say to mother, 'or did you read it (the book) for both?'. Father says 'You tell me a bit.' Mother replies 'But you switch off from me', 'I am listening', 'I know you are listening but you distance from me.' The couple thus outlined how each one handles emotionally distressing material, and how this plays out between them.

Henrie now tells me a story. 'To give you some idea, John. We lost our daughter in a cot death. It affected us all. Five years later when we lost our nephew through brain tumour I could not feel any compassion because it wasn't me who was suffering. It did not have the same calibre as loosing Angelique, or possibly loosing Pierre. It is nice that it is sometimes in someone else's court.' I commented 'You say – right that is the boundary of what I can cope with in terms of pain ... but does that become a problem when you (Marie) want to talk about things?' Marie nodded in agreement. She went on to describe how she faced the same issue. 'It brought Pierre's situation back to me and all the really painful times ... It was horrible. Horrible. I could not handle it. In the end I had to speak to my sister-in-law – look I cannot come to the hospital any more.' Polarisation between facing and avoiding pain does not mean that each cannot, at times, use similar strategies. The work of helping these two to see their common humanity had started.

I acted as narrator to the couple's process, often apparently reiterating what had happened or been said, but in my own words that reflected my view of what happens in relationships. It is only looking at videotape afterwards that makes me fully aware of that process. This is one way in which a more coherent co-constructed narrative emerges about the experience of illness and loss.

### *Each Parent's Pathway to Their Style of Handling Loss*

In the fourth session the parents came on their own again and genograms were drawn. Henrie, fifth in his family, had been put in Care in a children's home aged five together with his younger sister aged three, following a traumatic delivery of the youngest girl of the family that led to his mother being in hospital for two months. I asked him if he remembered it. 'Oh yeah. Yeah!' and gave a rueful grin. 'I remember hanging on the gate waiting for my father to visit ... (looking thoughtful) swinging on the gate waiting for him to come.' I commented, 'So there was still a bit of you hoping to get something from your Dad.' I now noticed that Marie was crying. As Henrie gave her some tissues he remarked with a grin, 'Wipe the sand out of your eyes' revealing his attitude to tears. She replied, 'No, I am feeling your pain for you.' A sad story told in a jokey or flat way invites others to feel the sadness. I can remember feeling sad myself at this story. Looking back on it I can see my personal overlap as I had waited in hospital for my father. I said 'So that could have been the time that you learned to cut your feelings off '. I spoke with inside knowledge having done the same when I went to boarding school.

When we talked about Henrie's adolescence he described how he had stormed out of the house following rows, shouting at his parents 'You do not love me! I will never come back!' I said, 'The way you deal with that (not feeling loved) is to say, I don't care because I am independent'. I went back to review the birth of his youngest sister, and discussed how he had had to compete with so many siblings that there could not have been much care available. He laughed and exclaimed, 'You had to queue for it!' Going back to the adolescent episodes I said, 'What impresses me is that there was a bit of you still longing for love. You did not kill your hope off all together. And you were still hoping that you would finally get something from your parents when you had your tragedy with Angelique.' (Henrie had cut himself off from his parents sometime before her birth) Henrie told me, 'They had a chance. They knew Angelique had been born and then died. We had a phone-call three months after she died. My mother said – I heard about

117

Angelique. It is just one of those things.' In this piece of work I had been working on establishing coherence within continuity over time, while also teasing out the remnants of his wish for care for himself rather than completely dismissing the importance of wanting to be looked after.

Marie had also had separations as a child. Her mother had been in hospital when she was one year old, and Marie had also been in hospital herself as an infant and then again when two and a half years. She thus had her own reasons for crying over her husband's 'swinging on the gate' story. She could not remember much of her childhood. She had different styles of attachment to each parent. Her father was very strict and hard. He had been wounded in the war when a shell hit a house that he was sheltering in and killed all his companions. He had been profoundly affected. She told me that the only time that he would be comforting to his children was when they were ill, but the incident Marie used to illustrate this was her father bringing her food once when she had flu'. In contrast Marie's relationship with her mother was close. Marie grew up to develop an Insecure/Preoccupied style of narrative, but also learned to use an avoidant defence when under considerable pain, as when not visiting Henrie's dying nephew. The two strategies are on a continuum; not opposites. A coherent story can link the two.

### Leaving Home and 'Familyectomies'

Both their families had histories of cutting off members of the family. Marie had been thrown out by her father when she was a teenager, as were some of her siblings. Henrie had been disowned by his family for marrying Marie as she was an unmarried mother. He had also cut himself off from his first family and had left his first wife and twin girls in France. He had not been in touch with them since, explaining he said 'Once you have gone it is best to go completely'. Later when Marie's family disapproved of something Henrie had done the couple cut themselves off from them. More recently Henrie had cut himself off from his family of origin (having made contact following the original disowning) because of lack of support over Angelique's death. I used the surgical metaphor of 'familyectomy' to describe this form of distancing. They understood it perfectly.

The couple also used to threaten to leave each other – 'maritalectomy'. Henrie also used to threaten to leave therapy as it was no help – 'therapyectomy', which I came to recognise was sometimes a test to see whether I had spotted that Henrie had in fact put a lot of effort into therapy. It was also partly an attempt to make me pull my therapeutic socks up. My story about this was that the threat of 'ectomies' were initially attempts to make others come closer, but if that failed could swiftly be put into action as self-protection against feeling very hurt and rejected. Both strategies could be woven into the same coherent story, to be found in both families of origin and within the here and now.

In the fourth session I learned that Pierre had to go to a boarding school for epileptics as he could not be educated locally. I had to struggle against an impulse to prevent this happening, which was hardly surprising considering my own experience of boarding schools. However as it seemed inevitable I decided to support this process. I used the metaphor of 'familyectomy' to help the family to avoid Pierre leave home feeling that he had been thrown out, or cut off angrily by his parents.

### Fifth Session: oedipal conflicts

The family had visited a potential school. Pierre started by telling me that he had had a dream in which he had been chased away. He then played a game in which two 'doll' men fought. Pierre smashed one down on the other in a what he called 'a 12 foot slammer' in which the brains of the attacked man was 'smashed'. I linked this to the previous work on having his own brain 'smashed' by the surgeon. However this did not seem to fit and he talked about the 'fat boss' whose head was being slammed, and how the 'slammer' was very very angry. I remember realising that the 'fat boss' was probably his stepfather, and the 'slammer' was Pierre turning the tables.

A little later Mother was telling me about how she was finding it difficult and embarrassing because Pierre was pushing his face into her breasts. She explained that Pierre had had to have injections of growth hormone since his brain operation, which had the side effect of making him sexually precocious. She described how she had been cuddling Pierre more as she had been desperately missing the dead Angelique and had been longing for another baby. I said to Pierre that it must have been difficult because he had to be two people for his mother, himself and his dead sister. And pointed out the muddle for mother who so much wanted cuddles with Pierre but then found it difficult, as he was now too grown up.

Henrie then described an incident in which he had been talking to his wife and Pierre had suddenly turned and smashed his hand into his face in a way that was painful. Henrie said 'There is a time and place for most things, but that was not a joke!' I then had a break the session in which I met with the group that were observing through the one way

119

screen. This gave me the space to put all these elements together. I came back and said that we had a story about Pierre's dream; 'We wondered whether the dream was about worries about having to leave home and being chased away from home, because he was going to be sent away to school.' Pierre corrected me 'Scare me away'. I went on 'You (to Pierre) may be frightened that if you get too close to you (pointing to mother), You (pointing at step-father) could get jealous and want to throw you (pointing at Pierre) out'. This was a way of making a systemic oedipal story.

Mother told me that Pierre sometimes tried to get into bed with his parents. Pierre said, 'I don't know why Mums and Dads have to sleep together.' It became clear however that Pierre knew that it was to make love, but what he was not sure about was whether that meant his stepfather hurt his mother (there was no evidence of marital violence). I said that I thought that it often looked as if making love was being aggressive. 'Maybe (to mother) Pierre wants to be there to protect you?' I was opening up the possibility of Pierre's relationship with his mother being both protective and Oedipal. I then returned to how being sent to boarding school could feel like being thrown out. Stepfather looked thoughtful and said 'Maybe it feels like rejection.'

### Diagnosis Narrative

It became clear that mother's certainty that Angelique's death had led to Pierre's tumour was disturbing to Pierre. In one session he was standing in the middle of the room and pretending to be his sister, and then took his finger from the chest (where he imagined Angelique had suffered her fatal illness) and made a buzzing noise as if a flying insect had left the chest and then flown around the room to land on his own head. 'Now I have worse troubles than she had.' He had, as would be expected at his age a very concrete version of the transmission. At the next meeting with the parents on their own I explored mother's beliefs. Eventually she came to understand why she had held on to that belief so tenaciously. It was less disturbing to her than her deep anxiety that she had caused it by taking an overdose while she was pregnant with Pierre. Her 'stress causes cancer' belief could now be seen as a defensive belief. This new explanation for her certainty about an illness whose cause is uncertain was made more plausible.

## 5. Toward a Coherent Story About Illness and Loss

### Care and Control Dilemmas

In one session Pierre was very restless, and came out with the idea that it should have been he who died and not Angelique. This revelation was of course a gift to a therapist, but as both I and mother, pursued this topic Pierre became more and more noisy and distracted until it was difficult to think. Henrie started to tell him to shut up, but Pierre escalated his behaviour and become very rude to his stepfather. Marie tried to explain to her husband why Pierre was so distracted, adding 'You just think he is being naughty.' I agreed with Mother although I did not say so. Henrie threatened to leave, and said that therapy was no good. It was Pierre saying 'Mum and me and John have brains, you have no brains!' that warned me that I now had an alliance with mother against father. In the break a senior GP family therapist asked what I would have done if Pierre had not had a tumour. I would, of course, normally have been helping the parents to work as a team to discipline Pierre so that he would settle and we could continue the session. Caring for children requires both understanding and discipline. It is particularly easy to disqualify discipline for ill children, and indeed try to protect them from it, as mother and then I had done. This was a pivotal session as it brought Henrie's authority into the family in a positive way, and Pierre's hyperactivity which had driven mother to feeling murderous towards him settled down. Trying to protect Pierre had been actually exposing him to greater risk.

### Marital Work: the dog story

After Pierre went to boarding school he did surprisingly well. Henrie had mentioned in the very first session that he and his wife were only staying together because of Pierre, so in my jargon Pierre was his parent's distance regulator (Byng-Hall, 1980). It was predictable then that trouble would increase in the marriage when Pierre left home. It did, and a period of work on the couple's relationship followed. One day they came with the news that things were much better. But Henrie said there was just one thing that could still wreck their marriage, which was Marie's request to have another dog. She wept as she described how desperate she was to have a dog to cuddle. Henrie seemed very cruel in opposing it. I asked about their last dog which was greatly missed by Marie when they had to part with it. Henrie had apparently been against having that dog, and he complained that she had just gone ahead and got it without planning it together. Something made me ask whether Angelique had been planned. This led into a powerful story about conception and its vicissitudes. When they first met Marie had had trouble conceiving and had an appointment to go to the fertility clinic. They did not take precautions because this appeared to be unnecessary. When they arrived at the clinic however Marie was found to be pregnant.

Henrie felt trapped into marriage by this, although delighted about the pregnancy. Soon after Angelique's birth Marie went for a consultation about sterilisation. She was put on a two year waiting list. However the next day they rang to say that they had had a cancellation and so she was sterilised almost straight away. After Angelique's death she went to have the sterilisation reversed. She became pregnant but it was ectopic and she nearly died. After that Henrie refused to co-operate on having another final try for a baby. This had upset Marie who could not understand his attitude. In this session however Henrie told his wife that he had seen how she had been devastated by the loss of Angelique and the ectopic pregnancy, and of course they had Pierre's uncertain future hanging over them. He said that he would never ever again expose her to the risk of being hurt by the risk of having another ectopic pregnancy. 'You would be in mental hospital for the rest of your life'. Henrie explained that he knew that the dog would be a substitute baby and that it would also die one day. 'That was the reason that it would not be a good idea.'

Finally it was possible to explore how Marie and Henrie each had the protection of the other in mind, although each suggested an approach antithetical to the other. He wanted her to give up the risk of getting attached. She wanted him to become more engaged. This acknowledgement of mutual care gave them a sense that they did live on the same planet after all. They then moved on to do some marital therapy. At a two year follow-up the parents were still together, with some conflict but it was manageable, and Pierre was doing well.

## References

Ainsworth, M.D.S.; Blehar, R.M.C.; Waters, E. and Wall, S. (1978) *Patterns of Attachment: A Psychological Study of the Strange Situation*, Hillsdale, NJ: Erlbaum.

Altschuler, J. (1996) *Working with Chronic Illness: a systemic approach*, London: Macmillan Press.

Bowlby, J. (1973) *Attachment and Loss* Vol. 2 *Separation*: Anxiety and Anger, London: Hogarth.

Byng-Hall, J. (1973) 'Family Myths Used as Defence in Conjoint Family Therapy', *British Journal of Medical Psychology*, 46: 239-50.
—— (1979) 'Re-editing Family Mythology During Family Therapy', *Journal of Family Therapy*, 1:2 103-16.
—— (1980) 'The Symptom Bearer as Marital Distance Regulator: clinical implications', *Family Process*, 19: 355-65.
—— (1982) 'Family Legends: their Significance for the Family Therapist', in A. Bentovim, A. Cooklin & G. Gorell Barnes (eds), *Family Therapy: complementary frameworks of theory and practice*, Vol 2, London: Academic Press.
—— (1990) 'Attachment Theory and Family Therapy: A Clinical View', *Infant Mental Health Journal*, 11:3 228-36.
—— (1995a) *Rewriting Family Scripts: improvisation and systems change*, New York and London: Guilford Press.
—— (1995b) 'Creating a Secure Family Base: some implications of attachment theory for family therapy', *Family Process* 34:1 45-58.
—— (1996) 'A family's Experience of Adjusting to Loss', in J.Altschuler (ed), *Working with Chronic Illness: a systemic approach*, London: Macmillan Press.
—— (in press, a) 'Recurring nightmares: heroic efforts', in S.H. McDaniel, J. Hepworth & W. Doherty (eds), *Stories of Medical Family Therapy: towards the practice of collaborative family health care*, Basic Books: New York.
—— (in press, b) 'Creating a Coherent Story in Family Therapy', in G. Roberts & J. Holmes (eds), *Narrative Approaches in Psychiatry and Psychotherapy*, Oxford University Press: Oxford.
Cain, A.C. and Fast, I. (1972) 'Children's Disturbed Reactions to Parent Suicide', in A.C. Cain (ed.), *Survivors of Suicide*, Springfield, Illinois: C.C. Thomas.
Dale, B. (1996) 'Parenting and Chronic Illness', in J. Altschuler (ed), *Working with Chronic Illness: a systemic approach*, London: Macmillan Press.
Fonagy, P.; Steele, M.; Steele, H.; Moran, G.S. and Higgit, A.C. (1991) 'The Capacity for Understanding Mental States: the reflective self/parent in mother and child and its significance for security of attachment', *Infant Mental Health Journal*, 12:3 201-18.
Judd, D. (1989) *Give Sorrow Words: working with a dying child*, London: Free Association Books.
Main, M. (1991) 'Metacognitive Knowledge, Metacognitive Monitoring, and Singular (Incoherent) vs. Multiple (Incoherent) Models of Attachment: findings and directions for future research', in C.M. Parkes, J. Stevenson-Hinde, & P. Marris (eds), *Attachment Across the Life Cycle*, London, New York: Tavistock/Routledge.
Main, M. and Goldwyn, R. (1985-1996) *Adult Attachment Scoring and Classification System*, unpublished manuscript, Department of Psychology, University of California: Berkeley.
Main, M. and Hess, E. (1990) 'Parent's Unresolved Traumatic Experiences are Related to Infant Disorganisation Attachment Status: is frightened and/or frightening parental behaviour the linking mechanism?' In M.T. Greenberg, D. Cicchetti, and E.M. Cummings, (eds), *Attachment in the Preschool Years:*

*Theory, Research, and Intervention*, Chicago and London: University of Chicago Press.

Main, M.; Kaplan, N. and Cassidy, J. (1985) 'Security in Infancy, Childhood, and Adulthood: a move to the level of representation', in I. Bretherton & Waters E., *Growing Points of Attachment Theory and Research*, Monograph of the society for research in child development, Serial No. 209, vol 50, Nos 1-2., University of Chicago Press: Chicago.

Pianta, R.C.; Marvin, R.S.; Britner, P.A. and Borowitz, K.C. (1996) 'Mother's Resolution of Their Children's Diagnosis: organised patterns of caregiving representations', *Infant Mental Health Journal*, 17:3 239-56.

Slade, A, and Cohen, L.J. (1996) 'The process of parenting and remembrance of things past', *Infant Mental Health Journal*, 17:3 217-38.

# Different Language/Different Gender

## Narratives of Inclusion and Exclusion

*Barbara Dale and Jenny Altschuler*

Illness is the night-side of life, a more onerous citizenship. Everyone who is born holds dual citizenship, in the kingdom of the well and in the kingdom of the sick. Although we all prefer to use only the good passport, sooner or later each of us is obliged, at least for a spell, to identify ourselves as citizens of that other place.

Susan Sontag, 1991, p. 3

### Introduction

This quote from Susan Sontag graphically introduces the politics of illness, the profound importance of staying healthy and not becoming a citizen of the other place. In this Susan Sontag stresses how it is impossible to take up a position in the kingdom of the ill unprejudiced by metaphors that include implications of shame and personal blame. The families that we have seen in therapy have shown us how costly it is for the ill to carry the responsibility of keeping the well safe. It is in the face of these pressures that ill and healthy parents have to find a way of renegotiating the meaning of parenting when they find themselves or their partners ill, in pain, incapacitated and facing the possibility of death. For this chapter we have drawn on clinical work with parents who are in heterosexual relationships where one member is seriously ill. We explore how illness can challenge the way in which men and women relate to one another, altering the stories of what can be known and understood.

We have elected here to look at specific aspects of heterosexual couple relationships: at how gender may construct the experience of illness. This chapter does not include the wider spectrum of families we have seen, nor does it include other major issues like race, culture, or on how sexuality/sexual preference influence ways in which people cope with illness. Whilst such a decision inevitably relegates important aspects of our understanding of these families to the margin, we have done so to have a clearer focus on the different experience of men and women in responding to parental illness.

We all select from different options in deciding how to talk or describe ourselves, ultimately establishing a view that becomes the dominant description of our lives (Reissman, 1990). Most families rely on long standing ways of coping in crisis situations, providing comfort and security when life seems most difficult. However, when a parent is seriously ill, both they and their partner are frequently pushed into new roles which denies them the protection familiarity can bring. Our work suggests that having to assume new roles when they are most vulnerable increases the pressure parents experience, and this in turn affects their ability to be supportive to one another.

Exploring these issues has not been one way: it has co-evolved between ourselves and the families, confronting us as well as the families with the limitations of our and their understanding, experience and ability to tolerate pain. Like the families we discuss, we are both parents, and members of couple relationships. As women, we have been confronted with the need to reconsider personal and professional views, challenging our responses to illness and to our own and the families' use of language.

The parents involved have allowed us to learn about the ways in which, at the most intimate and poignant moments, they can misjudge and mislead each other and so find themselves unable to provide or receive the support that was intended. We have also learned that couples can experience a new, intimate closeness at times of acute illness only to find that as recovery comes and they return to their old ways of relating, they loose the intimacy that was so special.

## The Project

As members of the Systems Family Therapy team, in 1994, we undertook, with John Byng-Hall, to see all families where physical illness was mentioned on referral to the Child and Family Clinic. Our side of the project was to explore the cases of parental illness. What emerged as we read the literature, was that whilst increased attention was being paid to the impact of childhood illness on the ill child (Eiser, 1994; Cadman et al., 1987), their parents (Greenberg and Meadows, 1991) siblings

126

(Lobato, Faust and Spirito, 1988) and peers (Spirito, DeLawyer and Stark, 1992), there was little research on parental illness. Despite the growing interest in the psychological implication of illness for families, ill adults are rarely asked about their children, or about the impact of their illness on parenting. Parents are almost never helped to think about sharing their diagnosis with their children, or how to prepare children for their hospital admission. Whilst health documents recommend parents remain in close contact with children during childhood admission (Department of Health, 1990), no similar encouragement exist for ill adults: with the exception of certain intensive care units, there are hardly any facilities for children in hospital units.

The avoidance of discussion about children by health care professionals can be seen as a way of protecting used by parents to protect themselves from further stress. It also protects professionals from experiencing the pain of children's distress about the illness of their parent. However, our experience is that far from protecting, it can compound their difficulties, leaving parents to struggle alone in thinking about how their illness might be affecting their children. Some parents' willingness to collude with this may well be based on a wish to minimise the extent to which their children are 'contaminated' by illness. Whichever choice is made, the role of the parent cannot be detached from the illness. We have found that in making the story more open, new strength in both parents and children can come to the fore.

In attempting to generalise from the families that we discuss here, it is important to recognise that they are a specific sample: families referred to a child and family mental health unit. They can be seen as representing people who have experienced particular problems with parenting, or those for whom parenting is of primary importance. However, most frequently they are both, their concern for their children allowing them to risk seeking help at this most vulnerable time in family life.

## Illness and Society

In recent years, medical science has begun to show increased interest in the connection between psychological attitude and physical well-being (Greer and Silberfarb, 1982, and others). For some people, this has resulted in their being able to challenge the sense of helplessness and hopelessness they had previously experienced. For example, the basis of current treatment of heart and coronary disease is an emphasis on a change in life-style and dietary control. Whilst this information can be helpful at one level, it can unwittingly add to the burden of being ill, creating pressure to behave in the so called 'right' way.

The nature of this pressure varies with the way in which each illness is portrayed by society. For example, cancer has been described as 'a disease of uncontrollable growth that invades the body' (Lupton, 1994, p. 69), as a 'demonic pregnancy' (Sontag, 1989, p. 14). The term is used to describe uncontrollable disaster, as when drug abuse is seen as the cancer of society, or in common with AIDS, it is frequently represented as a punishment for unhealthy living.

As one of us was diagnosed with breast cancer while working on this project, we do not underestimate the personal impact of these sorts of statements, particularly the global use of the word cancer as the description of evil in society. Obviously, this has had a profound impact on our work with families and our relationship with one another. It strengthened our resolve to take time to think about our own connections to the work and to use our personal knowledge when appropriate. The practical changes we had to make over the time when one of us was unavailable, allowed us to explore ways of using ourselves more interchangeably. This has resulted in some of the families talking to us about our different approaches and using us in differing ways.

Society and health care professionals support the idea that portraying a positive mental attitude can be seen as the way to achieve victory over illness, and thus essential in the battle for health. This however moves the idea from positive to negative, the idea that unless the patient remains positive they are in some way to blame. Representations such as these play a powerful part in influencing how both ill and healthy partners experience the illness, affecting the way in which they relate to themselves and each other.

We would not wish to devalue the importance of being able to retain a positive mental attitude in the face of severe illness: for many it has been crucial to sustaining a sense of future in the face of invasive treatments and progressive physical deterioration. However, keeping up the right attitude can in itself be exhausting, so that it should not be seen as an 'either or', but an 'as well as'. Helping families find a way of acknowledging exhaustion in the patient without being seen as giving up the fight has been an important part of our work. We have come to understand the idea of denial differently: it can be helpful and supportive until the time is right to explore a different position, which for some patients and family members may be never. We have had to learn to be very sensitive about pace: at times the ill person can go much faster than

128

the rest of the family. Part of our role as therapist is to hold the balance, which at times is a deeply painful position.

Many of the ill parents we have seen found that the invasiveness of the illness awoke earlier life experiences. Wambolt et al. (1995) reported a similar finding when working with parents of sick children. The return of these experiences may come in flashbacks or may be experienced as a pervasive sense of unworthiness, intensifying the suggestion of having brought the illness on themselves. Couples can then come to think that difficulties in their own relationship are a further demonstration that they are in some way to blame. What makes this even more complex, is that society frequently conveys the idea that families will 'pull together' at times of crisis, adding to their confusion and distress at finding themselves unable to do so.

Many of the couples we see face a Herculean task: responding to the demands of the illness, to parenting in the context of serious illness and anticipated death, and to changes in their relationship as a couple.

## Theoretical Constructs

The longitudinal research studies undertaken by Carol Gilligan, Jean Baker Miller and colleagues at Harvard and The Stone Center on the growth and development of women and their relationships in adult life have been very influential in the development of our clinical approach. Their work, together with other (Burck and Daniel, 1995) has highlighted how the model of autonomous independence as a definition of adulthood does not connect with many aspects of women's experience. Increasingly, it has been recognised that this understanding, researched on male undergraduate students, presents a restrictive model for the development of men as well (Real, 1995). This shift in understanding not only affects us as therapists, but has importance for the families we have been seeing. As the theory of autonomous independence supported the patriarchal values of our culture, it has been taken as a 'truth', and as such has silenced the voices and perceptions of women, and increasingly of men (Foucalt, 1980).

Our earlier work had led us to examine the influence of gender (Altschuler, 1993; Dale and Emerson, 1994). We had a speculation that women, if armed with the scientific 'objective' language of illness, may experience ownership of their knowledge and find their voices more clearly. This idea was supported by the work of Christine Eiser in her extensive research with parents of children growing up with illness (1994). She suggests that women who have become familiar with medical knowledge experience greater confidence and willingness to be assertive on behalf of their children (1997).

Whilst the examination of gender theory has been very helpful in assisting us in the development of a way of understanding relationships, we are aware of the risk of developing our own essentialist beliefs. In attempting to avoid this, we are indebted to the critical review of our colleagues who exemplify the 'both and' position. 'The assumption that no one observation is exclusively true means we have to struggle with the necessary contradictions' (Goldner, 1985, p. 21).

As we will later show in the case material, the language of men and women can be very different, and their differing reliance on subjective or objective ways of exploring their experiences can lead to deeply distressing difficulties. Developing an understanding that respects both ways of thinking can be a daunting task when placed against a background of the inevitably progression of some illnesses.

Three research projects have been particularly influential in developing our thinking about the dilemmas parents face in renegotiating an identity as parents in the face of illness. The first is Carol Gilligan's research on moral development (1982), and later longitudinal studies of the development of girls (Gilligan, Lyons and Hammer, 1990) suggests that while boys are encouraged to become independent at around seven or eight years, girls make their first real move for independence in adolescence. Until that time, they are encouraged to remain close and involved in relationships both within the family and friendship groups. This provides girls with greater opportunity to develop emotionally, placing an emphasis on their experience of themselves in relationships.

This faces girls with a dilemma. Up to adolescence, they have developed openly connected relationships. Their sense of self has evolved through the experience of being in a relationship. At adolescence there is an expectation that they will move into adult life, and the accepted mode for this is autonomous independence. Gilligan suggests that women are placed in a 'no win' situation. If they become autonomous and independent, they have to push their need for relationship away and become isolated or go underground and become a professional carer. If they declare their need for staying with relationships, they are seen as lacking independence, immature or even selfish.

Seeking relationships by including oneself, such as being selfless as a wife or mother is, Gilligan suggests, a strategy destined to fail. At times of great stress, such as personal illness, when the need for relationships is urgent, women frequently find that their family is so inexperienced at recognising their needs, that their sudden demand can be seen as irrational, over-demanding or even pathological.

The movement to revise understanding about men's development too has been growing. Real (1995) and others have begun to explore the limits of the model of disconnection for men's experience of fathering.

A second longitudinal research project, led by Jean Baker Miller (1989) focused on women and their relationships with their mothers and friends. From this, they formulated a theory of self-in-relationship, suggesting that women know themselves through relationships with others, rather than seeing themselves as separately autonomous. This approach emphasises the centrality of mutuality in relationships to women's development towards maturity. A sense of mutuality implies that both members of a relationship respects the integrity of the other person. The relationship is not based on one person servicing another's needs, but of providing personal space for difference, whilst at the same time retaining the committed security of the relationship. This highlights the impossibility of retaining a sense of mutuality in relationships where women are carers only, such relationships deny women space to own their needs, interfering with their ability to know who they are and what they think.

The third study of Belenky, Clinchy, Goldberger and Tarule (1986) examined how women learn and understand their right to have ownership of what they know. In interviews with women across a range of institutions, including universities and welfare agencies, they explored women's views on what is important about life and learning. They categorised the women into groups, ranging from the 'silent knowers', who gave no value to their own life experience but only learnt from others, to the 'constructivists': women who included the subjective with the objective, the rational with the relational.

When one partner is seriously ill, and risks having to alter previous forms of connection and intimacy, the demands placed on men and women's sense of self identity can be considerable. From our work with couples facing primary and secondary cancer, motor neurone disease, multiple sclerosis, heart disease and the effects of severe cerebral haemorrhaging, parents tend to adopt one of three patterns in finding a way of renegotiating their relationships. Clearly, this depends not only on the ill parent, but on the responses of the physically healthy parent as well.

### Solutions Taken by Men and Women Who Are Ill

The men who are ill seen in the project so far, have become much more central in their family lives. They have developed closer relationships with their children. However, the experience of being in the house throughout the day has brought its own pressures of isolation. One father who cares for his wife and is at home full time has tried to develop relationships with men in similar situations, as he has found it difficult to develop friendships with women who are full-time carers.

The position of ill women has varied much more. In some of the families, we met seriously ill women who had in many ways been able to voice their own needs. However, as primary carers within the family, they had also been trained to understate their own problems within the family. Many of these women attempted to separate their illness from their family. However, this was often damaging to their own need to be cared for, leading the family into confusion with distressing consequences for all. The mother did not receive the care that she needed, and, insulated from the sense of being required to respond to her needs, partners and children acted in a seemingly uncaring way. Alternately, women unused to voicing any of their needs within their families, relied on past experiences of support, often taking problems to where they knew they would be understood: to mothers or friends. For some, neither solution existed, and they kept their own needs to themselves at a high cost.

What many found most confusing was that the crisis of feeling their lives were at risk resulted in outbursts and accusations, creating the very tension and distress their caring behaviour was meant to avoid. Compounding this, few mothers and fathers had had any sort of rehearsal for meeting the situation they now faced. Moreover, where the family had already been struggling with problems, women tended to see their illness as linked with these problems, and had a sense that it might be believed that they or the family caused it. Men more frequently see a connection between their illness and their life style.

### Case Studies

Three case studies will be presented to illustrate these themes more fully.

### 1. The Illness Is Not the Problem

At the time of referral, the Williams family denied that the mother's cancer had any bearing on the problems they were facing. In speaking about her illness Alice (the mother) said:

> Occasionally I am visibly upset. I try to keep a stiff upper lip. I have to go out to friends and do other things.' When speaking about her all male family she said 'Men don't shift for themselves; I've got a tough shell because I've had very little protection. I can't ask for moral support, I'm carrying on as normal; its more encouraging. I find it hard to stay in bed.

Alice's words highlighted her attempt to silence her own needs, and comply with what she felt was a moral injunction to fight her condition in a positive, non-complaining way. She therefore took her relational needs to friends who accompanied her to hospital treatments.

There had been times however, when the pattern of meeting relational needs outside the family was broken, and her eldest son, Evan, acted as her confidant. Asked how his mother's illness had changed his life, he said:

> I've been made to change it. A decision I made I regret now – I was just determined, just to carry on and do what I usually did. Everyone in the household made me feel guilty. At the beginning I spent a lot of time pondering what I was going to do. I think that is what we all did, which affected mum.

Evan at this time was in his mid-teens, poised on the edge of adulthood. The model for adulthood conveyed by his parents and school, was one of autonomous independence, expressed in terms of rational argument and independent action. At times, he responded to his mother's relational needs, and at others, ignored them. As suggested by Real (1995), either option challenged his expectations of himself, expectations of how connected or disconnected to he ought be. While he might gain a great deal from being close to his mother at this stage, to respond in a way that was so different to his father challenged the family model of how to respond as a man. Furthermore, it could jeopardise his relationship with his father. His ambivalence about the lack of response in the family and also the unexpected surges in his mother's open emotional request for attention, is reflected in the following statement:

> It's made Mum a stronger person; she had to stand-up for herself, sometimes she has taken it a bit too far and gone over the top.

Like others in the family, Evan struggled with how his mother's distress about her illness would suddenly emerge within the family where it then became confused and distorted by existing family problems. Whilst Evan felt blamed, he too was able partially to justify his behaviour since previous problems were so entangled in their distress.

Christ, Siegel and Seber (1994), in their paper on the impact on adolescents of terminal illness in parents, suggest that there is a distinct difference in gender response. Girls are expected to be involved in the care of the parent, reducing their freedom to be part of their changing world beyond the home. However, they are entitled to stay close to their sick parent, retaining intimate connection at a time of maximum distress. Boys are freer to distance themselves and continue their lives outside of the family. This respects their need for independence, but leaves them isolated in dealing with their fears and anxieties.

There were many times when her husband, Albert, experienced himself as concerned about Alice's illness. However, when he demonstrated this by asking how she was, Alice responded she was 'all right'. She expected him to observe that she was unwell, but Albert responded to her verbal statement rather than the non-verbal process of interaction. This resulted in words rather than feelings being the dominant discourse. The outcome was that Albert felt his concern was heard, but Alice felt her experience was ignored.

Alice was an articulate, able woman and a good intellectual sparring partner. Much of the excitement of the relationship for both partners was found in intellectual exchange. Albert experienced failure in the face of Alice's emotional needs, finding it impossible to reconcile her apparent engagement with him in intellectual discussion with her statement that her emotional needs were not being met.

> Life can be quite normal, she can go to work [Alice worked all through her treatment]. It [the illness] keeps recurring as a thought. She was very ill for brief periods of time with the chemotherapy. Normal physical things are much as before, she says she feels tired now which may be as a result of the illness. If I didn't know that she had the disease I couldn't tell'. [At this time, Alice was still wearing a wig.]

For Albert, intellectual excitement was an emotional experience. He was essentially a solitary man, who was instrumental and caring in his job, gaining considerable satisfaction in providing structures that gave space for his colleagues to excel. He had therefore attempted to respond to Alice in a similar way: providing structural changes to the household. However, he failed to respond to her need for her distress to be heard, and her experience validated.

## 6. Different Language/Different Gender

Albert said:

> I don't express my feelings very much. It could produce a degree of stability, two people getting highly emotional might not be the best way of dealing with it.

While they had previously both valued intellectual sparring, this could no longer meet their needs as a couple: it had edged out all other discussion. Albert's fear of being abandoned by Alice had awakened his own powerful relational needs. Our sense was that in the past Alice may have responded to this at a non-verbal level, without Albert having to ask, or acknowledge them to himself.

At times, Alice's own fear became overwhelming to her, resulting in her expressing extreme anger.

> I lost my hair within three weeks. That was just the worst thing, I couldn't bear it. You wouldn't talk to me, you made me feel bad about it, only friends helped.

Both Albert and Alice were on foreign territory: their relationship had no prior repertoire for hearing and responding to such desperate needs. The caustic attrition that developed between them had a devastating effect on their children as well as themselves, affecting the extent to which Evan could acknowledge his own need to remain close to his mother.

We have noticed that several parents in families facing such enormous distress experience great difficulty in keeping their children's needs in mind. This is not dissimilar to what can happen during parental separation or divorce, where children may cease to make their demands heard as the only contribution they can make to reconcile their warring parents. Alice and Albert's shared construction of meaning had previously been based on intellectual constructs only: they had little capacity to co-construct meaning over areas of intimacy dependent on feelings (Weingarten, 1991). This left them exposed and raw when faced with the crisis of illness. They were unable to co-create a meaning that respected the integrity of the other's position. They had no facility to develop mutuality (Baker Miller, 1991).

## 2. Problems Caused by the Illness

The McNally family were referred to the clinic by their GP, as Jack was concerned about the effect of his wife, Betty's illness on their children. For this couple there was greater imbalance in the extent to which the mother and father used words to understand their experiences. For Jack, words were an important expression of himself, but Betty rarely used words to portray her understanding of her own experience. In Belenky's terms, she was a 'subjectivist': she seemed to depend on experience to understand the world, with little perception of herself as able to understand ideas that depended on objective language rather than observation.

Before her illness, Betty had devoted herself to her husband and children with little contact outside her home. Jack had worked long hours and spent weekends totally absorbed in his hobby of traction engines. Betty's illness meant he diverted his time to the care of the children. Whilst some parents develop a sense of mutuality over their parenting decisions, if not in their couple relationship, Jack and Betty had only one model of being parents: one which only minimally included negotiated or collaborative decisions and actions.

In sessions, questions directed at Betty were answered by Jack who appeared to 'own' his wife's illness (Belenky, 1986). It seems possible that Jack gained comfort and confidence in the scientific explanations he acquired about Betty's illness: in some small way, it gave him the feeling that everything was not out of control. This had been a long standing pattern as Betty had hardly ever voiced her opinions, particularly about herself (Gilligan 1982/90). She would talk with an animation about the children that was lacking when any discussion focused on her. With little practice in putting her own needs into words, one of the ways in which Betty responded to Jack was to demand more personal attention. Jack's mother suggested that Betty was now 'speaking' for the years of silence when Jack's views had dominated their decisions.

In therapy, Jack often questioned the actual words we used: for example, he corrected us when we spoke of their having decided to come to therapy, or how they had decided what their children most needed now. The word implied a sense of agency he no longer felt about his experience. The distress and intense isolation he himself had experienced in childhood meant that he had come to rely on words for providing him with the comfort of certainty in times of crisis, relying on books for understanding his experience.

His mother's decussion with him enabled Jack to hear his wife differently. His new experience of Betty's angry and critical outbursts led him to be more watchful of her non-verbal expression of feelings. As the couple's relationship had previously been centred around parenting this created an altered intimacy between them which may have awakened earlier experiences for Betty, experiences that were confusing to deal with in the present.

Jack's own earlier life had been greatly influenced by his stepmother's critical comments. What he had prized in Betty was her dedication to parenting, and her non-critical acceptance of the children and himself. Since her illness, Betty's need to be heard was at times expresssed in sudden outbursts of feeling. From Jack's view point, Betty's unexplained, 'explosive' outbursts had cut through the basis of their previous relationship.

As with the first couple, experiences of unrehearsed outbursts of emotion had left Betty and Jack struggling with new and disturbing dimensions in their relationship. Betty's illness had presented them both with a completely new set of problems.

Jack's new, more intimate, relationship with his children increased his ability to observe his experience in relationships. The urgency engendered by Betty's demands for more of her own space increased pressure on him to transfer this learning to his relationship with her.

We have seen a similar process in other families, where the father's illness has altered the father's intimacy with their children. Where a father is very ill or dying, their need to be close to their children highlights their lack of experience in staying connected in emotional relationships. Remaining at home for long periods whilst their illness is treated (or as a carer) can bring fathers into contact with their children in a way they have frequently not experienced before. Jack spoke with pleasure about his new relationship with his children as their primary carer. However, he struggled at times with the intensity of their needs.

### 3. The Illness as the Problem

The Cairn family contacted the clinic as they were concerned about the impact on their children of Graham's (the father) rapidly deteriorating secondary cancer. The couple's relationship seemed to have primarily been formed around parenting. This enabled them to retain a certain level of distance in their couple relationship. However, the demands of the illness and hopes for their children confronted them with a need to rethink this, allowing them to risk coming for therapy.

Whilst a great deal of our work involves meeting with the whole family, in common with some other parents, this couple chose to attend therapy alone first, to establish whether they could trust us in helping them speak to their children. In exploring what these parents wanted

137

their children to know, and later establishing what their children already knew, it became apparent that they each had different ways of articulating their ideas.

In a session with the parents only, Claire expressed her wish to anticipate Graham's needs without his needing to say them. She felt enormously distressed that she had not always been able to do this. Her comments took Graham by surprise, opening up their shared fear that when left alone, Claire would not feel confident in her parenting. While Graham saw her as a good, committed mother, he was frustrated that he had never been able to convince her of that. Claire was immensely critical of herself, and unable to experience herself as Graham saw her.

What we observed, was that Claire was thoughtful, protective and respectful of the children's wishes. For example, when one child became distressed about attending therapy sessions, Claire gave her daughter a clear message that she would have expected her to find it difficult talking about her father's illness, but she would not be made to come. She also respected her daughter's wish not to disclose to her friends at school that she was coming to the clinic. Throughout this negotiation, Claire showed herself well able to manage her children and they indicated they had confidence in her judgement and respect for their position. Although Graham was present for these discussions, it was Claire who took the active role in these complex negotiations. As we have learnt elsewhere (Dale and Emerson, 1994) as therapists, we could easily become drawn into praising Claire's parenting in the hope that this would 'empower' her. However, to do so would have risked adding to the disconnection she experienced from her own sense of self.

In order to explore the impact of Claire and Graham's differing styles of structuring their ideas, we shall discuss in greater detail one session with the parents on their own.

Claire had again voiced her doubts about herself and her 'stupidity', whilst Graham expressed frustration that she would not accept his view of her competency. Graham struggled to appreciate that Claire did not see herself that way: he battled with his sense of certainty that what he saw in her must exist as a truth for her as well as him. There was no experience of 'mutuality' in the way the ideas were being expressed. The more this happened, the more diminished Claire felt. Graham wished to respect Claire's view but could not understand why she did not see the (i.e. his) 'truth' (Baker Miller, 1991).

## 6. Different Language/Different Gender

Claire's distress at her experience being owned by others was not confined to her interactions with her husband. She later expressed anger at being spoken about by the therapist as well. We were able to use this experience in exploring how diminished Claire felt by articulate language.

> I can't do it, I can't formulate what I want and that everything kind of gets taken away from me and said for me, not necessarily in the way I want to say it. It happens a lot when we argue. It's always like a competition – he wins all the arguments because he finds it easier to articulate what he wants to say. Yes I got lost last week, I don't know if it was the words, I didn't know how I felt. I couldn't express it because within one sentence I'd feel a hundred different things. I find it so difficult to express myself. It's much easier to let other people do it for me, but it does not say what I want to say. I can't keep up, I feel really slow, really stupid.

In this statement, Claire identified her central dilemma: it was easier to let others speak about her, but this left her feeling they had not expressed what she had wanted to say. In speaking of her own needs, she said:

> I feel a hundred different things.

She showed that she had trained herself not to express these needs even to herself (Gilligan, 1992). So, confronted by the experience of Graham's illness, she was unrehearsed in a language to express her own experience. In not being able to own a language, she felt as though she did not exist: she was not able to recognize herself from other people's description. Her explanation was that she was stupid (Derrida, 1978).

Graham, on the other hand, remained perplexed as to why she avoided accepting her competence, and responded with interpreting her experience yet again.

> The point is you are the one with all the burdens on you. This is what [the therapist] is saying, I think. There are tremendous burdens, and the fact is that you feel inadequate to bear them and for myself I know that you can bear them ... It's a very deep issue; it has to do with your psychological make-up and the past, and that is why the focus is on you.

In trying to convince Claire of his respect for her, by explaining things to her and using terms like 'the point is', he represents his own view as if it were objective fact. However, this was the very language Claire

139

found so 'unknowable'. The more Graham explained Claire's behaviour, the more she became apologetic for remaining unconvinced. Despite intending to hold Claire in equal esteem, Graham's language, based on the rules of autonomous ownership of ideas, gives the understanding that he 'owns' knowledge of Claire. Claire's language remained subjective. However, as objective rather than subjective language is still more highly prized in our society, Claire's self knowledge gave way to the wider truth that others had an objective truth, and therefore a better knowledge of her than she does of herself (Harre, 1989).

'I feel really slow, really stupid'. She could not sanction the words that would express her 'hundreds of ideas'. As further confirmation of her stupidity, she expressed confusion that she was not similarly stupid when she is expressing other people's needs. Drawing on Gilligan's perspective (1990), we suggest that Claire had so subjugated her knowledge of herself, that she had not allowed herself a language to express her experience. The dominate discourse of articulate language she saw others use about themselves, rendered her speechless.

In exploring Graham's sense of self through the use of subjective language, the couple began to experience less difference about how they expressed themselves. Graham found himself with a much higher sense of uncertainty. His sentences became much shorter and less articulate. When asked what Claire may have found attractive in him, he said: 'I've no idea'. Asked to guess, he responded: 'No I haven't [an idea]'. Was he surprised? 'Not especially, I suppose ... didn't see anything profound in me.'

He went on to describe the relationship as 'companionship and pleasure, nothing more serious than that'. Later he reconnected with his experience and said that he was very serious about the relationship, that his experience of other relationships had taught him to compromise, and the importance of that.

Graham then moved away from emotion again and replied to the question whether their relationship had changed since he had become ill by saying he did not understand the question. After further explanation, he went on in distress, stating that they had become closer, and this had made an enormous difference to him: 'the supportiveness, to be loved and cherished.'

He had found new depths in Claire: 'The things I thought I knew were proven, just that she is very strong'. Asked whether it may have been risky before to get too close, Graham returned to minimalising, stating: 'I don't think that is really me, but it might be'. In responding to the same question, Claire said:

> I feel I have wasted an opportunity, I should have faced this years ago.
> Claire to Graham: It frustrates you that I don't.
> Graham: I'm sad about it, you shouldn't find it so difficult to overcome.
> Actually by accident by being ill.
> Claire: You give me a role.
> Graham: I'm sad. Perhaps I haven't tried hard enough and that's sad.

Whereas Claire immediately owns all her experiences, Graham still puts things at a distance. The language is stilted, and taken at face value, it can still sound accusatory. However, within the session, the touching and tears made the meaning very different and distinctly different from their earlier sessions. There was a much greater sense that they have co-constructed a different meaning in which there is intimacy, through mutual respect for their different experiences (Baker Miller, 1991; Weingarten, 1992). This placed the parents in a position to listen to their sons' more strident expressions of distress and their own more open emotional experience.

## Conclusion

In this chapter, we have explored how parental illness may challenge the narrative mothers and fathers have about themselves and their parenting. Drawing on clinical examples, we have attempted to illustrate how illness may result in rethinking the ways in which couples relate to one another and understand their own personal experience. Some parents found a way of reformulating their experience that felt satisfactory, both to themselves and their children. However, this was not always the case: many ill mothers in particular found it difficult to find a way of allowing themselves the opportunity of receiving the care they needed while remaining available to their children.

What we have grown to recognise in our clinical work, is the importance of listening to the story of how men and women construct their experience as parents and couples, prior to the onset of illness. Our sense is that listening in this way is central to joining with them to ensure that the illness does not become the description of the whole of their relationship. We have been able to explore ways of reintroducing previously obscured aspects of their experience, so enabling parents to reclaim their lives subsequent to and during illness. We have also explored with parents their own thoughts on how they could retain the new and special experience of intimacy that can come at times of acute crisis.

As stated earlier, we have placed particular emphasis on couple-relationships as a way of helping parents assume altered roles in the face of illness. Within this project, we have also worked with parents living in families that are constructed differently, and where parents have drawn on other relationships and aspects of their experience in creating new narratives of their parenting. Many factors other than gender affect how ill people respond to their children when ill, or how they experience their medical care.

Whilst some illnesses are very short and immediate, many illnesses are much prolonged. Children develop at a fast pace so that many stages of their development are greatly affected by the length and severity of the parental illness. Sick parents experience the dual sense of their own and their children's lives slipping through their hands. The wish to parent through creating an environment that both stimulates and protects their children is all too often at odds with the unremitting demands of illness.

An important aspect of the therapy has been to help parents place new value on their children's increased maturity, rather than to mourn their loss of innocence. Increased maturity can mean a loss of carefree childhood. However, it can also mean that a child has the chance to be close to the dying parent, to contribute to their care, and most importantly, to know their parents in ways that stay with them into their lives. The importance of having a coherent understanding that children gain from being able to carry a memory of their parents that includes illness and health is of the greatest importance for their development and their ability to make secure relationships in the future.

Working with parents to free the space for this to happen is painful. It can mean increasing the intensity of the session with a sick parent that seems to run counter to ideas of caring for the sick and dying. The contract with a sick parent and his or her partner needs to be made carefully. They need to be able to explore what the effect will be to put pressure on themselves as the work develops. Our experience is that many parents coming to the project are very clear that what they want is a way of helping their children through the experience, frequently being quite specific that they want the children to talk about the illness. For therapists this raises further questions about supporting a positive mental attitude for the ill parent. Is all stress to be avoided, and is a parent to marginalise the experience of illness in order to maximise his or her own chances of survival? Would this diminish stress when previously many parents have prioritised the needs of their children? How far can thinking of your needs as the sick patient be redefined to include some of your needs to parent, but at the same time give a much higher profile to your own needs than the family has experienced before?

As indicated with childhood illness (Eiser, 1994), parents' couple relationships are of central importance in helping children come to terms with their own illness. Here too, it is in helping families deconstruct the complex new and old needs surrounding the experience of being ill, that brings to light the centrality of couple relationships for two-parent families facing a serious physical illness.

As therapists, we have to hold in mind the request of the parents to explore the needs of their children. We have to respect the request so as to legitimise the need to put pressure on families to think more deeply. This respects the integrity of their wish to parent and does not allow the illness to be so dominant a discourse that it subjugates the parenting role, which in turn would undermine their sense of self as a parent and their children's profound needs. The quality of life for sick people who are parents needs to be understood in the whole or they are forced to put at risk the very aspect of themselves that they would give priority to parenting.

*The authors wish to add that all families have been significantly disguised to ensure confidentiality. In addition, they have given their written consent for material from these sessions to be used for the purposes of research.*

### References

Altschuler, J. (1993) 'Gender and Illness: implications for family therapy', *Journal of Family Therapy*, 15 (4) 381-402.

Burck, C. and Daniel, G. (1995) 'Gender Power and Systemic Thinking' in *Gender and Family Therapy*, Karnac Books: London.

Baker Miller, J. (1991) 'The Development of Women's Sense of Self ', in Jordan, J.V.; Kaplan, A.G.; Baker Miller, J.; Stiver, I.P. and Surrey, J.L. (ed.), *Women's Growth in Connection*, Guilford Press: London.

Belenky, M.F. Clinchy, B.M. Goldberger, N.R. and Tarule, J.M. (1986) *Women's Ways of Knowing: the development of self, voice, and mind*, Basic Books: London.

Cadman, D.M. Boyle, D. Szatmari, P. and Offord, D.R. (1987) 'Chronic Illness, Disability and Mental and Social Well-being: findings of the Ontario Child Health Study', *Pediatrics*, 79: 705-12.

Christ, Siegel and Seber (1994) 'The Impact of Parental Cancer on Adolescents', *American Journal of Orthopsychiatry*, 64 (4).

Dale and Emerson (1994) 'The Importance of Being Connected: implications for work with women addicted to drugs', in Burck, C. and Speed, B., *Gender Power and Relationships*, London: Routledge.

Department of Health (1991) *The Welfare of Children and Young People in Hospital*, London: HMSO.

Derrida, J. (1978) *Writings and Differences*, Chicago: University of Chicago Press.

Eiser, C. (1994) 'Social Support in Chronically Sick Children and Their Families', in F. Nestman and K.I. Hurrelman, *Social Networks and Social Support in Childhood and Adolescence*, De Gruyter: Berlin.

—— (1997) 'Growing Up with Childhood Illness', Tavistock Conference Presentation *Who Cares About Illness in the Family?*.

Gilligan, C. (1982) *In a Different Voice: psychological theory and women's development*, Cambridge: Harvard University Press.

Gilligan, C.; Lyons, N.P. and Hammer, T.J. (1990) *Making Connections: the relational world of adolescent girls at Emma Willard School*, Harvard University Press, London.

Goldner, V. (1988) 'Warning: family therapy may be hazardous to your health', *The Family Networker*, 9 (6) 19-23.

Greenberg, H.S. and Meadows, A.T. (1991) 'Psychosocial Impact of Cancer Survival on School-age Children and Their Parents', *Journal of Psychosocial Oncology*, 9 (4) 43-56.

Greer, S. and Silberfarb, P.M. (1982) 'Psychological Concomitants of Cancer: current state of research', *Psychological Medicine*, 12: 563-73.

Harre, R. (1989) 'Language Games and the Texts of Identity', in Shotter, J. and Gergen, K.J. (ed.), *Texts of Identity*, London: Sage.

Hoffman, L. (1990) 'Constructing Realities: an art of lenses', *Family Process*, 29: 1-12.

Jones, E. (1995) 'The Construction of Gender in Family Therapy', in *Gender Power and Relationships*, (ed.) Burck, C. and Speed, B., Routledge.

Lobato, D. Faust, D. and Spirito, A. (1988) 'Examining the Effects of Disease and Disability on Children's Sibling Relationships', *Journal of Paediatric Psychology*, 13 (3) 389-407.

Lupton, D. (1994) *Medicine as Culture: illness, disease and the body in Western societies*, Sage: London.

Parker, G. (1993) *With this Body*, Milton Keynes: Open University.

Pocock, D. (1995) 'Searching for a Better Story: harnessing modern and post modern positions in family therapy', *Journal of Family Therapy*, 17, 2: 149-73.

Real, T. (1995) 'Fathering our Sons; Refathering Ourselves: some thoughts on transforming masculine legacies', in Weingarten, K. (ed.), *Cultural Resistance: challenging beliefs about men, women and therapy*, Harrington Park Press: New York.

Reissman, C.K. (1990) 'Strategic uses of Narrative in the Presentation of Self and Illness: a research note', *Social Science and Medicine*, 30 (11) 1195-200.

## 6. Different Language/Different Gender

Ramsey, C.R. (1989) 'The Science of Family Medicine', in Ramsey, C.R., *Family Systems in Medicine*, The Guilford Press, London.

Sontag, S. (1991) *Illness as Metaphor*, Penguin Books: London.

Spirito, A. DeLawyer, D. and Stark, L. (1992) 'Peer Relations and Social Adjustment of Chronically Ill Children and Adolescents', *Clinical Psychology Review*, 11 (5) 539-64.

Weingarten, K (1991) 'The Discourses of Intimacy: adding a social constructionist and feminist view', *Family Process*, 30: 285-305.

# 7

# Making Sense of the Experience of Neonatal Intensive Care

## *Anne McFadyen*

### Introduction

Stories are told in order both to come to terms with and to shape experience, to pass on information, to re-edit, to share, to co-evolve, and to amuse and capture the imagination. They are tools in the task of meaning-making, serving both storyteller and listener or interpreter. As such, they lend themselves well to the task of research, the impact of which must be via a story of some kind.

In this chapter, I will describe a research project carried out while studying for an MSc in Family Therapy. My story about the project, which set out to examine developing mother-child relationships in a neonatal intensive care unit, will include an account of some of its many contexts, both personal and theoretical. I will consider the issue of 'systemic' research and, in keeping with the theme of this book, address the use of narrative as a research tool as well as presenting themes from the narratives of mothers of special care babies.

### Contexts

#### *The Personal Meets the Professional*

April 1989: I receive a letter requesting my attendance the following day at the course selection procedure. Somehow or other, the organisers have forgotten to communicate with me, or forgotten that I am on maternity leave and have a six-week-old baby. I duly arrange for a friend to meet me at the Clinic – she is to provide intermittent childcare throughout the day while I go through the process of goodness knows what. It all seemed rather bizarre. Even more so is my compliance with this request which I make sense of later by thinking (or indeed knowing) that at this time one exists only in the service of another, and that somehow I have muddled up my complete subservience to my baby with a sense of duty to my parent institution.

My friend is late, and so my son and I end up together in the large group which begins the day. He suckles, burps and farts his way through what could only be described as a large group experience (not the right terminology I'm afraid for a 'systemic' process), until a telephone call heralds the arrival of his substitute carer.

About two years later one of my close friends on the course told me that several candidates had come to the conclusion that my son was there for a reason, as part of the 'test' if you like. His presence had been strategic, and the candidates' response critical.

Of course, this was not the case. Nonetheless, the idea is worthy of further examination. Family therapists are not often found working with infants and their parents, and many of the candidates may well have found themselves on unfamiliar territory that day. For, while personally they may have been involved with babies in a number of ways, not least as parents themselves, their professional selves may not have been sure what to do. There is no doubt that babies evoke the most primitive of instincts and responses. Their vulnerability, the rawness of their emotions and their rather primitive communication of their needs often leave adults in their company feeling overwhelmed for a number of reasons, not least the resonance that this communication has with their own infantile emotions and needs.

*

July 1990: Almost halfway through the course – I am 28 weeks pregnant with my second child. Fuelled by my preoccupation with infancy and developing parent-child relationships, I have chosen to investigate the developing relationships of the premature baby. I now have to negotiate my way into a neonatal unit so that I can both observe the infants and carry out interviews with parents and staff. In order to do this, I have arranged to visit and meet with staff.

The nurse manager shows me around. She seems to want me to see exactly what I am dealing with. In retrospect, I appreciate the wisdom of this move. I find myself completely taken aback by my initial observations. Although I know theoretically that babies are born at 24 or 25 weeks gestation, I find myself quite shocked by the idea that my unborn child is older than many of the babies I observe. The nursing staff are either similarly disconcerted or unwittingly treat me as a mother who is about to deliver her baby. They are used to having pregnant women of similar proportions visit the unit in anticipation of a threatened early labour. I find myself quite daunted by the research task I have chosen in

147

order to complete my MSc. I feel awkward in the presence of the mothers on the unit, and quite anxious about my own baby.

\*

January 1991: My second son is almost 4 months old. I resume where I have left off. In the meanwhile 'the class of '89' has again appeared perplexed by the presence of a baby – this time in the form of my second son's attendance at seminars. Fortunately I am not too paranoid as a colleague's baby has also made the occasional appearance.

My next visit to the unit involves attending the psychosocial ward round. It is striking that most of the discussion focuses on infants who are doing less well, and about whom there is a lot of anxiety. One in particular became lodged firmly in my memory. The case was described as 'not atypical', although it should be noted that maternal death is rare. It serves as a dramatic example of the complex circumstances often surrounding the birth of these babies.

The baby was born at 25 weeks after a hazardous labour during which his mother had died. His medical progress was erratic, and there seemed little doubt that he would be significantly disabled as a result if he survived. His father, who was being threatened with expulsion from the country, was devoted to the baby, but had little materially to offer him. Social Services were planning to place the baby with foster parents on discharge.

The emotional context of the research was set in some ways at this point – I remembered the bad news, the horror stories rather than the success stories. This trend continued throughout my attachment to the unit and was later discussed with the consultant who felt that this was not a skewed perception but was part of the reality of the unit's memory. Despite having a prominently placed noticeboard with photographs of unit 'graduates' who were doing well, the talk was mostly about those who didn't make it or did less well.

There can be little doubt that one's own experience of a particular situation contributes enormously to how one interprets the relevant theoretical information about it. In this case, my own experience of having children, in the first instance in a relatively straightforward way and in the second by Caesarean section in rather precarious circumstances, and my experience both as a pregnant woman and as a 'new' mother experiencing the neonatal intensive care environment, undoubtedly coloured my view of what the issues for mothers in particular might be in such a situation. My babies did not need intensive care, other than from myself perhaps, but nonetheless my experience, and theirs as seen and felt by me, undoubtedly heightened my preoccupation with certain aspects of the experiences I had undertaken to research. Of course, this was not just coincidence. It is my experience that researchers often find themselves most passionate about projects to which they are connected at an emotional level rather than only a theoretical one. In my view this should be considered a good thing, but unfortunately there are many who subscribe to the idea that true research can and should only be concerned with a striving for complete 'objectivity'. The hierarchy of 'increasing sturdiness and sophistication in the level of scientific research' proposed by Garmezy (1986, p. 384), for example, suggests that some people believe that rated or digitalised descriptions are more valid than 'stories'. Others disagree. Bruner (1990), for example, has been critical of the way in which scientists have addressed the 'meaning making process' and has called for 'venture beyond the conventional aims of positivist science with its ideals of *reductionism, causal explanation and prediction*' (1990, p. xiii). He has appealed for a return to 'the *experienced* world of culture'(1990, p. 137) and for a recognition that 'whatever view one might take of historical forces, they were converted into human meanings, into language, into narratives, and found their way into the minds of men and women' (1990, p. 137).

This is a debate which is familiar to those in the world of family therapy, and one which in recent times has sought to include a discussion about the role of narrative in both research (for example, by Sherman, 1990) and therapy (for example, by White and Epston, 1990; and Sluzki, 1992). For researchers, the validity of a qualitative approach has in many ways now been confirmed, while for therapists the belief in the value of stories has recently been given credence by the development of a plausible theoretical foundation. In many ways this recent move has involved a revisiting of the past. Historically it seems that family therapists' early need for an identity of their own led to a disavowal of concepts previously held to be useful, namely those which had arisen from their relatedness to psychoanalysis. More recently however, under the influence of postmodernism among other things, the value of an individual's experience seems to have regained its rightful place and perhaps led to a re-recognition of common beliefs about the subjective nature of experience by family therapists in particular (McFadyen, 1997).

### Postmodernism and Research

Postmodernism is difficult to define. At its simplest, the term refers to the embracing of a 'new science' perspective, namely the idea that all 'knowledge' is relational. In some quarters, it has led to a reappraisal of the nature of scientific objectivity and a rejection of the mechanistic and reductionist approach to knowledge advocated from the 17th century onwards by Descartes and his followers. Its influence on the field of family therapy has most commonly been enacted through the discussion, and application to practice, of constructivist and social constructionist ideas. The latter, which 'posit an evolving set of meanings that emerge unendingly from the interactions between people' (Hoffman, 1990, p. 3), appears to have influenced researchers, particularly in the realm of the social sciences where it has led to an acknowledgement of the uniqueness of each person's experience. The use of narrative as a research tool and the development of discourse analysis as a research method could be said in some ways to epitomise this 'discovery'.

### Narrative

Narrative is also hard to define. As the editors of this book point out, the field seems rather confused because the concept has been used in a number of different ways, and appears to have led to the formation of several schools of 'narrative therapy'. The *Chambers Twentieth Century Dictionary* defines it as 'that which is narrated: a continued account of any series of occurrences: story' (1972). However, in recent literature, 'narrative' has tended to be defined by its context and its properties. From a systemic perspective, this is perhaps fitting. Bateson was highly critical of how and what children were taught about definition: 'they are taught at an early age that the way to define something is by what it supposedly *is* in itself, not by its relation to other things' (1979, p. 17). He described this as 'nonsense' and proposed that it was 'the context that fixes the meaning' (1979, p. 16).

The context of each narrative or story is a network of stories; it is also time, place and person. Each individual's construction of experience and events reflects their own belief system, which may be indistinguishable from that of their family or the society in which they live. There are different levels of stories which both influence and are influenced by current experience and the story about that experience In other words, the story defines the context, and the context defines the story. Sluzki has referred to this as an 'ecology of stories' (1992, p 218).

The temporal context of narratives has been emphasised: 'narrative incorporates the temporal dimension' and 'requires the location of events in cross-time patterns' (White and Epston, 1990, p. 3). Place can be interpreted in its broadest sense or in its narrowest. A similar set of events may be interpreted or storied very differently in one part of the world from another. The scene has to be set wherever. The context of 'the person' reflects the individuality of each narrative but also relates to the links which are made between different levels of meaning. For example, a person's religious, political or ethical views provide a context but are also owned at a very personal level, that is, they are that person. So that, for a woman, her story may be influenced by how she sees women in general in society, by her political beliefs about what being a woman means, but her story is also *her* story as a woman, and as an individual who happens to be a woman. Gilligan has suggested that 'development in women is masked by a particular conception of human relationships' (1982, p. 25), but goes on to acknowledge the reflexive relationship between the perspective of women, and the account of their development: 'since the imagery of relationships shapes the narrative of human development, the inclusion of women, by changing that imagery, implies a shift in the entire account' (1982, p. 25). This is a specific example of what Bruner refers to as the 'method of negotiating and renegotiating meanings by the mediation of narrative interpretation' which he sees as 'one of the crowning achievements of human development in the ontogenic, cultural, and phylogenetic senses of that expression' (1990, p. 67).

The specific acknowledgement of difference which has been introduced by those researching gender issues has impacted on social science research, in particular. The valuing of qualitative research methods is an example of this 'renegotiation' of meaning in the context of both postmodern and gender-sensitive perspectives. The recognition that human experience cannot only be made sense of by classification or digitalisation owes a particular debt to women and their influence on the world of science.

The potential of narrative to be used therapeutically and for research purposes seems essentially to hinge on the idea that the story told is only one of a number of possible stories which could be told. So that, 'those aspects of lived experience that fall outside of the dominant story provide a rich and fertile source for the generation, or re-generation, of alternative stories' (White and Epston, 1990, p. 15). Byng-Hall (1988 and 1996) uses the language of scripts and legends to apply a similar idea to the therapy situation where not only is past experience seen as shaping how current events are experienced, but current experience's potential to reshape the past is acknowledged.

'That it specialises in forging links between the exceptional and the

151

ordinary' is, in Bruner's view (1990, p. 47), one of narrative's crucial properties in relation to our drive for meaning-making. Not only are we able to find new explanations for things which don't fit with our well-rehearsed version of how the world is, or should be, but our ability to do this suggests that our view of the world is never fixed, and that we will always have in our head a possible world where the extraordinary *is* the ordinary. Our ability to generate meaning out of exceptions to the rule might be seen as the exceptional act which constitutes the rule of how to be a person. Bruner also describes narrative as having several other properties which include inherent sequentiality, power whether real or imaginary, and 'dramatism' (1990, p. 50), that is, an ability to invoke moral dilemmas.

The potential to use narrative as a research tool as opposed to just a way of finding out about how individuals and families see the world has been discussed by Reiss, who refers to 'the represented family', that is, 'each member's experience of the family' (1989, p. 199), and 'the practicing family' or 'the observable, external, and patterned coordinated practice in family life' (1989, p. 193). Sherman's account of an attempt to use narrative in research attached particular significance to the inability of some of the participants to recall stories about themselves as children, or 'to come up with any stories that touched family identity issues' (1990, p. 256). How people tell their stories as well as what they tell does seem important, and might be particularly so in relation to traumatic occurrences. In these instances, stories function 'to highlight, dramatise, and conserve the vividness of significant family transitions and stressful events' (Reiss, 1989, p. 208), and as such might be considered to be adaptive. Affleck, Tennen and Rowe (1991) have placed significance on the way that mothers, in particular, of special care babies tell their stories and attribute meaning, again seeing the ability to find meaning in such circumstances as an essential component of an adaptive response.

Workers in the field of attachment research, which might be said to act as bridge between psychoanalysis and systems thinking, have also recently focused on the use of narrative as a research tool to investigate the intergenerational transmission of psychiatric disturbance and disorder. The Adult Attachment Interview (AAI) (George, Kaplan and Main, 1985) is a semistructured interview which as its name suggests focuses on attachment and relationship issues. The form of narrative evoked by the questions is crucial to the rating of the subject's responses, in which particular attention is paid to the overall coherence of the 'story' and the 'fit' between the subject's evaluation of experience and their chosen illustrations of specific biographical episodes. The research of Main, Kaplan and Cassidy (1985) and Fonagy, Steele and Steele (1991), among others, has not only demonstrated the intergenerational transmission of attachment patterns, but has also established the predictive validity of the AAI in relation to future relationships and possibly therapeutic change (Main, 1995).

White and Epston see narrative not only as a key to meaning but also as the means by which we shape our lives: 'persons give meaning to their lives and relationships by storying their experience' and 'in interacting with others in the performance of these stories, they are active in the shaping of their lives and relationships' (1990, p. 130). Acceptance of the idea that stories are constitutive leads us to accept each individual's agency, and also implies a particular view about pathology. 'Thus the text analogy is distinct from those analogies that would propose an underlying structure or pathology in families that is constitutive or shaping of their lives or relationships' (White and Epston, 1990, p. 12). This view is in keeping with those of many contemporary family therapists, who desist from pathologising their clients and seek to empower them through conversations which lead to the coevolution of a new family story. The implications for research are at least twofold. First, there are no right or wrong stories, and second, narrative's function as a research tool cannot be divorced from its potential therapeutic role.

While it is 'true' that 'narrative can never encompass the full richness of our lived experience' (White and Epston, 1990, p. 11), it does seem to provide opportunities. Each story has its own validity and offers a momentary chance to capture that elusive thing called meaning.

## The Research

In this section I will briefly present a piece of 'formal' research, which I have continued less formally in my role as a clinician. In particular, my thoughts on how to carry out systemic research will be illustrated by the presentation of the research design and consideration of the role of systemic questioning as a research tool. Some examples of the narratives of mothers in the neonatal intensive care context will be used to illustrate the clinical relevance of the topic.

### 'The crisis of new-born intensive care'

The admission of a baby to a neonatal intensive care unit has appropriately been referred to as 'the crisis of new-born intensive care' (Affleck et al, 1991, p. 1). The baby, whose grasp on life is often fragile, is at the centre of a complex system of relationships which involve both family members and staff. The crisis is likely to have a different meaning for each participant, with institutional, cultural and family beliefs and history representing different layers of their individual contexts. The sense they make of their experience may depend on how they weave together the story of their current experience with these other stories of context. The baby's developing relationships will both influence and be influenced by other relationships within the hospital and family systems, while their parents' capacity to generate stories which are constitutive may determine how they cope with the crisis both practically and emotionally.

Earlier in this chapter, I drew attention to the fact that, even in a more ordinary situation, a baby's presence often leaves adults feeling overwhelmed. I have experienced this most dramatically myself as a new mother, when I often thought that nothing had prepared me for the task, or more importantly, the emotional experience. In the ordinary course of events, mothers do their job well enough because they are able to empathise with their babies, experience their experiences, help them to sort them out and give them meaning, and then let them get on with having them. The ability to put oneself in someone else's shoes is also important for both psychotherapists and other professional carers in the course of their work. But thinking about and trying to empathise with a 'special care' baby is a very difficult and often painful thing to do. Born too soon, often as early as 24 weeks gestation, these babies have the potential to stir up many very primitive emotions which may impede rather than facilitate the development of relationships. How can any of us begin to put ourselves in the place of these babies, some of whom are fragile, scraggy-looking creatures who may be naked and blindfolded, who are connected to tubes and wires to keep them alive, and who cannot be cuddled and loved in the same way as ordinary babies?

### Aims

The aims of my investigation were:

• to examine developing mother-baby relationships in the context of the neonate's admission to a special care baby unit;

- to consider the influence of other specified relationships on that relationship, and to consider the influence of the developing mother-baby relationship on those relationships;
- to consider the role of family, cultural and organisational beliefs about childcare, prematurity and the role of medical intervention in relation to the first two aims.

In Figure 1, I have attempted to represent the deconstruction of my main research aims diagrammatically. The mother-baby relationship in this context can be thought of as representing the interface of the two institutions, family and hospital. The key relationships around this couple have been expressed by using NURSE and FATHER as representatives of each. It was hoped that the close examination of the dyad and of this slightly broader subsystem by the method of psychoanalytic infant observation would clarify the nature of some of the interactional processes at this interface, and also generate hypotheses about the relationship of one institution to the other.

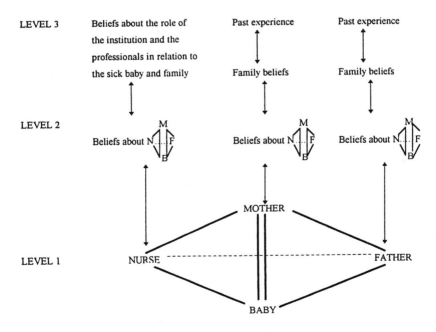

Figure 1 A representation of the relationships under investigation

## Methods

I wanted to find out about the experience of different participants but also wanted to attend to the subject from several different theoretical perspectives. In particular, I believed that it would have been difficult to study such early relationships without employing a theoretical model which permitted the meanings offered by psychoanalysis and child development research. I decided to use The Coordinated Management of Meaning CMM (Cronen, Johnson and Lannaman, 1982; Cronen and Pearce, 1985) as a framework for the project.

### The Coordinated Management of Meaning

The development of CMM Theory followed the acceptance, particularly in the field of social science, that social meanings were context-dependent. It was initially presented as a possible model by which to conceptualise the structural complexities of hierarchical systems, and as such represented a move forward from Bateson's initial insights (1972, 1979) that communication could be treated as a hierarchical system and that social meaning might exhibit reflexive loops or paradoxes. In particular, it proposed multiple levels of context, usually 5 or 6, which were governed by two key definitions:

1. Hierarchical relationship: two units of meaning are in a hierarchical relationship when one unit forms the context for interpreting the meaning and function of the other.
2. Reflexive loops: reflexivity exists whenever two elements in a hierarchy are so organised that each is simultaneously the context for *and* within the context of the other.

(Cronen et al, 1982, p. 95)

The property of reflexivity is helpful in that it permits the acknowledgement of bi-directional influence, but problematic in relation to the human drive to make sense of the world. As Bateson's 'double bind' theory (1972) illustrated all too well, the potential for different meaning to be inferred depending on which level represents the context can lead to confusion, if not madness. Cronen et al (1982) coined the phrases, 'charmed' loops and 'strange' loops, as they referred respectively to situations where either the interpretation remained the same or was different depending on which level was regarded as higher.

My analysis of the relationships between levels of meaning (as a researcher) therefore required the availability of information about three or more levels as its main aims concerned the influence of one relationship on other relationships, and included the participants' relationship with current experience and with higher order beliefs. To return to an earlier theme, it also seemed likely that the quality of the key relationship might depend on the parents' capacities to harness their own stories' reflexivity, that is, to make their own narratives constitutive.

The levels of information typically employed in relation to family research and therapy by Cronen and Pearce (1985) are illustrated in Figure 2. In this research project, I arbitrarily demarcated three levels to represent separate but overlapping theoretical perspectives (see Figure 3). Research methods included psychoanalytic infant observation, a relationship rating scale (providing information about Level 1) and semi-structured interviews with parents and staff (providing information about Levels 1, 2 and 3). Questions aimed at addressing and linking these different levels of meaning were developed as part of these interviews. As a whole, the stories that emerged from the interviews were seen as representative of the narratives of the participants.

| | |
|---|---|
| FAMILY MYTH refers to | high order general conceptions of how society, personal roles and family relationships work |
| LIFE-SCRIPTING | a person's conception of self in social action |
| RELATIONSHIP | a conception of how and on what terms two or more persons engage |
| EPISODE | conceptions of patterns of reciprocated acts |
| SPEECH ACTS | the relational meanings of verbal and non-verbal messages |

Figure 2: The CMM Model as represented by 5 levels of context
(Cronen and Pearce, 1985, p. 72)

The use of a hierarchical model in this study also reflected some of the issues raised in the ongoing debate about systemic research, where the concept of a truly systemic model of research has been considered with both scepticism (Goldberg and David, 1991) and confusion (Auerswald, 1987). Auerswald considered that confusion had been created by the strange loop which had arisen from the merging of ideas from Bateson's model of evolution and from the practice of family therapists. This loop referred to the conflict between the epistemologies of new and old science, the former embracing a both-and perspective and the latter, an

| Level | Hospital | Family | Theory |
|---|---|---|---|
| 1 | Beliefs about prematurity that inform practice, hospital policy, SCBU philosophy. | Beliefs about childcare, prematurity, hospitals, previous experience, role of medical intervention. | Systems theory and social systems theory. |
| 2 | Beliefs about this mother-child and her family. | Beliefs about this baby, its care by M, by staff, this mother-child relationship and family relationships. | Systems theory and attachment theory. |
| 3 | What happens at the relationship level? What happens between mother-child, nurse-mother, nurse-child, father-mother and father-child relationships? | | Systems, attachment and psychoanalytic theories, child development research. |

Figure 3: Conceptual model for a hierarchy of meaning analysis of relationships in neonatal intensive care

either- or one. The ability of the new science epistemology to theoretically permit the idea that there could be more than one reality, however, has the potential to lead to a resolution as the old (Newtonian) system is incorporated as a paradigm within it.

Interestingly Goldberg and David (1991) also resolved the dilemma of systemic versus linear by adopting a hierarchical model of explanation. Thus, a systemic theory at one level can be deconstructed to a number of discrete linear theories at another. In the authors' view this model effectively deals with a related dilemma, that between methods purporting to examine things from a position of neutral objectivity and those with a subjective view. The latter, often associated with the participant observer stance, are said to result in the generation of systemic hypotheses, while the former are more likely to be employed in hypothesis-testing research.

## Questions

In order to find out about how mothers and staff viewed their experience in the unit, I had to ask them questions. Of course, questions themselves have been the subject of research. In the context of systemic interviewing, Palazzoli, Boscolo, Cecchin and Prata (1980, p. 8) described circularity as 'the capacity of the therapist to conduct his investigation on the basis of feedback from the family in response to the information he solicits about relationships, and therefore about difference and change'. Tomm (1985) took this idea further, dividing circular questions into two categories: descriptive – whose aim was to lead to an understanding of the system; and reflexive – whose aim was to facilitate therapeutic change. My aim was the first of these, but as Tomm has also stated, 'the intent of a question does not, of course, guarantee its effect. ... Questions asked with a descriptive intent may, of course, also have a generative effect' (1985, p. 37). He recognised that questions could be addressed at different logical levels, and that 'there may be multiple levels of context. ... With each new level the number of connections that are possible increases enormously' (1985, p. 39). White (1988) has also discussed the usefulness of questions in eliciting family narratives. Again, this is seen as having therapeutic potential, and is in keeping with the view that narrative is constitutive.

My semi-structured interviews with mothers and professionals consisted of between 9 and 11 key questions. These questions sought to address different contextual levels; for example, I asked mothers about some aspects of both their own and the infant's behaviour as I had observed it; I also asked them about family beliefs and past experience. It had been my original intention to interview fathers too. This was not possible for several reasons, the main one being that only one woman was in a stable relationship at the time. Despite being randomly chosen, the sample shared a context of relationship difficulties and socioeconomic adversity in 4 out of 5 cases.

## Results

In this section it not my intention to report all my findings, but rather to leave aside details of my observations in the unit, and accounts of my interviews with staff. I have described these elsewhere (McFadyen, 1994). I will focus on the narratives of the mothers of five babies, each born between 24 and 28 weeks gestation.

## *The interviews*

The first interviews with mothers took place approximately 4 weeks after the birth and lasted up to 3 hours. I have referred to the use of psychoanalytic infant observation as a research tool, and at the time of my interviews this too provided a context, as I had observed the babies (alone or in interaction with others) weekly since their birth. Research interviews were tape-recorded and transcribed. Both the content of their stories, and the way in which they were told seemed important.

The response to my initial neutral invitation, 'Can you tell me what happened?' seemed particularly significant. In two cases, it resulted in an uninterrupted flow of information. Another mother needed no invitation. She poured out her story right from the moment I met her. I did not really need to ask her questions, even about some beliefs, past experience, and the impact of her relationship with her baby on other relationships; most of it came tumbling out. Where they chose to begin their stories also seemed important. Each of the five women interviewed began their story at a different point in time, and in three cases these related to the previous pregnancy – one began with the beginning of the previous pregnancy, one began with a previous miscarriage and one with the story of the previous labour. The others' accounts began more recently, one 5 weeks before the birth and the other with the labour which had been unexpected.

What is interesting here is that these women immediately contextualised their current experiences, possibly for me as a researcher, but probably also for themselves. They chose a particular marker from the past, and in the course of their stories the four who had had previous pregnancies often compared them, while the other compared the current event to her own experience as a premature baby. Similarly they introduced their beliefs about hospital care early on. This was often related to having had a sick relative and they detailed how this experience had informed their beliefs about health professionals. These stories about how they came to have their own particular views illustrated to me how they had used the stories of their own lives to make some sort of sense of their current experience. As a researcher it was beyond my remit to explore the constitutive nature of this in any therapeutic way, although it did seem that some were actively involved in a reworking of the past in the context of their present experience.

## 7. Making Sense of the Experience of Neonatal Intensive Care

### Themes

My context as an interviewer was influenced by both my personal role as a mother and by my professional struggle to make sense of the world. There is no doubt then that this brief account of the narratives of some of the participants in this research is as much my story as it is theirs. My comments about particular themes are also made as a clinician currently working in this context.

My impression of these infants was that they were fragile creatures whose struggle to survive both depended on and was potentially compromised by high-tech medical and nursing interventions. This presented a dilemma for staff and parents. Their fragility appeared to have led to mothers in particular having difficulties in knowing how to relate to them, and being afraid of damaging them. Research evidence (Field, 1990) suggests that this fear was justified as premature babies have been shown to respond to stressful stimuli with physiological changes which may be life-threatening.

Mothers' preoccupations more generally were influenced by their experience of the birth and of the unit, and appeared to impact on their developing relationship with their baby. Some common themes emerged from the interviews, which included a lack of preparedness for the birth of a live baby, concerns about communication with staff, a difficulty 'owning' their babies and an almost constant expectation of loss. For example:

> When the baby was born, I'd had 24 hours of pain, and I went to the hospital. I wasn't going to have a baby, I was going to have a miscarriage … the labour suddenly went very quickly, I was 7 centimetres and I could tell that they knew I was going to lose it. His heartbeat went down with every contraction. There was no paediatrician. Suddenly he was born, they told me it was a boy but no-one said whether he was alive or dead. And then they all went out of the room, they took him out of the room. I didn't know what had happened, I wanted to know, I thought if I shout I'll know, and then I thought it's better not to know.
>
> Later they came and said 'Would you like to see your baby?' I thought they were going to show me a corpse, but he was alive. I thought that he was dying. There was no explanation. I thought he's definitely dying. There will be no champagne and flowers. How would I tell his father? I was upset. I rushed out and when I came back a few hours later they'd moved him. I thought that he wasn't there, but he'd done so well they'd put him in a cot.

This mother had been sure that her baby would die, and even after seeing him alive, returned to the unit expecting him to be dead. Staff in the neonatal unit usually tried to let parents know in advance if a baby had been moved as they were very aware that parents' initial response to not seeing their baby was to imagine the worst even weeks after admission.

She had also feared for her own life. A number of women seem to think of their labour as a near-death experience. They have been frightened, not only for their babies but also for their own lives. Most will have been unable to confirm or refute this, unable to ask both at the time and later just what risks were taken. And, as is the case at the time of the birth and when the infant is in intensive care, they have often made assumptions that no communication means the worst of all possible imagined scenarios. Another mother shared this experience:

> I'd lost a lot of blood, I thought I was going to die ... I had a very rough time. I was afraid for my own life.

Lack of readiness for the birth of a live baby is common to both those who have threatened to miscarry for weeks and those who suddenly go into labour, but this may be experienced in different ways. As one mother put it:

> There will be a big difference between someone who just suddenly goes into labour with no problems before, and someone like me, who had lots of problems and was bleeding for months. I'm on the side of: isn't it amazing that I've got a baby out of all this. You know, rather than: what a shock it is that the baby's come early. Psychologically you sort of go through different processes if you're preparing yourself for a miscarriage.

Her experience of the time up until the birth was 'horrendous':

> The pregnancy was going on longer and longer, and as it did I was realising things I hadn't even thought about. I would have to deliver this baby normally, and it was going to be dead ...
> I got to 25 weeks ... I wasn't particularly expecting anything, I still wasn't expecting a live birth. The threshold was 24 weeks, at 24 weeks, I'd get the paediatrician.

The issues seem slightly different when there has not been a threat of miscarriage. Babies who arrive suddenly with no prior indication that things are not right will themselves be disadvantaged by the lack of opportunity to treat them for prematurity before birth. Their mothers too will not be ready. They have been deprived of time to prepare

162

emotionally for the event of delivery itself, and, in the case of first time mothers, to surrender their individuality and replace it with maternal preoccupation. For most of these women, the birth is accompanied by a sense of failure at some level, failure as a woman and as a mother. They experience the loss of a longed for and, in fantasy, perfect child, whether or not their baby is obviously disabled.

Of course, how ready any of these women are to be mothers will vary. It seems in some ways to be easier to take on the mantle of 'new' motherhood if they have already worn it. This will depend on what their previous experiences have been. For some women, the ability to be a mother seems to be invalidated in their own eyes if their infant is very small, fragile or obviously disabled. It is as if their mothering capability is suspended by the experience of having a baby who does not fit with their expectations. In this situation their capacity to generate a new story in which they are able to be a mother to *this* baby is crucial. I have referred to this earlier as 'our ability to generate meanings out of exceptions to the rule' (p. 152). In this setting, as Affleck et al. have reported, both the baby's developmental outcome and the mental health of the mothers are related to the mothers' capacity to 'restore a sense of meaning and mastery in the face of the profound challenges to their "assumptive world"' (1991, p. 129).

The spectre of disability also haunts these mothers. There is a real sense that the outcome may not be fully known until years later, and this, of course, is often the case. There is confusion about how to behave towards the infant, and a real feeling of not knowing what to do, both physically for and to the infant *and* emotionally. The expectation of loss, the feeling of inability to care for their child, the baby's physical appearance, and the sense of being peripheral and superfluous in the unit all contribute to a difficulty in owning their babies, which many say continues even after discharge. One woman, with whom I had kept in touch after discharge, said that even when she was walking out of the hospital with the baby, she kept expecting someone to run after her and say that he wasn't hers.

At an emotional level, it seems that the past is thrown into sharp relief by the current crisis. So that, for example, in the case of a mother who has already experienced loss, especially of a child, there will be a real question of how much commitment she can make to this baby. Other past experiences, for example of illness or hospitalisation, may both contextualise the current experience and be reinterpreted, especially at an emotional level, in relation to the current crisis. Similarly, perceptions of past and present relationships may be altered in the context of current stress and distress. New mothers, like those whose full-term babies are born in a straightforward way, may suddenly find themselves remembering their childhood and their relationship with their own parents. Many will feel judged by their internalised parents, and as a result may feel unable to accept support from their mothers. This dynamic also seems to impact on their relationship with staff, with those who have experienced their own mother as critical appearing to experience the staff as judgmental. In some cases, this suspicion appears to affect the mother-child relationship adversely as the mother's avoidance of staff leads to her distancing herself from her infant. In other cases, there is a determination to stick by the baby in spite of this feeling. In those cases where this relationship is experienced as comfortable, staff are usually able to influence the developing relationship in a positive way.

The support that mothers are able to obtain from their partners is also variable. A number of influences come into play. At a practical level, choices often have to be made about how the family will organise itself to cope with the crisis. The resulting division of roles between parents often means that they have little time to spend with each other. Mothers often find it difficult to make a commitment to both father and baby, and when there are other children too, their partner often comes last. The distancing in the marital relationship may also be affected by how the mother is feeling about her role in the events that have led either to the child being born too soon or with a disability of some kind. Many will feel that they have let their partners down, that they have not given him a fit and healthy child. They may also feel angry or depressed, and all of these things may make it difficult for them to allow their partner to comfort or support them. Of course, this is not always the case. Many couples may be brought closer by the circumstances, and may support each other very effectively, and this is likely to be associated with a strong commitment to the baby. The quality of their previous relationship is likely to be important; in some cases where the relationship has been shaky, and required a great deal of work to keep it alive, it appears that work is often put on hold temporarily while the infant is sick. It is as if the mothers make a decision about how much stress they can cope with; if the stress of their relationship with their partner outweighs the support they get from it, they may decide to separate or distance themselves for a while.

At another level, the influence of high-order beliefs is a powerful one, which often seems to have less potential for reflexivity than other contexts. By this, I mean that firmly held beliefs, particularly of a

164

philosophical or religious nature, may have been called upon through-out a person's life to make sense of their experience. Although these may be somewhat disabling in the current context, they are often clung to fiercely. One example of this relates to the relationship between 'fatalism' and agency:

> If they want to be alive they will be. No matter how much you attach yourself to them, they decide themselves if God says ... If the baby's destined to be alive, she will be whether you come to see her or not. Really. God takes care of little babies. He'll decide.

This mother, a refugee from a war-torn country, seemed to have used her beliefs to help her to survive separation from other family members and past miscarriages, among other adversities. She rarely visited her baby, and when she did she sat motionless at the side of the cot. She seemed to have surrendered any sense of agency to control both her own life and that of her baby. In contrast, a women of an infant of similar gestation, who believed 'that everything that happens is a result of your own actions', sat by her baby's cotside singing to him and trying to call him into life and into a relationship with her.

## Conclusion

In this chapter, I have described one aspect of a research project which sought to examine the developing mother-baby relationship in the context of the baby's admission to neonatal intensive care. In particular, the project addressed its relationship to other relationships or contexts. These contexts were both observed and in the minds of the participants. Although I have related *their* stories, this account is mine; this version of reality is the one which I have chosen to tell.

A hierarchical model was used in the study in order to differentiate layers of context and examine their relationships to each other. This model served the purposes of the research very well as it provided a framework which permitted the validity of different levels of meaning (Cronen et al, 1982), mirroring the way in which a 'new science' perspective affords us the potential to acknowledge the usefulness of different theoretical models.

Taggart sees 'truth' as 'connected intimately to our ways of looking for it' (1985, p. 118). As therapists and researchers, the meaning we ascribe to our patients' accounts of their lives and relationships, and the explanations we offer for their distress, depend heavily on our personal perspective and on the theoretical models we have chosen to adopt. I hope that by placing the story of this research in these two particular contexts I have made it a more meaningful and interesting story. But what is the relationship between these contexts? And how have they influenced my account?

My personal context as woman and a new mother brought both advantages and disadvantages to the research task, which I undertook with a keen awareness of my subjectivity. My own preoccupations fuelled my passion for the research and for ways of understanding early relationships. Coincidentally (perhaps) I had just rediscovered constructivism and social construction theory. I saw an opportunity to use the postmodern perspective to support my wish to carry out a piece of research which would be meaningful, which would connect rather than dissect, which would address relatedness rather than categorise, and which would tell stories rather than digitalise. Of course, postmodernism is not a theory of connectedness, but rather one which if taken to its extreme leads to chaos. However, it appeared to provide an epistemology by which I could tell a story about my way of knowing with some validity. The story, which sought to connect context and experience, might in fact be thought of as more typical of a women's story than a postmodern story.

The use of narrative as a research tool owes its debt to both contexts. In presenting some themes from the mothers' stories I have tried not to offer too many of my own explanations of their sense, hoping to allow them to speak for themselves too. Elsewhere (McFadyen, 1994), I have described my use of another research tool, psychoanalytic infant observation, in an attempt to hold on to the babies' sense of their experiences in this situation.

### A final comment

The task of describing this particular piece of research in one chapter has been a difficult one. This is not a new difficulty. The larger task of trying to make sense of the various influences on my professional self has been equally daunting, and my resolution to both in the first instance was not to write a paper but a book (McFadyen, 1994). This illustrates for me the difficult task we have as both researchers and clinicians of knowing how to edit the narratives of our subjects, or the conversations we have with our clients. Inevitably, the story we are left with is as much our story as it is theirs. For it is we who decide how to punctuate these stories in order to make our own sense of any experience.

## Acknowledgements

I am grateful to both the families and the staff who cared for them for giving me permission to carry out this project. I also thank Sebastian Kraemer for his helpful comment on an earlier draft of this chapter.

## References

Affleck, G., Tennen, H. and Rowe, J. (1991) *Infants in Crisis: how parents cope with newborn intensive care and its aftermath*, New York: Springer-Verlag.

Auerswald, E.H. (1987) 'Epistemological Confusion in Family Therapy and Research', *Family Process*, 26: 317-30.

Bateson, G. (1972) *Steps to an Ecology of Mind*, New York: Ballantine.

—— (1979) *Mind and Nature*, New York: Dutton.

Bruner, J. (1990) *Acts of Meaning*, London: Harvard University Press.

Byng-Hall, J. (1988) 'Scripts and Legends in Families and Family Therapy', *Family Process*, 27: 167-79.

—— (1995) *Rewriting Family Scripts: improvisation and systems change*, London: Guilford Press.

Cronen, V.; Johnson, K. and Lannaman, J. (1982) 'Paradoxes, Double Binds, and Reflexive Loops: an alternative theoretical perspective', *Family Process*, 21: 91-112.

Cronen, V.E. and Pearce, W.B. (1985) 'Towards an Explanation of How the Milan Method Works: an invitation to a systemic epistemology and the evolution of family systems', in: D. Campbell & R. Draper (eds) *Applications of Systemic Family Therapy: the Milan approach*, London: Grune & Sratton Ltd.

Field, T. (1990) 'Neonatal Stress and Coping in Intensive Care', *Infant Mental Health Journal*, 11: 57-65.

Fonagy, P.; Steele, H. and Steele, M. (1991) 'Maternal Representation of Attachment During Pregnancy Predicts the Organisation of Infant-mother Attachment at One Year of Age', *Child Development*, 62: 891-905.

Garmezy, N. (1986) 'Children Under Severe Stress: critique and commentary', *Journal of the American Academy of Child Psychiatry*, 25: 384-92.

George, C.; Kaplan, N. and Main, M. (1985) 'The Adult Attachment Interview'. Unpublished manuscript: University of California at Berkeley, Department of Psychology.

Gilligan, C. (1982) *In A Different Voice*, Cambridge: Harvard University Press.

Goldberg, D. and David, A.S. (1991) 'Family Therapy and the Glamour of Science', *Journal of Family Therapy*, 13: 17-30.

Hoffman, L. (1990) 'Constructing Realities: an art of lenses', *Family Process*, 29: 1-12.

Macdonald, A.M. (ed.) (1972) *Chambers Twentieth Century Dictionary*, Edinburgh: W. & R. Chambers.

McFadyen, A. (1994) *Special Care Babies and their Developing Relationships*, London: Routledge.

—— (1997) 'Rapprochement in Sight: postmodern family therapy and psycho-analysis', *Journal of Family Therapy*.

Main, M.; Kaplan, N. and Cassidy, J. (1985) 'Security in Infancy, Childhood and Adulthood: a move to the level of representation', in: I. Bretherton & E. Waters (eds) *Growing Points of Attachment Theory and Research, Monographs of the Society for Research in Child Development*, 50: 66-104.

Main, M. (1995) 'Discourse, Prediction and Recent Studies in Attachment: implications for psychoanalysis', in: T. Shapiro & R.N. Emde (eds) *Research in Psychoanalysis: process, development and outcome*, Madison: International Universities Press.

Palazzoli, M.; Boscolo, L.; Cecchin, G. and Prata, G. (1980) 'Hypothesising-circularity-neutrality: three guidelines for the conductor of the session', *Family Process*, 19: 3-12.

Reiss, D. (1989) 'The Represented and Practising Family: contrasting visions of family continuity', in: A.J. Sameroff & R.N. Emde (eds) *Relationship Disturbances in Early Childhood*, New York: Basic Books.

Sherman, M.H. (1990) 'Family Narratives: internal representations of family relationships and affective themes', *Infant Mental Health Journal*, 11: 253-8.

Sluzki, C. (1992) 'Transformations: a blueprint for narrative changes in therapy', *Family Process*, 31: 217-30.

Taggart, M. (1985) 'The Feminist Critique in Epistemological Perspective: questions of context in family therapy', *Journal of Marital and Family Therapy*, 11: 113-26.

Tomm, K. (1985) 'Circular Interviewing', in: D. Campbell & R. Draper (eds) *Applications of Systemic Family Therapy: the Milan approach*, London: Grune & Stratton.

White, M. (1988) 'The Process of Questioning: a therapy of literary merit?', *Dulwich Centre Newsletter*, Winter, 8-14.

White, M. and Epston, D. (1990) *Narrative Means to Therapeutic Ends*, New York: W.W. Norton.

# 8

# New Stories For Old?

## The Creation of New Families by Adoption and Fostering

### *Caroline Lindsey*

### Introduction

The time when this story begins is in the mid to late nineteen-seventies, when I started to work as a consultant to an inner city social services department, based in an observation and assessment centre. It was an exciting time for child care as important discoveries were being made. Family therapy was finding application in work with families in breakdown, where there was a crisis of the reception of a child into care (Lindsey, 1985). The development of the Milan Systemic approach (Palazzoli et al., 1978) provided the means to conceptualise the complex multisystemic interrelationships involved in the social services context. Systemic hypothesising allowed the therapist to include the interfaces between the therapist, child, family, social work and legal systems in her thinking and to consider, at any one point, where the most effective intervention might be made. For example, it might address the social work team, to enable the resolution of a difference of professional views. It might be focused on the relationship between the social worker and foster carer. By resolving a difficulty about the management of a child in care, the child might be freed from the conflict, thus leading to a reduction in symptomatic behaviour. The stance of neutrality, latterly termed curiosity, (Cecchin, 1987) made it possible to sustain therapeutic endeavour in the face of the pervasive sense of defeat and hopelessness, which often enveloped those who were struggling with the issues of child protection.

During the course of this work, when one of the area directors retired, I received an affirmation of the consultative method that I had developed to intervene with the families and their social workers. She told me that what had been important to her was that I had never said that a child or young person was untreatable. What this statement reflected was not that I had said that all their clients were treatable by conventional psychiatric or psychotherapeutic means. Instead, it meant that I had always been willing to have a conversation with whoever needed to come, to explore the dilemmas which faced them, the meaning they gave to their problems and possible solutions. I had learned that it was important not to do family therapy in the presence of the social workers. Instead, I offered a consultation to them and the families, empowering them in their roles with the families and avoiding, for the most part, the feared stigma of mental illness associated with consultation by a psychiatrist.

The other important discovery, which influenced the whole field at that time, was the increasing recognition that a substantial number of the children and young people, who until then had always been placed in residential care, when they could no longer stay at home, could potentially be found a family to care for them. This was underpinned by the research findings, which indicated how poor the outcome of residential care was (Tizard, 1977; Triseliotis and Russell, 1984). It was subsequently enforced by the rapid closure of children's homes. The extension of fostering and more particularly of adoption, to older, physically and mentally handicapped and seriously emotionally and behaviourally disturbed young people was (and remains) a challenge for the birth and substitute families, for the workers and, not least, for the children themselves. The enthusiasm and belief of the specialist fostering and adoption social workers in the potential existence of a family for every child who could not live with their parents, was inspiring. This passion for facilitating the creation of new families for children who need them has remained with me, despite the years of experience which have forced a recognition of how difficult a task it is and how much social, educational, financial and therapeutic help is required for success.

When I left the social services department, I, together with a colleague social worker, Lorraine Tollemache began a fostering and adoption project, offering consultation and therapy at the Tavistock Clinic. This chapter draws on our clinical experience in the project, which embraces systemic, psychoanalytic and attachment frameworks. The referrals are made, by social workers and parents, because of concerns about threats to the continuity of placement, anxieties about the suitability of placement and, with increasing frequency, because of

170

the need to resolve questions about ongoing contact between birth parents and the children. The children and young people whom we see cover a range of ages from birth to adolescence. In most cases, the decision that rehabilitation with the birth family is not possible, has already been taken. Some have been placed for adoption at birth; many older, pre-school or school aged children are in the process of being placed long term in the hope of adoption. For others, a decision may have been taken that they should be permanently placed with foster carers.

## Stories About Family Life

Another important social change over this period has been the move away from the idea of a normative family to the recognition of the great variety of patterns of relationship, family forms and structures that make up our multicultural society. Whilst each family is unique, thinking in terms of a 'family of families' (Lindsey, 1993) is a useful way of drawing distinctions between the experiences of birth, foster and adoptive families, two parent or lone parent families, and divorced, separated or reconstituted families. These distinctions between families of different form reflect an idea that there is a significance in the different ways in which they come into being, in how family life is sustained, how people separate from each other and the meaning of family life for them. Families who foster or adopt are very relieved to have their differences from other families acknowledged and this forms a crucial part of the engagement process, when they come for consultation. Beliefs about family life arise out of multiple contexts. The model of the Co-ordinated Management of Meaning proposed by Pearce and Cronen (1980) identifies six levels of interrelated, meaning – creating contexts. The contexts include the wider socio-cultural norms as well as local community life, the historical, intergenerational family myths and patterns, the individual's life script, the experience of current family relationships and specific family events (episode and content). There may, at times, be contradictions between the meanings created by each level of context, in this case about the meanings given to family life. These differences in belief and experience may account for some of the conflict and confusion which arise in the attempt to create new families.

The idea of a 'family of families' serves as a reminder that, despite the everyday experience of family life as real and stable over time, the meaning that people give to the concept of a family is created through their social interactions, expressed in language. In other words, it is socially constructed. Post-modern approaches to therapy have underlined the power that exists in the therapeutic conversation to co-create different constructions of relationships. New meanings for relationships emerge which carry unknown consequences, both of opportunity and risk for the participants. Nowhere is this idea more clearly illustrated than in the development of relationships in permanent foster and adoptive families.

In these families, who often have a mixture of biological, foster and adopted children, no assumptions can be made about the meaning carried by words as fundamental as 'mother', 'father' and 'family'. Neither is it possible to assume that they all attach the same person or group of people to those names. We are dealing with children like Jane who said 'It is possible to love more than one Mummy ... but I wouldn't tell Mummy that I love my foster mother, because she wouldn't like it and I wouldn't want to hurt her', and like William who declared to his social worker that he no longer wished to call his birth parents, 'Mum' and 'Dad' but to call them by their first names, to distinguish them from his adoptive parents. William, on a contact visit, resorted to pointing at the birth parent whom he wanted to address, to avoid the conflict created in him by their insistence that he call them by the names he was now reserving for his new parents. We see many children, received into care in infancy because of maternal mental illness, drug dependence or alcoholism, whose repeated experiences of failed rehabilitation and numerous disrupted placements with different carers, result in them having no sense of a mother or father or family, only the social worker's promise of a 'forever family'.

In one such case, a three year old who had been in care all her life because her mother's drug misuse had resulted in imprisonment, was being prepared for an adoptive home by her social worker. The social worker discovered that Sally had no understanding of the meaning of family relationships; mothers, sisters, aunties, grandmothers, neighbours were all indistinguishable for her. Sally had lived with foster carers in a somewhat chaotic household, where it was never really clear who was looking after her, the mother or her daughter. In addition, because of their sensitivity to her birth family's insistence that she remain a member of their family, they had taken particular care to prevent her from calling them 'Mum' and 'Dad'. There are other children, who, despite early traumatic and depriving experiences within their birth families, persist in a loyalty and identity with their original parents, which makes the idea of accepting alternative adults as parents intolerable.

In another case, the three children of drug dependent parents were placed together, with a view to adoption. The oldest boy fitted into the new family as a much desired son; the youngest, a sweet and attractive little girl, won everyone's hearts, but the middle child, Vicky, aged four kept alive the memory of her parents, constantly reminding her siblings of the past and challenging the adoptive parents by her clinging yet rejecting behaviour. Her dilemma was resolved by a placement with near relatives of her father, who felt able to take on the care of one child but not of three, whilst maintaining contact between all of them. Vicky's subsequent, smooth integration into the new home suggested that the 'family' relationships that they were able to offer her, satisfied her profound sense of identification with her original parents.

### Creating Families

There is a parallel story for the parents who come forward to create new families. Despite the variety of possible family configurations and the increasing numbers of reconstituted families following divorce, the significance of family history and intergenerational biological connections in the formation of the family remain strongly in people's minds. Using a social constructionist framework, it might be argued that the relationships in biological families, too, are created in language. Certainly, connectedness is maintained through conversations and interaction. However, the creation of permanent foster and adoptive families is entirely an act of social construction. Family relationships are brought into being in language, by discussions which take place between would-be parents, social workers, children and birth parents, during the course of introductory visits, in adoption and permanent placement panels and by the courts. The new relationships are later confirmed in writing. For children whose prior experience of life with parents has acquired a negative meaning, adoption provides the chance for the positive re-construction of the meaning of these relationships. In attachment theory terms, there is an opportunity to develop a new internal working model of relationships (Main, 1995). For adults, their own experiences of being parented have a formative influence on their internal working models of parent-child relationships. Research using the Adult Attachment Interview has suggested that what may be important for the quality of relationship developed with the child (in terms of attachment) is not so much the parents' childhood experience itself, but the coherence of the story which they use to explain what happened (Fonagy et al., 1995). Intending parents will have a positive expectation of forming a secure, satisfying attachment to the child who joins the family. This will arise out of beliefs about parenting, based on a realistic appraisal of their own experiences as children and possibly also arising from being parents to their own biological children. Nevertheless, the enormity of the task of creating new families cannot be underestimated. The child arrives at the new home, with uniquely personal stories of family life and familiar patterns of relationships, which are interrupted at the point of joining, almost, as it were, in the middle of a sentence. The same is true, of course, for the adults, whose way of life will suddenly change. Two siblings may have survived in a precarious home situation because of the parental role taken by the older one towards the younger. For example, stories abound of a four year old making bottles for a two year old and going shopping for a loaf of bread. But, in a context where there are parents able to take on their care and control, the older child's parentified behaviour may appear competitive, intrusive or controlling rather than protective. The child may feel bereft of her role, whilst not yet ready to accept the care which is also being offered to her. The task is to find the way beyond the punctuation, towards a newly developing narrative of family life.

However, the power of prior experiences to influence the meaning given to seemingly innocent interactions, puts relationships in substitute families at greater risk than usually exists in biological families, of being threatened by the content of conversations and consequent actions. These acts and conversations can arise in many ways, within families and with professionals. They may be precipitated by the persistent, apparently rejecting behaviour of the child, as in the case of four-year-old Mary, who screamed all the time. When she was asked about her screaming by the therapist, Mary was quite clear that it was to do with her distress at being rejected by her birth mother and not to do with the adoptive family. Later on in therapy, she talked about herself as rubbish, thrown away by her mother. But, her adoptive mother found it very difficult not to experience Mary's behaviour as directly relating to her and undermining, 'rubbishing' of her mothering. Another girl, Susan carried around a picture of her birth mother and talked about her idea that her mother might now have 'grown up' enough to look after her, once more. In this case, Susan's actions seemed to reflect the ambivalence felt towards her by the adoptive parents as well as her desire for the original family. The meaning created for the parents by this behaviour was of confirmation of the lack of fit between them, rather than an inevitable part of the process through which both she and they had to pass in forming a new relationship. Only once the placement is made, may parents and children recognise that they have made a 'mistake' in believing that they want to form or add to their family in this way. The act distinguishes the meaning of 'family' for them. One couple, where the father was an holocaust survivor, who had lost his original family, were asked to care for a challenging, eleven-year-old girl, Vicky, from a delinquent background. In the consultation, it was possible for the parents and Vicky to agree that their ideas about family life were so dissimilar that they could not live together.

The significant conversation, that leads to a reconstruction of the relationship, may emerge out of the social worker's experience that the child's emotional needs are not being recognised. The parents may have expressed disappointment that their (unrealistic) hopes and expectations for a reciprocal relationship with the child have not been met. They may complain of a 'lack of gratitude' and regard the seemingly endless demands for attention as hostile and attacking. Relationships may then be terminated abruptly and unpredictably, in a way that is far less likely in biological families, although clearly not unusual, after divorce and separation.

From the moment when a couple or individual sees an advertisement saying 'be my family', attached to the picture of a child, with a few biographical details, the process of creating a new family story has begun. People sometimes talk of 'falling in love' with the child at that point. This may predate or lead to a complex process of selection via conversations between social workers and would-be carers, known as a 'home study'. These discussions are powerfully affected by the desire to foster or adopt and by the need of social workers to find homes for children. The considerations differ depending on whether or not the carers already have children of their own and if so, on their ages and whether they are still at home and whether they intend to adopt or remain foster carers. Although the idea of the child or children that they might adopt emerges in the course of the conversation with the social worker, people often have quite a clear picture in their minds of the child who will fit into their family. It is essential that this *'Gestalt'* is respected, since one of the factors in breakdown of placements seems to relate clinically to attempts to persuade carers to take on, for example, a boy when they want a girl or an older child when they want a pre-schooler. There maybe an empty place to fill, but it may already belong to a child who died or who was miscarried and who should not or cannot be replaced.

It is likely that, in the home-study conversations, some aspect of the people's lives, which may have bearing on their capacity to parent may not be recognised or addressed. This may be because they are unaware

175

of its significance or because it is too painful or that it remains out of their consciousness until it connects with the experience that they have, once the child is placed with them. Not surprisingly, the impact of relationships which affect the carers' capacity to look after a child may come to light only when the placement is in jeopardy. There may have been the 'forgotten' abusive experiences remembered in caring for children, who have been similarly abused. They may have believed that their own trauma in childhood would enable them rather than hinder them in their care of traumatised children. At times, the wish that the unresolved pain of infertility will be assuaged by someone else's child may prevent the work being done to protect them and the child from the recurring confrontation with the fact that adoption is not a substitute biological family, but something different altogether. For others, it may have been too difficult to share the hope with the social worker that a child might heal a marriage that has run into difficulties.

Many people, however, end the period of home study confirmed in their idea of creating a new family. The result of these conversations is for the individual or couple to receive the accolade of being recognised as suitable to take on the role of 'public parents'; parents who will care for children on behalf of society, succeeding where others, the birth parents and, as is likely in late placement, other foster or adoptive families have 'failed'. The couple may be seen as successful parents already or as having the potential to form a family unit. One of the challenges of public parenting is that it requires the couple to share the responsibilities of parenthood with social workers. For some couples, this is felt as a loss of the autonomy, authority and independence which may have contributed to their previous success. The definition of success, too, requires renegotiation, if families taking on children, for whom past experiences of family life have been traumatic, are to feel satisfied with the outcome.

It is hard to convey the struggle involved in forming a family which must also contain within it, the story of the child and the birth family. One mother, when faced with the idea that the loving but incapable birth mother would always remain a significant person for the three-year-old girl she hoped to adopt, responded by asking 'How will she ever be my child, then?' Gradually, over a period of time following a meeting between them, which included the child, the adoptive parents were able to reach out to the birth mother, whom they no longer saw as a threat. She had been able to convey to them that she was choosing them to look after her child. She could acknowledge that she was unable to care for him, although she continued to love him and wanted to hear

176

about his progress. This allowed all the parties to attend the adoption hearing together and for the adoptive parents to undertake to keep in contact with the birth mother. The possibility of future direct contact between the child and birth mother was no longer ruled out.

## Stories About Stories

Families often say to us that they were not told the full story about the child by the social workers. One explanation is that their eagerness to adopt prevents them from taking in the significance of the stories about the child's damaging prior relationships. It is certainly not possible to anticipate the impact of the child's way of being on their ongoing lives. Neither is it possible to be sure about the way in which the child's behaviour will be affected by their explanations and responses to it. The physical and emotional demands of the deprived and abused child are often exhausting and seemingly never to be satisfied. In one case, a young boy who had been starved, continued to eat each meal as if it was his last. His table manners prevented the parents from feeling that he could eat in company. Unlike some other families in this predicament, the couple were untroubled by his behaviour, which they could tolerate because of their understanding of its origin and their belief that he would eventually feel satisfied by their 'feeding'. Others, more constrained by beliefs about socially acceptable behaviour or who experience this voracious eating as a sign of an insatiable need, will respond very differently to such a child.

However, the story which the social worker does tell about the life of the child will have also been very much influenced by her personal beliefs about family life and adoption. It will also be influenced by her agency's ethos concerning child care, by her sense of responsibility for the predicament of the child and by professional beliefs about the need for family placement and the significance of family identity. Sometimes, when social workers have attended meetings without the case file, we have thought that it is a metaphor for their wish that the child's history could also disappear, because of their fear that, if anyone heard the 'true' story, a placement would never be found. On the other hand, if much work has gone into the attempt to make the rehabilitation work, then the worker's identification with the birth family and sense of failure may create a sense of rivalry and make it difficult for the new family to feel confident in her wish for their success.

### Story-time

Time is a crucial ingredient in the creation of new family stories. The introductory meetings are the nearest equivalent to the psychological preparation period of pregnancy. After this, there is sometimes a 'honeymoon' experience when it feels as if the child has always been there, and there is a sense of fit. But this may also represent an attempt on the child's part to leave behind the past and a fear of further rejection. The 'honeymoon' may be followed by a period of testing out of the ability of the parents to cope with the worst aspects of the child's behaviour. Unlike a biological family, which will have some idea of a family life-cycle, based on their own social and cultural norms, the family adopting an older child struggles with time in a variety of ways. There is the question of when the child will at last accept that they are here to stay and begin to see the adoptive parents as their own. For many children, the past is ever present. For example, they may continue to feel afraid and to fear violent responses to their misdemeanours. The children's experience is also that the past is easily re-evoked, driving out the security of the present, so that changes like holidays represent a threat rather than pleasant enjoyment. Families always find that this process of family integration takes much longer than they expect. They are shocked by the professionals' ready acceptance of a time frame of several years for this adjustment, which may be intolerably long for them. They would like the children to forget the past.

Our consultative work often focuses on helping families to understand that, rather than forget the past, the past has to be remembered as part of their present and future. The child's past needs to become part of the family's ongoing story, newly understood, so that it no longer carries the same risk or danger. Even when this process has been successfully undertaken, at each new developmental stage and particularly in adolescence, there is a re-working of the old traumas and losses. This is often accompanied by the young person wishing to search for the birth family, if they are not still in contact with them and by their challenging behaviour, which may be experienced by the adopters as rejecting.

In one case, the parents of two boys sought help. The eldest, Jack had been adopted within a few months of birth. The younger boy had been born one year after Jack had come to live with them. Jack's mother had chosen the adopters. They had met on several occasions, having gone to some length to reassure themselves that she was clear about her decision. The parents had not wanted ongoing, face to face contact and the Judge had ruled in their favour. They had agreed to keep in contact by letter. However, they had been aware all along that the birth mother had never really accepted this and, as the years went by, she let them know how much she now regretted her decision. They talked very little to the children about Jack's adoption as they grew up, regarding their lack of expressed curiosity as evidence that they had no interest. They were open about their desire to create a tight boundary round their family, wanting to appear as far as possible like the families of their friends. They were increasingly worried about the impact on their lives, as the children grew older, of letters and telephone calls from the birth mother. The referral was precipitated by an episode in which she had made a visit to Jack's school and approached him in the playground. He put his suspicion that she might be his birth mother to his father, who had dismissed the idea. Both parents were distraught at the idea that they might lose their dearly loved child to the rival mother. They had a powerful belief that if her existence was acknowledged to Jack, somehow all the significance of their relationship with him would vanish. He would leave them. They hoped that this would be an isolated incident and could be forgotten. I worked with them on the meaning that their silence would have for Jack. We discussed the effect of his not being able to talk to his parents about something so important as his birth mother and the impact of the meeting at the school. We looked at how he might construe their response as meaning that he had to deal with this by himself and to protect them from his own anxieties, rather than being able to rely on them for help with something unknown and threatening, as he had been able to do up till now. We talked about their contradictory feelings about being parents. Was it really possible that their experience of bringing Jack up all these years could be wiped out by the mother, who had brought him into the world but had not taken care of him? Was she really such a threat to them that she could not be acknowledged as significant in Jack's life. Was it not possible that Jack already knew about his mother and needed their assistance and permission to recognise her existence. They would take a risk either way – by denial or by admission. Gradually, over a period of weeks, they gathered their courage to talk to Jack about his mother. He was relieved that the story was completed. He wanted to meet her. But, he also made it very clear to his birth mother and to his adoptive parents that his home was with them and that he saw them as his parents.

There is also the issue of time for development that has been missed, through the disruptions to the care and lack of attention to the needs of children in the care system. They often function socially, educationally and psychologically as much younger children so that there is a discrepancy with their chronological age and sometimes with their physical maturity. This leads to conflicting expectations for the children and their new parents, of each other and by others, such as teachers and friends, of their needs and of what they will be able to achieve now and in the future. At home, ten year olds may need to be put to bed and to be read bedtime stories, given bottles and dressed in the morning as they develop a relationship of trust with new parents, whilst at school, age-appropriate behaviour may be expected, even if their special educational needs have been recognised.

Not only is present time confused with the past and the future lacking in the predictable milestones that biological families can usually anticipate, but the experience of daily routine is often distorted as well. Children whose early lives have been disrupted by episodes of care and changing caregivers frequently fail to develop a sense of personal time that can guide them through the day. They seem never to be able to remember what to do in the morning, and in which order and they have to be constantly reminded of their routine. Families often find it helpful to discuss the mismatch of societal, chronological, biological and psychological time, which they experience. It frees them from the socially constructed time constraints, so they feel more satisfied by doing what is possible within the time available and with the children they have.

## The Therapist's Story

The Children Act 1989 has emphasised the abiding importance of the family of origin by renaming ongoing connections as contact rather than access. The change of language, with its physical connotation creates the idea of a mutual experience, between parents and children, including the possibility for physical intimacy as well as emotional relatedness. (Lindsey, 1995). It contrasts with the word 'access' which suggests a more linear concept of parental rights to the child. Adoption continues to be recognised as the most successful alternative, when children cannot remain in their own families. But, the Children Act, by insisting on consideration of contact in all cases of permanent placement, has legislated for the recognition given by professionals to the ongoing significance of the birth family to the child, even when placed as a baby. This significance may, of course, not always be of positive nature, as in cases where the child has suffered severe abuse. The enduring quality of the meaningfulness of the birth-family relationships has been underlined by the experiences with searching and 'reunions' of adult adoptees with their birth parents. (Feast and Smith, 1993)

In the group of families whom we see in a clinical context, the question of whether the relationship with the birth family should be maintained in reality, by contact, rather than by the inevitable fantasy, is regularly asked. I have found it useful to conceptualise the transition that the birth parent needs to make, so that contact can be helpful for the child, as becoming a 'non-parental parent' (Lindsey, 1995). They have to go through a process of relinquishing their role as a parent to the new carers. This involves the acceptance that the daily tasks of upbringing and the making of major decisions for the child are no longer for them to undertake. Without this acceptance, there is the danger that they will undermine the placement, by challenging the right of the foster or adoptive parents to care for their child. The child will feel a conflict of loyalties which may be expressed by disturbing behaviour around the time of contact visits and may be confirmed in a belief that a return home is still possible. There is also the danger that the child may experience the contact as a disturbing threat to a newly established security, after their previously abusive treatment by the birth parent. On the other hand, contact may provide the child with the reassurance of the birth parent's well-being and a sense of not having been totally abandoned by her. It may result in a sense of continuity of the relationship over time, preventing its total denial, denigration or idealisation, by both sets of parents and children. In such a case, the stories of family life might be able to develop together. But, for this to be possible, the birth parent would need to have a belief in their value to the child and this would have to be shared by the substitute carers.

In the case of William, the little boy mentioned earlier (p. 172) who no longer wished to call his birth parents 'Mum' and 'Dad', his parents wanted to maintain the level of contact they had with him when he had been in foster care. They found it difficult to understand why they were being deprived of his company, now that he was placed for adoption, with their agreement. It was hard for them to make the same connection as the adoptive parents, that his tantrums and tears were related to contact visits with them, since he spent so little time with them now. They were suspicious of the care he was receiving. They brought fresh clothes for him to wear and fed him continuously, throughout the meetings. They wanted to share him with the new family although they could not offer him a home. The adoptive parents had not been able to see the value of the visits and we discovered that they had never prepared him for them. Following our suggestion that this would be helpful, the next visit was not so fraught. Their original wish to terminate contact was modified as they heard about William's desire to stay in touch. When we met with the birth parents to share our thinking about the question of contact, they became angry at the proposal of contact only twice a year, saying that it was insulting to them. Instead of accepting this as an invitation to a fight, we spoke with them about their love for William, their loss and his evident fondness for them. By describing his behaviour in the contact, when they insisted on being called 'Mum' and 'Dad', they, in turn, could acknowledge their awareness of his confusion. They could also acknowledge that they, too, had been aware of his exhaustion by the end of the meeting, which he had found too long. They began to separate his needs from theirs, once we had recognised their significance in his life. They enquired what he would like to call them. Although they departed sadly, it seemed as if they had begun to redescribe their relationship with William, as people who were important to him, but not as parents. This was further supported by the knowledge that our proposals for contact had been accepted by his adoptive parents.

This case highlights the intensity of the emotional pain experienced by all the individuals in the family systems involved in fostering and adoption. In working with families, the therapist is always in touch with her experiences of being a member of her own family. Work in this field entails having to recognise the meaning for parents and children of family life not succeeding to the point of loss of parenthood, and the loss of being parented. It is inevitable that the therapist identifies with their anger, frustration and sadness and feels anguish at the emotional damage being done to the children in their journeys through the care system.

Working in teams gives therapists the opportunity to consider the meaning that these therapeutic encounters have for us in our family life. In particular, being parents to our own children, whose needs we try to meet is constantly evoked by this work. In our consultations with the front line social workers, it may sometimes be appropriate to recognise the impact that these powerful emotional experiences may have on them, as they hold on to the hope for new relationships, which will meet the children's needs.

### Concluding Thoughts

The story of adoption is still evolving. From offering couples without children of their own the chance to become parents with a family, adoption has become a way for children to be offered another chance to make secure bonds of attachment in a family. Now by attempting to keep the links with the birth family, open adoption or adoption with contact may give some children the best of both worlds, by commitment to a future and connection to the past. This is importantly different from permanent foster care, since it does not include the involvement and support provided by social services for foster carers. Therapists need to continue to discover ways of helping families to create themselves.

## References

Cecchin, G. (1987) 'Hypothesising-circularity-neutrality Revisited: an invitation to curiosity', *Family Process*, 26: 405-13.

Feast, J. and Smith, J. (1993) 'Working on Behalf of Birth Families: the children's society experience', *Adoption & Fostering*, 17, 2, 33-40.

Fonagy, P.; Steele, M.; Steele, H.; Leigh, T.; Kennedy, R.; Mattoon, G. & Target, M. (1995) 'The Predictive Specificity of the Adult Attachment Interview and Pathological Emotional Development', in Goldberg, S.; Muir, R. and Kerr, J. (eds), *Attachment Theory: social, developmental and clinical perspectives*, Hillsdale, NJ: Analytic Press.

Lindsey, C. (1985) *Consultations with Professional and Family Systems in the Context of Residential and Fostering Services: 'in and out of care'* in *Applications of Systemic Family Therapy: the Milan approach*, (eds) Campbell, D. & Draper, R., London: Grune & Stratton.

—— (1993) 'Family Systems Reconstructed in the Mind of the Systemic Therapist', *Human Systems: the journal of systemic consultation & management*, Vol 4: 299-310.

—— (1995) 'Systemic and Developmental Aspects of Contact', in Argent, H. (ed.), *See you soon: contact with children looked after by local authorities*, BAAF.

Main, M. (1995) 'Attachment: overview, with implications for clinical work', in Goldberg, S.; Muir, R. and Kerr, J. (eds), *Attachment Theory: social, developmental and clinical perspectives*, Hillsdale, NJ: Analytic Press.

Pearce, J. and Cronen, V. ( 1980) *Communication, Action and Meaning: the creation of social realities*, Praeger: New York.

Selvini Palazzoli, M.; Boscolo, L.; Cecchin, G. and Prata, G. (1978) *Paradox and Counterparadox*, New York: Aronson.

Tizard, B. (1977) *Adoption: a second chance*, Open Books.

Triseliotis, J.P. and Russell, J. (1984) *Hard to Place: the outcome of adoption and residential care*, Heinemann.

# 9

# Rewriting the Story

## Children, Parents and Post-Divorce Narratives

### *Gill Gorell Barnes & Emilia Dowling*

Each year during the early 1990's about 160,000 families with children under sixteen went through an experience of their parents divorcing. Of the children one in three were under five years old and a further seven thousand between five and ten years old (Haskey, 1995). Research from many countries has shown how aspects of the divorce experience has both short and long term effects for many children and in this chapter we will focus on how the stories parents tell themselves about the divorce process, contextualises different kinds of childhood experience.

The chapter is based on our experience of having set up a clinical service for families living through processes of separation and divorce as well as subsequent family reconstruction. The service was set up for any child referred with psychological difficulties relating to a parental divorce. It was based on former clinical experience that at a time of family breakup there would be a number of different stories surrounding the lead up to the divorce and to the divorce event itself. The way a story is told offers a particular meaning given by each individual to his or her lived experience; in conflict ridden situations, stories made by each of the child's parents are often not possible for the child to reconcile. We therefore organised the service so that each person's differing views and the differing stories held within different subsystems in the family would be taken into account by offering individual interviews to each parent and to the children. We made it our goal to develop an ongoing overall post-divorce family narrative which would allow the acknowledgement that there are many different views of equal validity. Our hope was that children would no longer then be required to falsify their own experience in the service of each parents' reality in

184

order to maintain their parents 'illusion' of the truth. We paid particular attention to the child's view, knowing from former work how it might be different from either of the parents, and how the child might be required to privilege other views above his or her own. When we felt we understood something of the different and competing realities, we saw as much of the family together as could be reconciled within one meeting to share the differences we had experienced.

Out of a range of presenting problems described briefly below we have identified three main groupings of post divorce parental relationship presenting themselves for psychological disentangling.

The first group contains ongoing conflict laden relationships, which include narratives that disqualify the child's experience in favour of a personal slant preferred by one parent. The children have to develop parallel narratives to 'fit' with each parent, and are left with a loyalty dilemma as to which to believe and therefore whom to please. A higher order organising construct of their experience becomes 'not to upset the other parent'.

The second group lacks narratives or deny the children in the family the right to a story. The main features of this group are an intransigent silence involving a refusal to talk about areas of the child's experience that relate to the separated parent and the refusal to clarify or attempt to develop explanations for the child about the processes taking place around them. The absence of shared meaning between parent and child about their daily lived experience and the falsification of family memory contribute to unmanageable confusion in the child's mind.

The third grouping consists of parents who have remained entangled with their spouses, preoccupied with anxieties about the care offered to their child in the context of contact visits. The perceived failures of parental care often re-arouse previous experiences of 'being put down' by the other spouse with highly charged consequences for the present. Stories may be full of reproach and the ongoing desire to reform the other and re-engage them with the preferred view of the storyteller.

The children take on the task of 'keeping conflict at bay' carefully filtering information from one parent to the other. Their primary concern becomes to 'keep the peace'. Their efforts take up a considerable amount of mental energy which may result in difficulties in concentrating and learning. Their own wishes and views become submerged.

In this time of family transition we find ourselves working not with coherent family stories, but with individuals whose subjective meanings emerging from a shared life are widely different. Although we began the project four years ago with our own illusion that we would be working towards 'coherent' stories, we have since changed our views in two important ways. The first is the recognition that some parental narratives contain irreconcilable differences. Since the project began we have seen a number of children whose parents have made bids for their loyalty in oppositional ways over the larger part of their childhood. Children who have been subjected to persistently discrepant stories over time experience 'oppositional voices', each making a claim for their loyalty. They are likely to find it of more use to have these drawn out of their own confused accounts rather than have strained attempts at reconciling the differences imposed upon them. The second view we hold is that coherence itself, as an attribute of post divorce life, is an inappropriate metaphor for the complexity of the narratives that develop. We prefer therefore to think of multiple stories, in which the element of coherence is the parent's joint desire to do the best for their child(ren). Our work has emphasised the importance of the child's perspective while paying ongoing attention to the differing dilemmas affecting mothers and fathers in the evolution of the idea of ongoing 'family' life after divorce. In relation to the clinical work itself this has led to a tighter focus on the hierarchy of discourses in a family; the ways in which certain stories about children's lives and parental functioning dominate over other stories, and the effects of such dominance on potential other stories about life which become silenced or submerged. This approach has been of particular value when unravelling the oppressions of power driven stories in which either parent tries to assert their moral superiority, as well as the oppression created by silence and omissions of information which does not allow the child to think freely about what is going on.

We have seen 30 families to date. 24 families and 38 children have been seen on more than two occasions. The average number of sessions has been six to ten, but with some families our contact has spanned over two to three years. It is not possible to make generalisations from this sample of clinic users to the experience of all troubled families living through the transitions that follow divorce. However, the variety of patterns encountered, both of family structure and family culture, lead us to believe that what will carry wider relevance to the post-divorce family experience of others is focusing on the subjective differences emerging from the accounts of mothers, fathers and children and the different ways they understand the events that they are living through.

We are also interested in looking at the different resources for coping that parents developed, both for themselves and on behalf of their children. Although this will not form the major focus of this chapter, the relationship between accounts given of coping with stress in adult life, and the parents account of stress in their childhoods and in the course of their earlier adult lives, is an important part of their narrative about current troubles in family life and resulting transitions and change. The way in which parents have developed a sense of identity and effectiveness; as well as the coherence of the accounts they give of their experience have formed part of an earlier study of post divorce and stepfamily life (Gorell Barnes et al., 1997, forthcoming). In describing the lives of young adults who had lived through widely differing divorce experiences as children, drawn from their own subjective accounts, it was found that identity derived not only from structures of the immediate family and home in childhood, but was negotiated continually within the extended family and subsequent intimate relationships. An ongoing narrative also had to be negotiated within daily worlds that changed, and where meanings between households often conflicted.

## What Research Shows

Hostility and acrimonious rowing long after divorce are shown to be a common feature in divorcing families in the UK, whether in the north or south of the country. In the studies carried out by Walker and colleagues in Newcastle at least a quarter of the 400 families studied were unable to co-parent harmoniously (Simpson et al., 1996). The Exeter study published in 1994 showed that from 152 children whose families were reordered, fewer than half had contact with the non resident parent two years later (Cockett and Tripp 1994). The intense pressure that the wish for ongoing contact with a child can set up between parents who have parted bitterly and continue to war, plays a major part in such ongoing rows.

Research in this and other countries has highlighted that divorce affects children in the short term (Isaacs et al., 1987; Ochiltree, 1990). Can the effects of the divorce itself be distinguished from the effects of other social change that may amplify the loss of a parent from the home? Studies from both the USA and Australia have shown that children show more difficulties at school in the short term, have increased health problems including a range of psychosomatic problems and have an increased negative self image and low self esteem. Not all children are affected in this way when parents separate, but most studies show a high temporary increase in disturbance which drops after the eighteen-month to two-year period. In Sweden, where economic factors following divorce affect mothers and children less (due to high welfare benefit maintaining family income at 85 per cent of pre-divorce income level) effects appear to be much lower, since children's social milieu remains much the same. Homes do not have to be sold, schools therefore remain unchanged and peer groups also stay the same. The emotional climate is not further clouded over with arguments about money (Wadsby 1993).

Other research showing how the effects of divorce can be amplified by the concomitant circumstances accompanying parental separation such as loss of income, changes in home school and peer group has been documented elsewhere (Gorell Barnes et al 1997).

### Our Own Experience as a Contribution to the Project

In what ways has our own experience led us to become involved in the discourses that surround divorce, and how do they influence us in our orientation to the complex task of unravelling the post-divorce knots entangling, and sometimes strangling the children caught within them?

Gill Gorell Barnes experienced the consequences of divorce in her adolescence, when after many unhappy years her mother decided to separate from her father. Though unable to assess how this would affect any of the parties involved she was aware at the time of great relief that the decision had been made, following years of hostility and unresolved rowing between the two of them in which inevitably, although without the intention of either, she had become caught up. As the time was the early 1960s the processes of the divorce involved lies and subterfuge in order for speedy arrangements to be carried out. Following the divorce itself she acquired a stepfather, with whom she subsequently became very close even though they disagreed on almost every social and political issue. More relevant to her research and clinical work has perhaps been her awareness of the isolation of the post divorce situation for the parent who moved out of the home; and the way in which children can become caretakers of unhappy and isolated parents under the guise of 'contact' in the 'best interests of the child'.

A child psychologist, Emilia Dowling has always focused on the child's perspective. Although her parents never divorced, there were times during her adolescent years when she experienced the uncertainty and loyalty dilemmas related to the possibility of her parents' separation. In terms of her clinical work these experiences have heightened her awareness of the dilemmas for the children, on the one hand having to understand and sympathise with the parents' feelings and on the other hand feeling angry and sad as a result of the threat to the family's stability.

Both from their respective points of view therefore share an interest in the voice of the child, and in separating out the narratives of father, mother and children as these need to represent different positions at a time when the coherence of the family is fragmented.

### Following the Narrative Theme: in the short term

#### *Arguments or Conflict*

Arguments alone have been shown to affect children in the long term. Work in the UK by Jenkins (1988) as well as by Elliott and Richards (1992) has shown that long term quarrelling has negative effects on children's emotional behaviour and academic performance. Following acrimonious divorce, successful adaptations to new family arrangements are less likely. Children are also more often left with distorted, or disqualified and partial accounts of their own lived experience, which it is hard for them to make sense of. They may not be allowed to own what they know, and may be required to falsify their own experience in the service of loyalty to different and competing parental realities. The family as a safe base for both children and adults (Byng-Hall 1995) is likely to lose its original meanings in the divorce process, and in order to evolve has to develop some new and workable ideas about the arrangement of ongoing relationships. In mourning the loss of a former life together 'successfully', new constructions of the story of 'family' can emerge for men, women and children which allow the idea of 'family' and 'self in relation to family' to evolve rather than to be denied and destroyed. In acrimonious circumstances this process is impeded by the *maintenance* of former patterns of argument and the attempt by one or other parent to dominate the discourse with their own versions of the truth.

In the Exeter study (Cockett and Tripp, 1994) many children did not understand the reason for their parents divorce, were given little explanation at the time and were left confused and bewildered, often hoping for a reconciliation far longer than their parents imagined. Some children did not perceive an improvement in parental functioning following the divorce. Whether or not a parent shows themselves as 'coping' may make a significant difference to the post divorce experience for all the family.

The Exeter study points out how conflict may actually rise in some

189

families following, not preceding the decision to divorce. The New-castle Study (Simpson et al., 1996) has also highlighted the relationship between men's wish to maintain contact with their children and a high level of conflict in the parental relationship. This is more likely to happen where parents separate through 'incompatibility' or because one of the partners wishes to live with someone else. Conflict, or a higher level of conflict, may arise in those circumstances as a direct result of the decision to separate rather than being the cause of it, and such conflict may persist for many years. Children may then become more involved in the conflict taking a more central role as message carrier and identifying with each parents version of the other.

The Exeter study showed that in angry situations, children, moving on a regular basis between two homes, reported that they sometimes had to suppress talking to one parent about enjoying time with the other, or had been asked by one parent to keep something secret from the other parent. Only one in five children reported being able to talk freely about one parent in front of the other. Nor did they feel free to talk about the divorce and about changes in family life. Where children saw parents infrequently, they reported that they never mentioned either parent to the other, and also concealed facts about any new relationships the parent might have.

The study of young adults who had grown up in re-ordered families (referred to above) showed that in many families high degrees of silence had been maintained into adult life (Gorell Barnes et al., 1997). Many of the respondents said that they still felt the subject of the 'other parent' was taboo. As one young woman whose mother had left said 'I should imagine if I ever asked about her, he'd just completely blank the issue, he wouldn't talk about it. Or he'd get very cross with me, I can imagine him getting cross about that.' Another young woman for whom the interparental conflict had never ceased twenty years after the divorce, said, 'I think a parent should never forget that the child has two parents, the original parents. My mother totally cut my father off from her and I felt she wanted me to do the same as well, but they were still my mother and father.'

## Lone Parents and Children: honouring
## intergenerational intimacy

Children tend to establish more intimate peer-type relationships with lone parents after divorce. This fact, now proven many times over from different studies, still requires further deconstruction with each family.

In relation to violent and acrimonious divorce such attachment poses special questions. Do children form more intimate attachments because they are scared of losing another parent, one already having gone? Have they been 'parent watchers', especially mother watchers, in the face of interparental violence where they may have felt passionate but helpless. Have children living with opposite sex parents realised the Oedipal dream? What is the impact on this enduring tie when the parent forms a new adult attachment? Is this at this point experienced by many children as unbearable betrayal? What is it like to be asked to 'honour' this new adult-to-adult-bond as the most important 'relationship' in the household when in the child's own experience the mother's relationship to a man may be both treacherous and dangerous? Moreover, children may feel that such relationships are less enduring than mother's relationships to themselves. Ultimately, the enduring tie is not that of adults who separate but of mothers and children who do not. Which loyalty is to be privileged over which?

## Predictability, Competence and Self-Esteem

How does the move into post-divorce life validate or undermine a positive sense of self for those who are involved? What helps children in particular survive transitions in positive ways? We can now think with some confidence about the way in which external ongoing experience and internal experience mutually influence one another and reciprocally interact. We have conceptual frameworks for thinking about the relationships between sets of relationships, new ways of conceptualising a young child's development in relation to different kinds of secure and insecure experiences. A secure base may be considered not only as a single parent 'mother' but as sets of reliable relationships with family and intimate caregiving others, constituting bases of more or less security from which to explore. The changing milieu of a developing child can be conceptualised as a number of overlapping social systems of which each provides elements of identity or ongoing sense of self. We also need to ask how many changes, and of what quality can a child manage and still retain a coherent sense of self? When we consider divorce and remarriage this frame of 'child in interaction with reliable sets of relationships' is valuable in relation to the questions we ask about her daily life. What proportion of daily life is disturbed by the transitions of divorce, how insecure does the child become and how do the multiple adjustments required then prevent, for a time, other exploration? The school can play a crucial role as a reliable alternative context in which the child can develop a sense of self as competent. Desforges (1995) points at the legitimate and increasing need for teachers to become interested in separation and divorce as they affect children's social and emotional development as well as their ability to learn.

Given that such frameworks of security or insecurity also connect to the internalised emotional and cognitive maps for adults we can usefully ask similar questions of them, leading us to evolve the unique understanding of the meaning of a divorce and its associated transitional experience for each individual and family.

### The Child's Perspective

How does our study from a clinical group gain weight from comparison with non clinical studies? The Exeter study showed that even though children who had been part of a violent marriage were glad to be removed from that situation, they remained concerned about their non-resident parent. Even where children were fully aware of the conflict many were sad that the conflict had resulted in separation and a dramatic alteration in their own relationship with one of their parents.

In looking at the words of a boy aged nine from a family where both parents were violent, we can see this concern for the maintenance of the marital relationship as the child's overriding concern; placing his awareness of the marital discord at a lower level of reality than the fear of separation.

| | |
|---|---|
| Boy: | Mummy, I just want you both to stay together. |
| Mother: | I know but ... |
| Boy: | Please ... |
| Mother: | You see we were staying together darling ... |
| Boy: | Please, pretty please, pretty please, pretty pretty please ... |
| Mother: | You're a bit of a baby. I'm trying to tell you something. |
| Boy: | I just want to know if you and Dad will stay together. |
| Mother: | Well, I've decided ... |
| Boy: | Yes or no! |
| Mother: | I've decided not to stay together with Dad because ... No, no. Dad and I have decided not to stay together as well. Firstly because Dad and I don't get on and because, in fact, when we were staying together and we weren't getting on, you were having a lot of problems. |
| Boy: | But you were getting on. |
| Mother: | We were not getting on, Darling. One of the reasons we have decided, I have decided to leave Dad, is because I want to give you a chance to have a nice calm home where you can |

grow up and can learn things and you can have friends and
at the same time you might be able to visit Dad and make
sure that you have fun with Dad and that Dad won't hit you.

Reporting on her attempts to tell her son at home about the impending
divorce, another dimension of his social reality is again placed above his
awareness of the parental fights.

I don't want you and Dad to divorce because none of my friends is
divorcing, and then he said to me, I said, it that's why what's bothering
you? Things are bad between Mum and Dad ... He said, 'Yes that worries
me a lot.'

## Different Contexts: different stories

The families we have worked with in our half-day-a-week commitment
to this project contained a number of different family constructions;
they did not consist of just one post-divorce family organisation, but
displayed the following permutation:

1. Divorced: still living together with children
2. Divorced: living as lone parent with children: other parent out
3. Never married: living as a lone parent with children
4. Re-ordered: resident parent cohabiting (part or full-time)
5. Re-ordered: non resident parent cohabiting full-time
6. Re-ordered: both parents cohabiting (part or full-time)
7. Not yet divorced: living in house with children
8. Not yet divorced but one or other parent cohabiting elsewhere

Families were of diverse ethnicities and countries of origin: in half the
families, one or both parents moved to this country during their
lifetime. All but three of the residential parents were mothers. The
subtext of our discussion therefore must include questions relating in
wider ways to how divorce may be different for men and for women;
who has lost, in what respect and who has gained in what respect. For
men as non-resident parents two dimensions of their stories stand out.
The first is the dimension of loss; loss of self as it was formerly
constituted in the family over time, and loss of former intimacy with the
mother of their children and secondly the development of new but
definitely precarious skills in relation to the tasks of parenting.

For women stories following divorce also included loss. However
these were in active dialogue with new aspects of self, including release

from marriages formerly experienced as abusive and oppressive, depression resulting from the withdrawal of intimacy with a partner and the tasks of living alone in intimacy with the children (Burck et al., 1996). This loss was followed for many of the women, but for none of the men, by the declared experience of developing new or higher order skills which were storied as the exhilaration of survival (usually accompanied by exhaustion). An ongoing worry about the well-being of the children in relation to the irresponsibility of their other parent formed a part of women's narratives at both the initial interview and the follow-up two years on, although to a less intense degree at that point if things were going better by that time. Two fathers had not been in touch from the beginning, one had severed contact since leaving and two who were maintaining contact were causing both their wives and children ongoing (although more resigned) concern.

What was the effect of telling individual stories about the divorce experience? For some people to narrate their stories of divorce in a therapeutic context seemed to offer a way to move between past, present and future and to develop new possibilities even as they talked: in the act of talking about an old event new meanings and potential changes in patterns of relationship emerged. These carried the possibility of different actions developing in the future and some changes of position from helplessness to effectiveness could be achieved in a relatively short time. Below, we consider the differences between two stories of marriages which contained violence to see how descriptions of the self in relation to former negative relationships were able to change over time.

Flynn aged five, drew himself standing at the door witnessing his father strangling his mother while she hit him in the stomach. While such an event is stark when described and discussed, his mother did not wish to conceal the meanings in which the events were embedded, but to understand better the effects these had both for her and for her son. For Cathleen the powerful meaning of his drawing lay in its intergenerational repetition ... she too remembered such fights in her childhood and her own sense of impotence. Her wish however, was that Flynn should be able to continue to see his father, following the separation, as she had not been able to see hers following her mother's. Her goal was to become strong, to feel safe enough to allow the father-son relationship to continue in spite of the marital violence. She was able to be clear with her son that the separation was not his fault; 'You're too little, darlin' it couldn't be your fault in no way.' She handled his father's recent attempted violence by taking out an injunction to prevent him

194

coming to the house and negotiating contact with him outside the house until she felt safe. Over a period of a year she transformed her own story from being at risk to one where as a result of different kinds of affirmative action (which lasted and amplified), she felt in charge of the family and the risks involved.

For Ray however the story his parent's told contained powerful binding elements in which the participants seemed to be trapped, the accounts being full of blame, distortion and a sense of victimisation. The narrative of either parent often had repetitious immutable features, which the couple found very hard to change, caught it seems in a timeless web of stock phrases of description of self as victim, and other as bully, tyrant or persecutor. Exaggerated and distorted accounts of the other's behaviour might typically characterise such a story. He was also faced with learning to manage his father's violent tempers; familiar for years, but intensifying in the protracted divorce negotiation. This disciplining of his son was never called 'hitting' but was known as 'giving him the hand' or 'a clout, a box, a whack or a thwack; never a smack or a hit'. Raymond was passionately attached to his father but frightened of the hitting. He did not understand the cues that meant he was in for one of these attacks, intended as 'corrective teaching'. He had formerly relied on Mum, but now on contact visits, he had to manage Dad on his own.

A short segment from an account given by his mother, Mrs Finlay, gives the flavour of a violent episode:

> His father took him into the bedroom, grabbed him by the neck, twisting his collar while he felt choking that he was almost choking, lifted him into the air and then started hitting him while he was in the air, at random and he said fifty times just absolutely hitting out at him, shaking him up and down and then he threw him to the ground and ...

One of the difficulties for Raymond in facing a way of dealing with his father's violent behaviour was that his parents had started to use 'police' language about it. Punching, kicking, hitting, strangling had begun to be referred to as 'incidents'. The first thing that seemed to be important was to de-neutralise the language; and 'unpack' the incident into details of what actually happened; then to link it to bodily feelings of hurt, upset, tears, blood, and then having broken it down or 'deconstructed' to think about specific ways the violent spiral could be broken into, so that it did not escalate. Mr Finlay always denied that the incidents occurred at all. Our attempts to disentangle 'truth' and 'reality' in this situation as with others have led us to recognise 'truth' may remain hidden, but persistence in holding onto our experience of the child's reality must always remain in the forefront of our practice.

A key feature in reducing violence in this family involved working with father to allow the expression of his loving and protective feelings towards his son to be validated and to have them as part of the acknowledged conversation about his ongoing commitment to him.

> And I mean, to me, a father's role, from the sort of society I come from, was the sort of the tough, bluff, let the mum look after the kids sort of thing, you know, and I'll go down to the ale house and that sort of ... mmm ... And that's not the sort of role that I'm playing, or have played. It's mum and dad role that I'm playing. You know I find that instead of saying now look, get up, you're going to be okay, be a man, I've got to go over and cuddle him.

The way in which children have to learn to manage anger following divorce, in a situation unmediated by the other parent and the degree to which they themselves learn anger as a habitual response to every day problems is an important area of the child's development that we were often concerned about. Holding in our minds the concept of internal working models, a concept originally put forward by Bowlby (Main et al., 1985; 1992 Byng-Hall, 1995) defined as effectively laden mental representations of the self, other and of the relationship derived from interactional experience, we were concerned at the way children carry the patterns they have learned forward into other contexts in their lives. Other studies (Sroufe and Fleeson, 1988) have noted how children repeat both aspects of the abusive behaviour they live through, being able to play the role of both abused and abuser in contexts away from home. This we found constantly born out in Ray's school report. Yet other studies have noted how a good relationship with one parent may mediate the negative effects of the violence from another. But how does the child who has to co-exist in two modalities which are separate and of equal emotional power, and which also actively disqualify one another learn to free himself from a dominant discourse of violence, and relate in different ways to other contexts such as school, peer groups or their own subsequent family life?

Such concerns and how to 'unpick' the knots through therapy brings us some way between the 'two ways' of looking at theory: the 'internalisation' of experience held by individual therapists, or 'mental map making' or 'representations of relationships' held by systemic family therapists. How a child living and witnessing adult behaviour takes aspects of parenting into their own models of constructing family life, which will be available for action replay when they in turn become parents, is not only important to keep as a question in the mind of professionals, but useful to openly discuss with parents and children. Where the current patterns have potentially aversive consequences other ideas about resolving family issues can be introduced, and tried out within the ongoing clinical work with the family.

Conversations about violent behaviour have to take place in the therapy context so that there is a language in which it can be spoken about in each of the parental contexts and within the child's mind. While language alone does not change behaviour, it introduces the idea of the relationship 'becoming' something else which is not violent. Once settled as a new theme or part of the discourse about learning or discipline it can be elaborated in a number of ways.

Where children also have to learn to manage certain forms of interparental conflict, the question of who protects them or mediates the situation on their behalf is crucial to making a therapeutic difference. Divorce itself may not make a difference, as research has shown. The ongoing disturbance, which may have been contained in the marriage will have to be handled in a different way as the child confronts two parents each with their own separate constructions of reality, and each with their own acute and possibly rigid version of how their child should be. What may also happen in this situation is that the child will be temporarily annexed to form the 'other person' in the mental representation of either parent whose own self definition as 'good' or 'capable' requires a couple in their minds (Gorell Barnes, 1991). The function of the other person in the 'couple' may be to be assigned the part of 'bad' or 'incapable' someone who has to be punished or shaped correctively. Where a parent has resigned from this ascribed role through divorce, the child may in the other parent's mind take up the understudy position. This can put the child at additional risk. New communication skills have to be developed between parent and child, since the child can no longer rely on the other parent to defuse or distract from an escalating conflict or spiralling 'madness'.

An interesting aspect of family narrative is the way in which children might hold an 'official' version of the parental breakup at the expense of their own perception of what has happened. This official version might change depending on which home they were in (the residential home or the contact parent's home) at which point the 'other' version would have to be held 'unofficially' and silently in their minds until a new context allowed it once more to be brought forth. This switching of truths was something the therapeutic context of the clinic could challenge, 'all stories have recognition here' until the differing parties could refocus on a story that was in the interests of their child, rather than their own wounded or warring feelings. In one case a father gave the authors his sympathetic congratulations for 'trying to sort us lot out', and has also written to thank us for our persistence more than once. This raises interesting questions about the amount of time such family work may require and highlights the inadequacy of current provision.

### Silence, and the Elision of Memory

However it was not only 'war' which made narratives of family life difficult for children but also deliberate silence, the elision of memory of the parent who had gone and a refusal to discuss their ongoing life in another place. A key function of the interviews was to challenge such a silence. Silence was also contextualised by a lack of clarity in parental arrangements stemming from uncertainty about whether the marriage was ended or not, or as one mother once she had gained some sense of distance re-described it 'having your cake and eating it ... he knows I'm always here to come back to'.

For Ben the changes in relationship between father and mother were hidden over a number of years; and the absence of explanation led to an inability to think which was reflected at school. It seemed that to ask questions or display open curiosity was too dangerous.

> Ellie:  When Stephen (father) does come back ... he ... we, sort of fall into him being one of the family. He is like one of the family you see. And on Sundays, its like it always was ...

In this situation a child may not only worry about the meaning or absence of explanation for himself, but also for a parent who he observes to be unhappy.

> Ellie:  He (Ben) says "You know I sometimes worry that you haven't had a very nice life, Mummy", you know and I have to re-assure him ... and I have to say to him, look we are very fortunate, and we've got a lovely home and we've got enough money and we're really very fortunate ... more than most people really are. We, you know, see Daddy twice a week, even though you know he doesn't live with us any more ... I know that it upsets and has upset him very deeply obviously, seeing me unhappy.
>
> Gill:  It seems to me that in order to help Ben regain his own sense of his own mind and his own confidence, these are things

| | |
|---|---|
| | that may have to be talked about, so I guess its important for you to think about whether you want that to happen. |
| Ellie: | You see, I don't know what they spoke about (son and Emilia). I think maybe she (Emilia) made him *see* things. But he doesn't like to admit, you see ... |
| Gill: | What might he have seen that he doesn't ... |
| Ellie: | I don't know, maybe he realises ... |
| Gill: | Hasn't seen before ... |
| Ellie: | That there is another woman. |
| Gill: | Had you talked about that before with him? |
| Ellie: | He's refused to talk about it with me. |
| Gill: | Have you just ... |
| Ellie: | Broached ... I broached the subject. |
| Gill: | And you said it ... |
| Ellie: | Yes. |
| Gill: | What did you say? |
| Ellie: | We know what Daddy is, I don't know why Daddy's left us, or something like that you know, I said well you know Ben, You know that there is another ... I've told you that Daddy left because there is some other woman. |
| Gill: | Does *she* have a name in his mind? |
| Ellie: | No, probably not. |
| Gill: | Would he have an opportunity to talk to his father about that? |
| Ellie: | Doesn't want to ... Stephen's tried ... |
| Gill: | And if he insisted? |
| Ellie: | I would get upset. |
| Gill: | You would ... |
| Ellie: | Upset, upset ... I mean I can't feel terribly civilised towards her, I'm afraid ... I hate the idea of her becoming friendly with the children and everything, I really do ... and I think Stephen always kept us in separate compartments ... he's liked to do that as well, and he's the one whose always said, "Oh look I'll get over it, I'll come back, you'll see". He cries a lot. It's not just me ... it's him. |

A year later Mrs Johnson is still hoping that her husband may return although he has now bought a flat with his girlfriend:

| | |
|---|---|
| Ellie: | I hope that once they start living together, some of the magic will go out of their relationship ... I mean, that's what I'm hoping. |
| Gill: | How many years would it take for you to believe he wasn't going to change his mind? Would you be happy to live like that hoping for the rest of you life? |
| Ellie: | I suppose it won't be that much longer now that they are living together. |

| Gill: | You are very genuinely involved with this man still and emotionally connected ... perhaps coming here has given you an opportunity to explore that a bit more. |
|---|---|
| Ellie: | I know, it's awful really. |
| Gill: | But I also think not to explore it and to preserve the stale mate for ever is maybe partly holding you and Ben in this locked position. Are there conversations you might like to have with Stephen in the security of a setting like this ... which you might not have felt free to have at home ... on behalf of you and the kids? |
| Ellie: | Well, I suppose the only thing he could say is look, I'm now making a new life with this woman.<br>And then one could feel, really I suppose, I could start letting go, because I'd have to wouldn't I? |

In an interview with Mr and Mrs Johnson together their sorrow at the marriage ending is explored and the couple mourn the loss of intimacy:

| Ellie: | I miss that terribly, and I miss when I read things in the papers I mean, its like a loss, I think, oh that would amuse Stephen, and I used to say, you know, I read this or I heard that on the radio, or and I miss, you know television programmes that we used to share and I still watch that and I think I wonder whether he's seen that. |
|---|---|
| Stephen: | ... The pleasures of simple, sort of, family life really. And nothing wildly exciting, just, ... uhm ... doing simple things together and obviously we were all happy in that setting, and my knees start trembling ... it's a sort of feeling, you know, sort of like, the fall, like, if you know what I mean. |

Following the *parental* conversation between Ellie and Stephen, it becomes possible for Stephen to talk more openly with Ben about his living arrangements and Ben also expresses his anger more openly with his father.

| Gill: | What's your understanding of where your dad is planning to live? Do you believe he is going to come home again, or do you believe he is not going to come home again? |
|---|---|
| Ben: | Not going to come home again. |
| Gill: | Have you talked about that with him? |
| Ben: | He said I've got to accept the fact that he is living with someone else. |
| Gill: | Is it new for him to say that clearly? |
| Stephen: | You did say ... that you hadn't really understood that I was living somewhere else until you'd come here ... and he wished that Susan and I had been more forthright with him |

... because it would have helped him to accept it, and I think
he's absolutely right. I think we both felt we were somehow
making life easier for him by not involving him in it all, and
I think you're right, I think we're making things more
difficult for him.

## *Using Whole Family Sessions*

Does it sometimes need the original pre-divorce family to re-gather
together for certain issues to be mediated between the members? We
would argue that it does. Meaning as an intersubjective experience is
created in conversations and actions between people in particular
contexts. Sometimes the same significant others between whom the
problems were originally constructed need to be regathered so that the
original forum in which misunderstandings were developed can be
newly opened. We would suggest that this forum contains not only
language but powerful and intimate affect. As a result of the work in
subsystems we have found that it may be possible to develop new
meanings which will shape subsequent understanding and action in
different ways. Where mothers and fathers are painfully at odds, it is
not only the children who suffer, but often the alienated parents in
role as mother and father, even if no longer sexual partners. For
example a father who had built up the belief that his former wife was
trying to keep the children from him was helped by the children
clarifying with their parents, their own understanding of their mother's
misgivings.

| | |
|---|---|
| Jimmy: | Dad, remember when you said that thing about Mummy is trying to keep the wall around us? I don't think that is right, Dad. |
| Jonathan: | Well, it's what I felt. |
| Jimmy: | I think ... |
| Jonathan: | It's what I felt. |
| Jimmy: | At that moment. |
| Jonathan: | At that moment. |
| Jimmy: | But you don't feel it now? |
| Jonathan: | Perhaps less so now because we are all here talking openly and your Mummy is here and ... |
| Jane: | I don't think exactly that Mum wants to keep a wall around us ... I think she wants us to see you but only if you are in a good mood and not drinking ... and you'll be nice to us. |

201

## The Organisation of the Work

Work of this kind requires attention to be given both to the former family system and its ongoing bonds and loyalties as well as to the disequilibrium and necessary adaptation of those connections in the newly reordered family. It involves drawing on what we know about couple work, individual work and family work as well as the skills derived from the child psychologist's understanding of children's different perceptions and grasp of process at different ages.

The goal of our intervention is to contribute to family members becoming more secure observers of their own lives, moving from a reactive to a reflective narrative. The notion of 'reflective self function' (Fonagy et al., 1991) in adults, the ability to take into account the mental states of self and others, has been found to have a predictive value for secure attachment in children. As professionals intervening in the current context of a child's *life*, we use our different positions as clinicians to enable a context for a reflective mind to develop. A milieu where reflection rather than angry reaction becomes a more normal mode in previously oppositional couples, or a milieu in which thinking about what is going on and speaking about it is an open part of life rather than taboo, may create significant differences in moderating discord and denial. In reaching a more reflective position, children can themselves then help parents address some of the more complex questions of post divorce life, and its contradictions.

Couples need to be freed from entrainment in an ongoing pattern of acrimonious and competitive parenting. We would argue that no significant change may be made without some move towards the sorrow underlying the anger and some recognition that things were once good. We hazard a belief that there has to be some mutuality of purpose in the parenting couple, however minimal, before they can co-parent successfully over time. The focus made to move away from a preoccupation with righteousness towards a concern about children and parenting.

To this aim we have offered individual space to the parents so that old stories can risk being told in new ways. New connections can also be added, 'I loved you passionately ... and then there was war ...', rather than the denial that there was ever any love or connection. The former meaning of family life can then be held onto during the divorce process because former experience is seen to have potential new meanings for the future. It is as though individuals (adults/parents) take aspects of the whole family system into themselves in a positive way as well as acknowledging the negative.

## 9. Rewriting the Story

The individual interviews with the children represent the first time that many children have been able to voice their own subjective experience. The opportunity is created for them to give their unedited story which will be by no means coherent. Such sessions provide the opportunity for children to speak to someone outside the family who is skilled at listening, who is neutral and eliciting what is of concern to the child. In the process, the child's understanding of the many differences involved is clarified. Subsequently, in family interviews the child's voice can be more clearly heard sometimes via the therapist, and the child can then be absolved of the responsibility for holding all the differences.

### The Family Interviews

Having individual space for both parents and children acts as a precursor to bringing parents and children together. Each therapist takes the freedom to stop the old grooves of quarrelling. A more directive approach in family sessions is taken because of each therapist's prior knowledge of the individual concerned. Having provided a secure base, the therapists can take risks and redirect the session into more useful frames.

The interviews are usually very focused and address the different versions of controversial aspects of the divorce process. Family members are encouraged to listen to each others' views as distinct, divergent and sometimes oppositional. The paradigm of difference replaces the paradigm of right and wrong. The aim is a negotiated agreement of very *concrete* things which concern the children in full acknowledgement of the effectively laden nature of the small details of family arrangements and the powerful personal meanings these can hold.

Some questions remain unanswered: for example, the way in which in the course of therapeutic work, the narratives of the different members successfully transform memories of family life and the part played by the self in creating stories which appropriately connect the past with the evolving construction of post-divorce identity. However, it is a beginning. We have sketched some of the aspects of working with parents and children, separately and together, which create a sense of agency rather than a sense of helplessness. We hope to learn more about how this experience is different for parents and children by further analysis of the work undertaken as well as following up the families involved.

## References

Burck, C., Hildebrand, J. and Mann, J., 'Women's Tales: systemic groupwork with mothers post separation' in *Journal of Family Therapy*, 18(2): 163-182 (1996).

Byng-Hall, J., *Rewriting Family Scripts*. London: Guilford, (1995).

Cockett, M. and Tripp, J., *The Exeter Study*. Joseph Rowntree Foundation, (1994).

Desforges, M. 'Separation Divorce and the School' in Best, R. et al (eds) *Pastoral Care and Personal-Social Education*. London: Cassell, (1995).

Dowling, E. and Gorell Barnes, G., 'Children of Divorcing Parents: a clinical perspective' in *Journal of Clinical Child Psychology and Psychiatry* (forthcoming 1998).

Elliott, J. and Richards, M.P.M., 'Children and Divorce: Educational Performance and Behaviour Before and After Parental Separation' in *International Journal of Law and The Family 5*. 258-276 (1992).

Fonagy, P., Steele, M., Steele, H., Higgitt, A. and Target, M., *The Theory and Practice of Resilience* (1993).

Gorell Barnes, G. (1991) 'Ambiguities in post-divorce relationships' *Journal of Social Work Practice*, 5, 143-150.

Gorell Barnes, G., Thompson, P., Daniel, G. and Burchardt, N. *Growing up in Step-families: life story interviews*. NCDS Cohort 1958. University of Essex, Department of Sociology and Institute of Family Therapy. Oxford, Clarendon Press (forthcoming 1997).

Haskey, J. Population Trends No 74. 'Divorces in England and Wales'. *OPCS/HMSO* (1993).

Hetherington, E.M., 'Coping with Family Transitions: Winners, Losers and Survivors.' *Child Development*, 60, 1-4 (1989)(a).

Hetherington, E.M., 'Marital Transitions: a child's perspective' in *American Psychologist*, 44 2, 303-312, (1989)(b).

Hetherington, E.M. and Stanley-Hagman, M.M., 'Parenting in Divorce and Remarried Families' in Bernstein, M.H. (ed.) *Handbook of Parenting*. Hillsdale, NJ: Erlbaum, (1995).

Isaacs, M.B., Leon, G, and Donahue, A.M. 'Who are the 'Normal' Children of Divorce?: on the need to specify a population'. *Journal of Divorce* 1987 pp 107-119, (1987).

Jenkins, J., Smith, M., Graham, P., 'Coping with Parental Quarrels'. *Journal of American Academy of Child and Adolescent Psychiatry* 28 182-189, (1988).

Main, M., Kaman, N. and Cassidy, J., 'Security in Infancy, Childhood and Adulthood: a move to the level of representation' in Bretherton. I. and Waters, E. (eds) *Growing Points in Attachment Theory and Research*. Monographs of the Society for Research in Child Development, 50, 1-2, 66-104, Serial No. 209, (1985).

Main M., 'Metacognitive Knowledge, Meta-cognitive Monitoring and Singular (Coherent) vs. Multiple (Incoherent) Model of Attachment. Findings and directions for further research' in Murray Parkes, C., Stevenson Hinde, J. &

Mains P. (eds) *Attachment Across the Life Cycle*. Routledge, London, (1992).

Ochiltree, G., *Children in Stepfamilies* (Sydney, Prentice Hall, 1990).

Simpson, B., McCarthy, P. and Walker. J., *Being There: fathers after divorce*, Relate Centre for Family Studies (Newcastle, 1996).

Sroufe, L.A. & Fleeson, J. (1988) 'The Coherence of Family Relationships' in Hinde, R.A. & Stevenson-Hinde, J. (eds) *Relationships Within Families: mutual influence*. (Oxford Scientific Publications, Oxford, 1995).

Wadsby, M., 'Children of divorce and their parents' in Linkoping *University Medical Dissertations* No 405. (Linkoping Department of Child and Adolescent Psychiatry, Faculty of Health Sciences, Linkoping University, s.58185 Linkoping Sweden, 1993).

Walker, J., *Family and Community Dispute Research Centre*. (University of Newcastle upon Tyne, 1990 ongoing) (see Simpson, McArthy and Walker 1996).

# Is Home Where the Heart Is?

## Narratives of Oppositional Discourses
## in Refugee Families

*Renos K. Papadopoulos and Judy Hildebrand*

### Introduction

As long as human beings have had homes, they have always been at risk of becoming refugees, uprooted by natural disasters, interpersonal and group conflicts, war and territorial competition. The refugee condition affects many facets of life from the most tangible external aspects such as shelter, food, health, education and often even physical survival itself, to a wide spectrum of psychological dimensions. These can range from subtle and often initially imperceptible experiences of a lack of safety, disruption, abandonment, displacement and disorientation, to more noticeable and obvious experiences of destruction, violence, loss and disorganisation. Similar to many other potentially painful events in the life cycle, such as the onset of illness, bereavement, leaving home, family relocation, and divorce, becoming a refugee engenders stressful experiences which may lead to temporary or permanent psychological dysfunction in individuals, families and communities. However, such experiences, despite their painful nature, may also have positive consequences in so far as they may lead to the development of more appropriate coping mechanisms, deepen a sense of identity in individuals, strengthen cohesion among family members, and offer an opportunity for a more fundamental re-evaluation of one's life. It is not uncommon for members of refugee communities to become extremely successful in a wide variety of activities and careers in the receiving country and to lead creative and fulfilling lives (Knox, 1997).

Comparing the refugee condition with other stressful events within the 'normal' life cycle raises an important and most sensitive question: how to create a context within which refugees are not pathologised whilst, at the same time, the conditions which lead people to become refugees are clearly condemned? On the one hand, this comparison enables a focus on the normalisational aspects of this condition thus de-emphasising inappropriate pathologising, whereas, on the other hand, it may also imply an acceptance that to become a refugee is a 'normal' fact of life. Although the latter proposition is obviously unacceptable, the former has a significance which is usually ignored. Becoming a refugee does not and should not imply that a person has developed any form of psychological pathology and, hence, he or she should not be treated as such. Capturing the essence of the refugee condition is not easy. For example, although there are some similarities between becoming a refugee and experiencing the loss of a parent, or the onset of a chronic illness, the refugee condition cannot be understood exclusively in terms of the psychology of loss nor in terms of any other single psychological model. This whole question highlights the subtlety and multidimensional nature of the refugee condition in which psychological considerations are only part of the totality of the situation (Cohon, 1981 and 1985; Holtzman and Borneman, 1991; Mollica et al., 1987, 1989 and n.d.; Mollica and Jalbert, 1989; Vernez, 1991; Williams and Westermeyer, 1986). Essentially, people become refugees as a result of political factors and thus the political dimension should not be forgotten even when approaching refugees from a psychological perspective (Rutter, 1994 and 1996). To paraphrase Lynn Hoffman (1989), the infiltration of politics into daily life acquires a particularly poignant meaning in the case of refugees. Due to its multifaceted and complex nature, the refugee condition requires a correspondingly multidimensional approach so that we avoid crude pathologising and psychological labelling.

## Locating the Refugee Experience

There is an implicit tendency to construct theories of change in psychology on the basis of either individual psychological factors or, when we do include the wider social system, of predictable interactions within our social network. This means that theories of the life cycle are based on expected transitional milestones with bereavement possibly the only unexpected phenomenon included. However, appropriately, within the last few decades, separation and divorce have also entered our conceptualisation of predictable changes. The relatively recent phenomenon of the increased rates of separation and divorce in the Western world has forced mental-health professionals to appreciate its *de facto* significance in the lives of an increasingly high proportion of our population. Accordingly, the way in which we describe families who have experienced separation and divorce has changed. For example, we no longer talk of 'broken homes' but of 'single parent families' and our stories no longer treat divorced parents as 'abnormal' instead we talk of 'incompatibilities', and of the effect of 'circumstances'. In other words, we have managed to normalise the experience of divorce without diminishing its disruptive effects.

However, it seems that this process has not happened with reference to war. Central to any psychological approach to refugees lies a key confusion which has to do with the way we conceptualise war and its place in our lives. Despite the fact that millions of people's lives have been affected by war and its consequences, we have not yet found an appropriate way of recognising its place in the life-cycle. After each military conflict, there seems to be a recurrence of optimism that the world will finally settle into a more peaceful mode; yet, time and time again these expectations have been shattered by new outbreaks of hostility. Following the recent collapse of the communist regimes, people looked forward to a more open and peaceful society free from the suspicion, divisions and animosity that the *cold war* had produced. Instead, they were confronted by the outburst of a most violent *hot war* in the former Yugoslavia. It is remarkable that people reacted as if their current situation and stories of previous war atrocities were not on the same historical continuum. It seems that there is a protective function in human beings which enables us to 'forget' painful memories of war and react with the wrath of naive ignorance when conflicts recur. It is as if humanity needs to keep cleansing itself from the horrors of war by constantly 'forgetting' them and thus renewing its virginal innocence. Thus, we may be destined to keep wishing that we could learn from history while reacting with fresh and genuine abhorrence whenever the excruciating absurdity of war recurs.

Stories about war appear to have a rather paradoxical position in the Western world, where they are portrayed either as if they are distant and irrelevant phenomena or noble and heroic events. Painful stories of terror and atrocities are related as if they belong to the past or as if they provide abstract moral lessons. This is why when new conflicts emerge, as in Bosnia, we seem to need to distance ourselves, denying or minimising their relevance to us, and attempt to rationalise their ferocity ('the war is so vicious because there is a long history of animosity between the combatants') or we perceive the warring factions as vastly different from ourselves ('horrific events happen there because those

Balkan/African/Chinese etc. are different from us in the civilised Western world').

This paradoxical stance seems to create an epistemological confusion between moral and theoretical perspectives. In other words, from moral and political standpoints, we cannot and would not wish to accept that war is part of our lives; yet, we cannot deny the fact that it has been so throughout history. Our abhorrence of war should not affect our comprehension of it; we need to maintain a recognition of its apparent inevitable existence. The direct implication of this paradox is that when war breaks out, mental-health professionals may find themselves trapped in a disabling syndrome. This consists of a powerful and yet fuzzy mixture of political and moral considerations, attempts at psychological theorising, disbelief, numbness, relief that we are not the victims, shame and guilt, impractical idealism, omnipotent phantasies, etc. This syndrome sustains its powerful grip on us with the help of two important elements — the media and the 'specialist care industry'.

The media and the 'specialist care industry' constantly produce new stories which inadvertently seem to maintain this paradox as well as the epistemological confusion and ultimately the inertia. Although, logically, one tends to think that the media and this type of 'industry' are a response to, and therefore a consequence of the war, in effect, systemically speaking, they are interdependent and feeding off each other. This means that as mental-health professionals we should constantly endeavour to consider the nature and effect of our own position within the overall refugee care system. As part of the 'specialist care industry' and as media consumers, we are shaped in imperceptible ways often to the detriment of our effectiveness (Bell, 1997).

Given that our theories of change are based on norms in peace time and that war is seen as an aberration or abnormality, it is almost inevitable that we tend to regard most suffering due to war also as within the model of abnormality. In other words, as yet we have not developed a model, comparable to that of divorce, which would enable us to normalise the suffering due to war (which includes the refugee experience) without diminishing its disruptive effects as well as its abhorrent nature. Thus, it appears as an unavoidable consequence that the stories that are told about refugees both by themselves and by professionals tend to be formulated within the context of a pathology and deficit paradigm.

### The Mental Health of Refugees

Statistics show that the refugee population in the world has recently been growing almost in geometrical progression and reaching alarming proportions. For example, in 1970 there were 2.5 million refugees, in 1983 11 million and in 1993 over 18 million (UNHCR, 1993). More recently, the catastrophic events in the former Yugoslavia, Rwanda and Zaire have augmented these figures even further. As Papadopoulos (in press) commented, 'world attention on "trouble spots" comes and goes but the refugees generated from each one of them do not vanish with the same ease as the news headlines. The gradual accumulation of refugees and traumatised people in different parts of the world affect increasingly more aspects of people's lives in more countries'. Nevertheless, the overall approach to refugees seems to remain the same. Marjorie Muecke identified two approaches to refugee health, which she argued dominate the field today; these are 'the objectification of refugees as a political class of excess people, and the reduction of refugee health to disease or pathology' (1992, p. 515). Muecke goes on to argue for the inclusion of a new paradigm based on her understanding that 'refugees present perhaps the maximum example of the human capacity to survive despite the greatest of losses and assaults on human identity and dignity' (p. 520). This view is similar to the sentiment expressed in the most recent guidelines issued by the United Nations High Commissioner for Refugees: 'the single best way to promote the psychosocial well-being of children is to support their families. Refugees bring with them their personal resourcefulness and they come with other refugees — relatives, friends and neighbours — who have a tradition of helping each other. A family that is split apart or under serious stress may not fully meet the physical and emotional needs of their children. These families may need assistance in using their own coping techniques and rebuilding their support links' (1994, p. 43).

These guidelines offer a close link between resourcefulness, resilience and the family. Evdokas (1976), in a large scale research of Greek Cypriot refugees following the Turkish invasion of Cyprus, found that what refugees valued more than anything else was being together with members of their family (cf. Hirschon, 1989). Hirschon's study based on long-term anthropological field work is one of the few known to us which portrays the resourcefulness and resilience of refugees, instead of locating them exclusively within a pathological context (Hitch, 1983; Holtzman and Borneman, 1991). Such a positive and non-judgmental approach would be consistent with current perspectives of the systemic model. In this chapter, we attempt to develop some ideas about how we could begin to conceptualise the refugee condition from a non-pathologising and systemic perspective.

In examining the relatively limited specialist literature on psychological approaches to refugees, one is struck by two facts; firstly, as Muecke remarked, the majority of studies are based on the pathology model (in its various shapes and forms, ranging from crude to subtle and benevolent pathologising); in other words, refugees are approached in terms of their psychological deficits which are defined in a variety of different ways. Secondly, there is a striking diversity among these studies; this is understandable because although there may be common features to most refugee conditions, every situation is nonetheless different, and therefore unique. In particular, issues of race, culture, language, religion, political affiliations, geographical proximity and history directly affect the refugee experience. For example, in many ways the Somali or Vietnamese refugees in the UK have had a different experience from the Bosnian or Cypriot refugees, in so far as they have had to face the additional problem of looking physically different from the majority of the British population. In addition, there are many other circumstantial factors which determine the specificity of the refugee experience: these include the degree of traumatic exposure (whether they were subjected to physical torture or had witnessed atrocities), the overall context of their plight — whether the situation in their country attracted media attention or not, whether it was considered an internationally relevant issue or an isolated incident in a local conflict, whether the receiving country was sympathetic or critical towards the refugees. Accordingly, studies differ depending on which aspect of the refugee condition they focus upon.

The most usual way of approaching the mental health issues of refugees is by using the diagnosis of Post Traumatic Stress Disorder (PTSD). Workers found that by offering 'hard evidence' that refugees suffer from an identifiable 'disorder' which is included in the standard nosological nomenclatures (e.g. the DSM IV and the ICD-10) they were able to secure support and funding for their refugee projects. However, using the PTSD model is not without difficulties (Friedman and Jaranson, 1994; Marsella, 1996a and 1996b). After a critical examination of the application of the PTSD category, Marsella et al. (1994), argued that 'the PTSD model is useful in conceptualising the traumatic experience of refugees, but it must be broadened to incorporate ethnocultural differences in the expression of traumatic stress' (p. 216). Moreover, suggesting that the emphasis on 'disorder' is inappropriate, they pro-

211

posed its replacement with 'the general construct of PTSS [Post Traumatic Stress Syndrome]' which, they believe, 'may offer a more useful conceptual approach to the psychological impact of the refugee experience' (p. 215).

Also critical to the inappropriate uses of the PTSD concept, Judith Zur (1996), an anthropologist and psychologist who worked with war widows in Guatemala, used the concept 'experience-near' to create a coherent context to appreciate the predicament of these widows. She borrowed this concept from anthropology where it was proposed to describe the way one refers to something 'naturally and effortlessly — to define what he or his fellows see, feel, think, imagine, and so on, and which he would readily understand when similarly applied to others' (Geertz, 1986, p. 124). This is contrasted to the concept 'experience-far' which is understood as a concept employed by specialists to further their own understanding about something. Zur discussed the positive value of using 'experience-near' concepts which have local significance and are based on the belief systems of that particular community rather than resorting to the PTSD categorisation.

The PTSD has emerged as a powerful tool in approaching refugee mental health issues because of its seemingly objective nature (de Jong and Clarke, 1996; Goderez, 1987). Marsella et al. (1994), in the same paper mentioned above, maintained that despite its limitations, the 'PTSD model permits us to search for psychophysiological and neuro-biological abnormalities associated with PTSD that may be independent of ethnocultural factors' (p. 213). This means that they believe that there are some clear indicators, i.e. some psychophysiological re-sponses, which do not depend on cultural variations and other circumstantial factors; they mention 'autonomic reactivity, startle reflex, sleep disturbance, adrenergic hyperarousal, hypothalamic-pi-tuitary-adrenocortical dysregulation, and endogenous opioid system activity'. However, despite the fact that even though these phenomena may be measured objectively, they are still experienced and interpreted by individuals in different cultures in different ways. Thus, it would be difficult to argue for the existence of culture-free indicators of the refugee experience.

Mindful of this difficulty, instead of the PTSD, Eisenbruch (1990 and 1991) advanced the concept of 'cultural bereavement' as a more ade-quate model for understanding the refugee experience. Based on research findings, he argued that one of the key predictors of refugees doing well in the receiving country is the continuation of their cultural contacts, networks and practices. Within the context of the model of 'cultural bereavement', the refugee reactions are appreciated as normal and healthy responses towards normalisation. Building on Eisenbruch's idea, Papadopoulos (1997a) suggested that the concept of 'nostalgic disorientation' could provide a more appropriate framework for appreciating the refugee condition because it is not only 'culture' that refugees might lose but their whole home environment with all its practical and symbolic components and functions. Referring to the classical Greek meaning of 'nostalgia', (i.e. the pain experienced in the yearning to return home), Papadopoulos emphasises the importance of 'home' as the key construct which interconnects three overlapping realms — the intrapsychic, the interpersonal and the sociopolitical, as well as containing conflicting archetypal polarities such as joys and sorrows, love and discord, proximity and distance. Thus, he likens the destruction of homes, as in the refugee experience, to nuclear explosion when all the contained forces erupt creating widespread devastation. So, what the refugees yearn for may not be just the specific cultural practices which they left behind but the restoration of the holding functions which the home symbolised and actually performed. Therefore, Papadopoulos argued that home, as a Bowlbian 'secure base' (Bowlby, 1988; Marris, 1996), provides more than physical safety and can positively or negatively affect development within the three interconnected realms.

In searching for appropriate analogies to the refugee experience, Loizos (1981), in his study on refugees in Cyprus after the Turkish invasion in 1974, turned to other situations which he termed 'deeply disruptive change' (p. 196). This seems to be an apt expression of the core of the refugee condition in so far as it identifies the radical and deeply disruptive change in their lives and it is formulated in a neutral way (in terms of pathology). In this category, which essentially is based on the idea of loss, Loizos compared refugees to (a) bereaved persons, (b) disaster victims, and (c) people who had been forced to migrate. In his careful review of these studies, he emphasised the differences as well as similarities among them, repeatedly cautioning against inappropriate comparisons and observed that under all these circumstances people display variations of grief reactions. However, as Wortman and Silver (1989) emphasised, 'coping with loss' is an issue fraught with many inappropriate perceptions and expectations.

## Stories of the Refugee Condition

Although, as described above, the bulk of the literature has addressed the refugee experience within the context of a pathology or deficit framework by focusing, in different ways, on the problems around the refugee condition (ICIHI, 1986; United Nations, 1960), there have also been several attempts to conceptualise it differently by emphasising the perspective that refugees are 'normal people reacting to abnormal circumstances'. In so far as systemic ideas also move away from pathologising phenomena by placing them within the context of interactional experiences of meaning, a systemic approach to refugees could provide a suitable framework along the same lines (cf. Arredondo et al., 1989; Papadopoulos, 1996 and 1997b; Reichelt and Sveaass, 1994; Woodcock, 1994; Zur, 1996).

The narrative metaphor which has emerged relatively recently within systemic therapies also affords a useful method of conceptualisation and technique. Based on the contention that human experiences are organised in the form of stories (Bruner, 1990), the narrative metaphor focuses on the ways in which experiences are shared among members of certain groups of people, e.g. families and communities. In other words, people interact not only on the basis of instantaneous feedback but also on belief systems which shape their perceptions of themselves, of others and of their relationships. Moreover, these belief systems do not exist in a vacuum but form part of shared narratives (Epston and White, 1992; Parry, 1994; White, 1989; White and Epston, 1991). In a sense, it could be argued that in so far as our lives are shaped by storied narratives, we can affect them to a considerable degree if we modified the way we represent them in our narratives. There is a reciprocal relationship between the stories we tell about ourselves and our lives; one affects the other in a way that we are both actors and authors of our stories. This is the basic rationale behind the recent movement in establishing 'narrative therapy' as a distinct form of psychotherapy with individuals and families (Parry and Doan, 1994). The refugee condition would be a most suitable area in which to apply the narrative approach (not necessarily the 'narrative therapy' as such) as it would provide a wider perspective to examine the multiplicity of interactional factors involved.

### The Current Project

The opportunity for developing these ideas was offered to us when the Systems Team at the Child and Family Department of the Tavistock Clinic created a number of specialist research groups. Consistent with the systemic view that interactions between internal and external worlds are essential in order to understand the complexities of human problems, we decided to focus on individual families who had become refugees as a result of a major upheaval in the wider system. Both of us head this small research group which also includes postgraduate students who are actively engaged in various research projects with refugees. We have also been involved in teaching of specialist courses for refugee workers, clinical work with refugee families and consultation to relevant individuals and organisations.

We believe that our own previous personal experiences of the refugee condition have affected us in various ways in our work; this became increasingly clear the more we worked together on this project. Therefore, we found most fitting the editors' request to the contributors of this book to provide a personal connection with the presented material. Writing this chapter has helped us systematise our thoughts and feelings and assisted us in organising our experiences thus clarifying further for us the relevance of our own history to what we brought into our work.

## Our Stories

In 1940, Judy and her two older sisters were part of an exodus of Jewish refugees from Britain sent to the United States to escape from a feared and threatening Nazi invasion. As a child of 5, without her parents, little sense could be made of the sudden uprooting overseas, to unknown distant relatives whose rural life-style, on a small holding in Connecticut, was a far cry from the familiar bustling extended family life in London. This unexplained and incomprehensible sudden change from the known and predictable to the completely unknown and unpredictable had a profound psychological effect on her over the years. Overall, being English and therefore 'different' and having to adapt to many changes in terms of new host families, new towns, new schools led to both a persisting sense of uncertainty and impermanence as well as to a capacity to acculturate to a variety of contexts, even though she only spent five years in the USA.

Renos was born in Cyprus and his early schooling was dominated by the liberation struggle against the British colonial power. School demonstrations and patriotic enthusiasm were part of his early experiences. In addition, the conflict between the Greek and Turkish communities on the island began developing and even before the British left Cyprus (1960), violent clashes between the two communities produced small groups of refugees. Renos remembers families of relatives and friends huddling together in safe houses, fleeing from the fighting zones. Three

215

years after the independence of Cyprus in 1960, the intercommunal strife blew up into a civil war and thousands of people were left homeless, looking for safety. Renos, as a teenager, witnessed atrocities and was involved in helping refugees. Finally, the invasion of Turkey which divided the island in 1974 created the biggest human disaster in Cyprus' modern history. Although Renos was not in Cyprus during this last tragedy, he became actively involved in helping refugee families whilst residing abroad. The effects of these experiences were deep and Renos has remained involved with social issues throughout his professional career, working with victims of violence and disaster.

Both of us have become acutely aware of how the refugee condition can disrupt and reshape family stories. Families have many sets of assumptions which are expressed in terms of narratives (stories) which account for similarities and differences, hopes and aspirations, joys and sorrows, achievements and failures etc., all of which fall within the range of predictable and expected developments and changes. However, the advent of traumatic and unexpected changes disrupt narratives, leaving people's stories in limbo. It takes time to make sense of the unexpected.

From our own experience we realised that, in time, people do modify their stories and develop new ones to help them make their predicament intelligible. Those who are unable to do so seem to remain psychologically stagnant.

## The Setting

The choice of working with Bosnian refugee families was based on our joint concern and involvement with refugee work as well as Renos' connections with a group of Bosnian ex-camp prisoners who were brought to this country by the Red Cross as medical evacuees.

In September 1992, shortly after the discovery of the prison camps in Bosnia by western journalists, the Red Cross negotiated the evacuation of the first group of 69 Bosnian Muslim male camp-prisoners and brought them to the UK as medical evacuees. Before their evacuation from the camps, the Red Cross promised these men that their families would be allowed to join them in the UK. On arrival, the men were distributed by the Department of Health to hospitals in England and 18 of them were taken to a hospital in the South East of England. As this was the first group of medical evacuees from those notorious camps to arrive in the UK, they attracted considerable media attention and continue to do so.

216

The men were suffering from a variety of serious medical conditions ranging from scurvy to physical exhaustion, from malnutrition to various physical injuries; some were even in a coma (Papadopoulos, 1996). In addition to providing medical treatment, the hospital authorities immediately approached the Tavistock Clinic requesting 'psychological help' for them. Thus, Renos' first visited their ward within a few days of their arrival in the UK. The men seemed to have found him acceptable because, although he spoke their language and was familiar with their culture and country, he was seen as neutral, not being a member of any hostile Yugoslav ethnic group.

Gradually after their physical recovery, most men were joined by members of their families and moved to council accommodation where Renos continued his therapeutic contact with them. This stage of families re-grouping was often very difficult. Each reunion contained a mixture of powerful feelings. Both the men as well as their families had changed a great deal in the months that had passed since their forcible separation. Their reunions, although in themselves happy occasions, were taking place against the backdrop of the catastrophic destruction of their country. Not only had their personal circumstances radically changed but the arrival of their families in the UK confirmed beyond any doubt that the unthinkable had indeed occurred, they had become refugees abroad and as such their future in Bosnia was no longer predictable. Together, they were faced with sharing the horrors and misery of their past experiences whilst trying to cope with the current and daily practical arrangements — from housing to financial realities, from schooling to medical care, from basic travel to shopping. Their survival has been further hindered by the fact that only a handful of adults managed to learn to speak some basic English, although, of course, the children picked up the language more quickly in their interactions with their peers at school.

Following Renos' connections, we approached Bosnian refugee families and asked to interview them in depth for about one-and-a-half-hours on two occasions with an interval of more than six months in between. All interviews were tape-recorded, transcribed and analysed. The focus of our investigation was to identify core dilemmas and the way in which they impacted on family systems in the context of being refugees. We wanted to see how these dilemmas affected them currently, and how they described them. We were interested in how their narratives accounted for their past and present life events, their future plans and aspirations and the sense they made of the radical changes in their lives.

## Theoretical Framework

One of the major dilemmas refugee families seem to experience is expressed in a constant underlying tension between two polar opposite tendencies: on one hand, to privilege and remain loyal to the past, not to forget the home country and its ways, to honour the home culture and belief systems, to value the old, the pre-war relationships and connections, and to emphasise the previous styles and modes of being with their corresponding perceptions, values and aspirations; and on the other hand, to focus on the benefits of their current place of safety, to value the adjustment to their new life, to emphasise their new modes of being, to ensure maximum gain from new relationships and connections, to explore and benefit from the new life styles found in the receiving country, and to look towards the future ensuring that they make the best of their new opportunities.

Each one of these tendencies is not a mere preference or view or orientation but much more than that; far from being an abstract notion, it is a living reality which determines where and how the refugees locate their own sense of identity and how they position themselves in relation to other family members, their own refugee community and the wider network of institutions and society of the receiving/hosting country at large. These living realities are more than belief systems; they form interwoven systems of meaning which are expressed in the way people talk about themselves and others. In this way, the refugees' narratives formulate their perceptions of their predicament and of what they perceive as being predictable developments in the future. However, each one of these two tendencies/realities/narratives has its own *intertextuality*. Shotter understood intertextuality as the fact that communication 'draws upon people's knowledge of a certain body of *already formulated* meanings in the making of its meanings' (1993, p. 26). This means that each tendency carries a whole body of shared and unspoken meanings thus forming a distinct *discourse* along with corresponding realities, perceptions and resulting relationships. For example, within the discourse of 'honouring the past', refugees are likely to perceive as positive everything that goes along with that tendency, e.g. retaining the relationships in the way in which they were structured before they had to flee their homes, remaining within the scope of their home cultural values and norms, and focusing on ways to achieve successful repatriation. However, these tendencies would not only be incompatible with the other discourse but indeed antithetical; one would exclude the other.

Daniele Joly (1996), in a comparative study of Chilean and Vietnamese refugees in the UK and France, found two distinct patterns in the way refugees deal with their refugee condition. It is quite striking that her observations regarding these patterns correspond with our model which posits two opposing discourses. According to Joly, the 'overriding' feature of Chileans was 'a collective project identified with the society of origin' which 'influences their process of settlement and their relationship with the society of origin ... Their primary goal was to regain their power as social actors in the society of origin, albeit from a distance. Time and events in the homeland modify the expressions of this identification and a diversification takes place but the homeland orientation never disappears totally on a collective level' (p. 184). In contrast, the 'main orientation' of the Vietnamese 'is that of the society of reception ... all their efforts tend to address adaptation and settlement in the host society ... Their aim is to gain social power in the host society ... The concrete desire for return is not part of their strategy' (pp. 184-5). Although Joly's 'two distinct categories' refer to the collective and cultural level emphasising the socio-political and not the psychological context, her study offers a clear example of the two oppositional discourses (proposed by our model) as identified by empirical research.

It is important to appreciate that, at the conceptual level, these discourses are antithetical to each other and, logically, cannot coexist as one contradicts the other. The intertextuality of the one organises the family in ways that privileges the pre-refugee world, whereas the other discourse organises the family around the new context of the refugee reality in the receiving country. Thus, if both opposing discourses are 'activated' simultaneously in a given family, then the roles, perceptions, relationships of family members and, ultimately, the stories (which combine together all the aspects of each discourse) could be expected to result in disruptive conflict. It is precisely these issues that we wanted to investigate in our project. More specifically, we were interested in finding out about the implications of these two oppositional discourses and how families negotiate their conflictual and antithetical directions. Ultimately, this approach was more in line with both our systemic framework as well as our concern for finding a meaningful way of investigating the refugee condition outside the pathology paradigm.

## Concerns

Given our personal experiences with the refugee condition we had several concerns about our contact with these families in the context of our project.

Van der Veer (1994) offers one of the best discussions on the consequences for the helping professional of working with refugees; he highlights issues of burn-out, countertransference and vicarious traumatisation. He also acknowledges that long-term work with seriously traumatised clients can have deleterious effects on the functioning of the professionals; certainly our experience in this area, and in the field of sexual and other forms of abuse, suggests that to sustain a healthy balance with regard to human nature, it is essential that professionals have a structure in place for discussion, consultation or supervision about their work and its effect on them. This provides a protective factor for the professional and also monitors the nature of the work undertaken with clients. In this project, we discussed the content, the process and the impact of the refugees' narratives on us after each interview. This routine practice helped us to achieve a wider understanding of the material and provided a context for expressing and digesting our own emotional responses; both of us benefited from this process and from making personal connections with the refugees' narratives.

Another shared concern about the project was that in our conversations with the refugee families we could be raising hopes and expectations of additional help, which we would be unable to provide. It was therefore imperative for us to clarify our boundaries and our role in our contact with the families as clearly and promptly as possible. Professionals often forget that some of our clients tend to invest us with powerful roles which ignore the complexity of functions that we have in a given situation, resulting in a confusion between authority, responsibility and resources. Like many other workers we also experienced the inevitable discomfort of having some assurance and control about our own lives compared to the refugees' uncertainty. We did feel however that by 'bearing witness' (Papadopoulos, 1996) we were facilitating a valuable process. As systemic clinicians, we recognised that the way in which we asked questions and responded to the families' comments were in themselves a form of therapeutic intervention, which we hoped would not only produce information for us, but would also lead to providing alternative new perspectives for them. Nonetheless, we remained uncomfortable about not being in a position to provide them with resources and the full range of services they required.

Finally, we are aware that not all refugees find it easy to communicate openly about their predicament; most of them are under pressure from various concerns and dilemmas which affect them at a variety of emotional levels. These concerns range from fears that they may be perceived as being disloyal to their own country or ungrateful to the receiving country, to suspicions about the implications of their honesty or the gains they could derive from their contact with 'official' people. Ultimately, we recognise that open communication as a possible mode of dealing with stress and trauma may reflect our theoretical framework and culture rather than that of the refugee.

### Special Circumstances

It is important to note that our interviews were conducted during the period when all the families were uncertain about their continuing presence in this country. Their legal status as ELR (Exceptional Leave to Remain) meant that they were unable to plan for the future and were, thus, ambivalent about returning to Bosnia. In addition, travelling abroad was not easy and employment possibilities were virtually non-existent. All this created a most volatile and unstable situation. For many asylum seekers this period of waiting leads to a psychological hiatus in which personal, familial, social and economic status are all contingent on apparently arbitrary decisions taken by powerful external authorities.

### The Interviews

The standard procedure we followed included an explanation of our purpose in contacting them and asking for permission to use an audio-tape to record our interviews. We emphasised our interest in learning about their experiences and how they saw their situation. We hoped that what we gleaned in this project would be of some use to others in the field. The initial contact at the first meeting was generally not difficult because Renos had met most of the families on their arrival in Britain. His credentials with them were well established and he was knowledgeable about their conditions and overall culture. Some clarification of Judy's role was required, however. On one occasion, no doubt exacerbated by the use of the audio-tape machine, her presence produced a hostile and suspicious response. It seems that the way she was listening intently and following the non-verbal clues in the conversation between Renos and the hosts (although not understanding the Bosnian language at all) coupled with her dark hair, made the hosts suspicious — they thought she spoke their language and feared she was a Serbian spy.

Unfortunately, our follow-up interviews proved more difficult to

221

arrange than the first ones. Some families had become busier and more involved with daily life, they developed different priorities and some were reluctant to be reminded of their predicament. The obstacles we had to overcome in re-establishing contact with some families testify to both the degree of adaptation some had made, as well as the transitory nature of some refugees' lives and, hence, how tenuous their connections can be. This was exemplified by one worried and unsettled man with whom all the agencies had lost contact.

## The Interviewees

As previously mentioned, the families we saw already had a non-clinical connection with Renos through his work with the Bosnian refugee community. The refugees were chosen on the basis of availability, and an interest in participating. We hoped that Renos' ability to speak their language and his previously proven interest in their plight would help to sensitise us to at least some of the transcultural gaps we would inevitably encounter in the process of the interviews. Our aim was to try and locate a variety of families representing the different ages, life-cycle stages, culture and social status among the refugee population.

## Translation

The interviews were in the refugees' homes and were mainly conducted in the Bosnian language with Renos being both the interpreter and one of the interviewers. Judy's lack of previous contact with them helped to bring a fresh approach and to ask questions which may have been more difficult for Renos to address, given his previous contact with them. The advantage of two systemic therapists working together in this way meant that we would have more opportunity to learn about the subtleties of conversational interactions and the nuances of both spoken and body language. The fact that one spoke their language and the other did not, created an interesting structure. On many occasions, Judy's role was comparable to that of a reflecting team in so far as she was one step removed from the direct conversation. When painful material emerged and one of us became too involved in their narrative, the other could maintain a more systemic role, keeping in mind the whole family system. This tended to occur around details of torture.

## Types of Heterogeneity

Ultimately, there is a serious difficulty in referring to refugees as if they were a homogeneous group of people in the same way as one refers to persons belonging to a set psychopathological category. In other words, when referring to 'psychopaths' or 'schizophrenics', one discards all the other characteristics of a person and focuses only on those aspects of their personality which fit into the diagnostic category because, presumably, in certain contexts it may be meaningful to do so. However, the descriptive category of 'refugee' refers to the external circumstances that a group of people find themselves in, as in 'employees', 'consumers', 'sports fans' etc., and does not address any personality characteristics as such. Refugees, not belonging to a pathological category, may have little in common in their personalities; the only characteristic they definitely share is that they have all had to leave their homes. Thus, it would be inaccurate to subscribe to any description of labelling of refugees as if they were a psychologically coherent group of persons. As Baker put it, 'to assume homogeneity and create stereotypes of refugees is likely to lead to misunderstanding of their needs and to further depersonalisation and dehumanisation' (1983, p. 74).

Unlike other groups of refugees in this country, the families we interviewed were not noticeably different from the rest of the population in terms of physical appearance, manner of behaving, clothing, or because they followed any unusual customs. Being white European was, for them, a mixed blessing. For example, they did not attract unwanted attention in so far as they were not visibly recognised as foreigners; however, they experienced their different circumstances and their cultural 'otherness' without evoking sensitivity to their needs. Although we may make general comments about the refugees within the project, we are mindful of important differences among them. Our interviewees were a most heterogeneous group: they were different in relation to class, education, previous family functioning, rural or urban dwelling, types of employment, aspirations and expectations, financial position, political affiliation, degree of religious belief, level of cultural involvement, etc. Two of the families we interviewed were of mixed ethnic background: one family included a Serbian husband and a Croatian wife, and another a Muslim wife and a Croatian husband. These mixed families faced additional difficulties because it had proved harder for them to maintain links with their extended families and friends. They had little hope that they would be welcomed back by either side.

## The Families

The theoretical framework informing this project explicated two opposing discourses. In the narratives of refugee families the tension between these discourses was apparent throughout the interviews and the first visible division along these conflicting tendencies was in terms of generational subsystems and life-cycle stages. The grandparental generation seemed more focused on the past, the middle generation most divided between their loyalty to the past and concerns to establish a future for their families, whilst the children, although they talked of missing aspects of their previous home world (e.g. their friends and familiar places) were already acculturating in terms of learning English, attending school, following the current fashion and pursuing their sports interests.

Several grandparents expressed how bereft they felt, having no motivation to settle here. They had expected to spend their late-middle and old-age 'at home' in the company of those with whom they had shared a past. In one family, the elderly grandmother described feeling isolated, and how affected she was because she lost her role as a provider, with no visitors or extended family to cook for. On the other hand, her daughter and son-in-law had become involved with the NHS when their child was seriously ill, and as a result had become actively involved in the community. One middle-aged widow of a paediatrician summed up this contrast: 'My daughter and son-in-law are orienting their lives completely in the British way, I am living my life in the hope that I am going to return. So they are looking forward to the future and they have a completely different attitude from me. I am still orienting myself towards returning home and my whole attitude towards life is based on those values. They have already adopted the different values of England and they want to move on in that direction'. This woman had lived a comfortable bourgeois life-style before the war; she was now acting as cleaner and housekeeper for her daughter, son-in-law and grandchildren. When she returns to her own flat after taking care of the family, she goes to bed to keep warm, since she cannot afford heating, and reads Croatian newspapers. Although an educated woman, she has no wish to learn English. This is a woman desperately loyal to the past, who sees no possibility of starting life afresh here.

Another young couple, who expressed their confusion and uncertainty about maintaining loyalty to the past or placing hope in a future here, said 'It would be much better if we knew exactly the conditions; how long are we here, whether we're going to begin to earn some money for our own house, or start to learn the language. I don't know whether this is going to be my home, and whether it's worth spending money and effort, or whether I have to abandon this and go away again'. However they also provided an example of how they were struggling with these two discourses, when they said 'We believe that the system of life here does not correspond with our mentality'. But they also added, in relation to their new baby, 'The only nice thing is that he is not a refugee. It's nice to have a second homeland in reserve'. So, they were able to break the dichotomous antithesis of these discourses by conceptualising a two-home existence.

This same couple experienced flashbacks and dreams of their past, sometimes these were painful and sometimes comforting, providing an opportunity to slip back in time and place. The wife often used to dream of her home whilst the husband rarely did so and never in pleasant contexts. Characteristically, he said 'I told her the night before, that I would like sometimes in my dreams to go back to my house also. I say to her, "I don't want you to sleep tomorrow night, you are not allowed to keep going home without me! I also want to dream that I went to my house".'

A Bosnian man who had recently got engaged to an English woman he had met in London illustrated how circumstances can affect the oppositional discourses: 'Here I want to start a new life with a wedding and beginning a family, here in this country. I don't want to return there and get involved in the killing, kill anybody or be killed. But before [meeting my English fiancée] I was praying to God to allow me to go back and get involved again and now it is completely different. The only difficulty now is the uncertainty whether they will allow me to stay here or not'.

The childrens' situation seemed rather easier with their structured daily routine. It appeared that their adaptation was less fraught. Despite expressing occasional concerns about what they had left behind, they were more inclined to talk to us about what they were currently doing rather than relate stories of the past. However, many did express concern about their parents' physical and emotional well-being. As one insightfully commented about her mother, 'We have our goal in front of us, she hasn't'.

We gathered from our contact with these families, that the childrens' attitudes to settling down were largely affected by their parents' views. We also noted that boys appeared more resilient and demonstrated no active symptomatology; they were less parentified and appeared to be emotionally protected by their mothers and sisters. Not all the children fared so well. Two of the adolescent girls were struggling to achieve academically and socially, to cope with the new language and to cope with the contradictions inherent in bridging two cultures. It seems that the oppositional discourses here contributed to actual symptomatology. Both were the eldest in their families, one was 17 and the other 13; both were discovered to have eating problems and low self-esteem. Despite some similarities, the contrast between their family situations was marked, demonstrating yet again the inappropriateness of talking about refugees as a homogenous group. The first came from a successful middle-class business family from Sarajevo. The daughter had come to London as an au pair in order to learn English shortly before the outbreak of hostilities. Financially, they were reasonably well off and her mother and younger brother were able to join her here when the situation at home became unsafe, while their father remained behind. In contrast, the second family lived in a rural area and had been deeply affected by the fighting; the mother and children had not known of the father's whereabouts for 18 months and they had all spent time in a variety of camps, suffering serious material deprivation and emotional abuse. In both these situations the daughters responded to their family situation by assuming adult responsibilities for their younger brother and by trying to emotionally support their mothers in the absence of their fathers. In the first family, the father had to stay in Bosnia and in the other, the father had insisted on returning to Bosnia, driving trucks on aid missions. This second man was determined to remain actively involved in the conflict and to try to rebuild his country despite suffering from considerable physical and mental symptoms following his imprisonment and torture during the conflict. His family was left uncertain with regard to dealing with the split caused by his passionate loyalty and dangerous connection to his country and their wish to try and start a new life here. This pull between the two polar opposites led not only to extreme disruption in the couple's relationship, already damaged by the enforced separation during the war, but inevitably to distress and uncertainty in the whole family.

The first family had an agreed goal for the adolescents to complete their education here and then for them all to leave and return home to be with their father. The mother experienced the time here as 'living in limbo'; despite her good knowledge of English, and her previous training as a lawyer, she chose not to develop contacts here: 'There is a sense of temporariness here. I don't have opportunities and perhaps I am not even looking for opportunities to meet other people. I am here because of them [my children]'.

However, on closer examination, the generational hypothesis is not

226

entirely accurate. Grandparents are extremely keen that their grandchildren do well and make the best of the opportunities in the UK. They encouraged them in every possible way; for example, one grandparent offered to do housework which the parents were asking their children to do so that the children would have more time for their studies. Grandchildren were also not exclusively oriented towards their new world in the UK but also had moments when they privileged their pre-refugee world. Despite the fact that a grandchild would wear a London soccer club jersey, speak with the local English accent and begin to forget the nuances of his mother tongue, he would spend time with his grandfather encouraging him to talk about their home town back in Bosnia and to relate stories from the good old days; a teenage girl, although she seemed preoccupied with fitting in with her school friends in appearance, mannerisms, music preferences etc, also spent time with her grandmother learning to cook Bosnian specialities. In several cases, the parents were preoccupied with trying to find work or study here and seemed less motivated to encourage their children to focus on their old culture whereas the grandparents were in a better position to activate connections with their home culture.

Therefore, although there is some evidence that grandparents seem to be the main representatives of the first discourse (i.e. honouring the past) and grandchildren of the second discourse (i.e. valuing the new life in the UK), these divisions in reality are much more complicated and less clear-cut than it first appears.

In order to examine the details of this complex picture we need to focus on some additional themes in a more specific way.

## Language

For many families an obvious basic disadvantage of the refugee condition is the literal inability to communicate verbally, although some minority groups do deliberately maintain their separateness and their loyalty to their own culture by maintaining a linguistic ghetto. As one Bosnian woman said 'Language is not only a means to communicate, but also language is much more than that'.

Learning the host language could be seen as a capitulation to acknowledging that the future lies here rather than in their homeland. One woman, who travels 16 stations on the London Underground to buy a Bosnian newspaper in an effort to keep in touch with her own culture, also sadly related that her granddaughter no longer tells her what she is doing but instead writes her diary in English in order to keep secrets. So whilst the host language offers more opportunity for external contact, it can also be used to distance family members.

Eva Hoffman (1989) describes a process whereby having to speak in a new language not only inhibits the range and depth of what you can talk about but also inevitably affects the way in which you present yourself, limited by lack of vocabulary, metaphor and perhaps insensitive to nuance. In an effort to try and accommodate to the host country's ways, many non-English speakers may feel that they have to alter their natural exuberance and their customary patterns of relating, in order to become acceptable. In this way they may lose their idiosyncratic and cultural forms of expression, feel inhibited and self-conscious, losing a sense of their own identity.

A minimal knowledge of language can also evoke misperceptions and misunderstandings. A Bosnian talked specifically about his attempts to communicate and use humour in a relationship he was trying to establish with an English woman. It seemed to us that their lack of a mutual language had allowed two emotionally needy people to attribute falsely to each other qualities and capacities they were searching for. In this instance, misunderstandings, stemming from an inability to speak their thoughts, led to disappointment, arguments and finally to a breakdown of the relationship.

Finally, it is important to acknowledge that among the many changes the people of former Yugoslavia experienced (which included changes of country boundaries, names, value of ethnic and religious sentiments) was one which passed almost unnoticed — language. In the former Yugoslavia, the language spoken in Bosnia was called Serbo-Croatian. As the name implies, it was a combination of Serbian and Croatian and it was the same language which was spoken in the former Yugoslav republics of Serbia, Croatia, Bosnia and Herzegovina, and Montenegro. Currently, no language is called Serbo-Croatian; instead, now in Serbia they call their language 'Serbian', in Croatia 'Croatian', and in Bosnia 'Bosnian'. Thus, 'Bosnian' is a completely new name for the same language which was spoken before the war. The impact of the change of the name of their language is difficult to assess at this stage. What impact would it have on the English if one day their language was no longer called English?

### Hierarchical Organisation and Parentification

The tendency for the older generation not to accommodate to learning a new language may serve to distance them further both from the community at large and from other family members. This phenomenon can also have a major impact on hierarchical roles within the family whereby different members assume different roles and additional responsibilities which would not have been the case prior to the war. Since children learned English more quickly, many of them had become the interpreters for their parents in most situations, thus taking on an important role and additional responsibilities. They had become the conduits for exchanging information and in this context at least the usual generational roles had been reversed. Their parents were now partly dependent on them. One formerly powerful executive in Bosnia was now sitting at home frightened to venture out because he did not speak the language, and waiting for his eleven-year-old son to come back from school so that he would take his father out to the park. A complete role reversal.

Our impression was that although the children had clear narratives to relate about their past, they were mainly actively caught up in the day to day issues of learning and adapting to their new way of life. As mentioned above, the children, who were aged between 9 and 17, related their worries about their parents, especially about the mental health of parents who had been traumatised by torture and deprivation in the war. In one family, the two children said they were worried about their mother, who was often physically unwell and emotionally distressed because of her concern about their father.

In another family, the grandmother, who originally had only helped by playing with the children when they came out of school, was now responsible for all the household menial tasks. The children no longer spent time with her or chatted; they preferred their technical toys, TV and videos or their privacy. Perhaps this was an inevitable outcome of the children growing older, but she certainly experienced it as a reflection of their wish to get on with their new lives and leave her behind. That grandmother told us very emphatically: 'Nobody is happy here, do you understand me? Nobody is happy. They think they are happy. It's just that I know that I have no choice at all'.

One general comment about most families is that the majority of the relatively younger parents when they were in the former Yugoslavia were both in employment, following the socialist ideal of the working mother. As a result, it was usually the grandparents and the extended family who looked after their children. In the UK, most parents had much more time to spend with their children and for a lot of them it was the first time they had to play an actual parental role. This created some interesting situations where some parents relished their new role, whereas others found it frustrating and demoralising not to be able to become financially independent and pursue their chosen careers.

In one family, both parents, determined to settle here and progress from their refugee status to the well-paid and respected white-collar positions they had held in the former Yugoslavia, were working extremely long hours in menial jobs and had to accept remuneration far beneath the minimum wage. They were rarely both at home at the same time and there was virtually no time during the week which the family could spend together. The parents felt so guilty about this as well as about the fact that, as a result, their children had to cope on their own (at home and at school) that they compensated by meeting all of their childrens' excessive material demands. This created a vicious circle because the parents had to work even harder and the children became even more powerful within the hierarchy. When asked whether they ever said no to their children, the mother replied 'Sometimes at home [i.e. Yugoslavia], but never here. I know this is a big mistake, but I always feel very guilty here'.

In this family there was an apparent split between those who wished to return and those who wanted to stay; the parents and their son were planning their future careers in England but their adolescent daughter and her grandmother wished to return. However, as it emerged, they all took it in turns to represent each one of the two oppositional directions, without being aware of it.

### Gender Roles and Responsibilities in the Couples

Some of the younger families have also shifted their patterns partly in response to their experiences in the war, but also as a result of living in a country with changing attitudes towards gender. The following are examples of the confusion that this can evoke.

One father told us, 'the mentality there [i.e. in the former Yugoslavia] is that the husband is the dominant one, and I didn't particularly want that myself. I always expected some equality but here it seems to me that my wife wants to be always dominant over me. I cannot possibly accept that'.

Another father had become completely preoccupied by his traumatic experiences of torture and his compulsion to return to his country on humanitarian missions: he was no longer able to occupy himself in the daily life of his family which he had enjoyed before the war. His wife now took on all the decisions and responsibilities, despite her own precarious physical and mental health. She felt he had changed so much that she no longer recognised him, at times his aggression and intensity of feeling frightened her. The children were clearly aware of this and open about their worries about their parents; they said they were doing well at school and were anxious not to do or say anything which would upset their parents. The joint-parental role had disappeared, the maternal role had become confused and the children took on what would have been adult concerns.

A disturbing episode was revealed when the father related to us how frightened the children had been on Guy Fawkes night when they heard the bangs and whistles of the fireworks. We asked if he had suggested that they go to the window so that they could see the spectacle and confirm that it was not part of any military conflict. He had refused to let them look, presumably because he could not bear the reminder of the war himself, thus leaving them with their anxieties intact. When this man painfully described his horrific prison camp experiences in detail, his children tried to watch the television, but he insisted that they listened too.

The only couple who did not talk about the stress of being together virtually 24 hours a day was an elderly farmer, completely absorbed in politics, and his ailing but hospitable wife. Despite the fact that their lives had changed radically, they managed to retain a division of roles comparable to what they had back in Bosnia. Their long and solid relationship helped them to survive their refugee upheaval and although they wanted to return home, they were very realistic about the difficulties involved and they coped remarkably well with their new conditions in London.

It seems that the women, even if they had had careers previously, could manage to occupy themselves more than the men who said they were demoralised and appeared to have a rather low self-esteem. All men felt ashamed and humiliated about receiving social benefits, when all they wanted was a chance to earn a living and provide for their families as they would have done in their own country. Their identity as providers for their families was damaged and therefore they felt that their own status in the community was diminished.

Another gender difference we noted was that the women and men had different language for expressing emotion (Riessman, 1993.) The men we spoke to seemed more factual, talked about political aspects of the war and dominated the conversations during the interviews. The women were hospitable ensuring that we were comfortable; they attempted to talk about feelings and their uncertainties and throughout were aware of the children being present and how they were responding (cf. Cole, Esprin and Robinson, 1992). Overall the mothers and grand-mothers prioritised the needs of the children and men, before considering what would be important for themselves.

## Reflections

Perhaps the most important finding of this study is that the two oppositional discourses (despite their logical incompatibility) do not have to cease their antagonistic pull nor do they divide the family into two distinct, static and permanent factions. What we observed in practice is that in the internal dynamics of the family there is a constant process of containing these contradictory discourses

What emerged from this work is that refugee families embrace both oppositional directions most of the time although, due to circumstantial factors, they temporarily may privilege one against the other. It is understandable that families hold onto both of these perspectives be-cause both of them are valid. The most succinct expression of the two orientations was given in their own words as follows: the first discourse as 'We shall always remain Bosnians and we shall never fit into this society here in England', and the second as 'We cannot turn the clock back, what has happened cannot be undone. Let us look forward towards the future now.' Each view offers a sensible and realistic perspectives. Therefore, what matters most is not to attempt to eradi-cate the tension created by the antithetical nature of these discourses, by eliminating the one and imposing the other; instead, what emerged as being of greater importance was the ability of the families to contain the tension which is created by the presence of both oppositional tendencies. Families that find it difficult to hold this tension and choose one direction only, are likely to lose their vitality because both tenden-cies are psychologically and pragmatically indispensable.

As far as the family division is concerned, although there is some evidence that the grandparents and grandchildren represent the two polar opposite directions, the situation is far more complex than this. There seems to be what could be called a 'systemic arbitrariness' as to who represents which direction at any given time. It is as if the family system needs to ensure that both tendencies are represented, regardless of who is enlisted to uphold them. Each family member may challenge allegiances and champion a different direction at different times accord-ing to the overall systemic scenario, the sole aim of which is to ensure that both tendencies are represented in the family and held in a balanced tension. Thus, far from having detrimental effects, the oppositional discourses may enrich and assist families to live more creatively. We noticed that we often got caught in these family tensions and would be in danger of becoming more interested in either their present adaptation in this country or the value they placed on their cultural roots. Inevitably, we temporarily became part of their system.

By focusing on the oppositional narratives, we were able to expand our perspectives and increase the complexity of our understanding beyond the identification of stereotyped patterns or assessment of pathological behaviours. Using a systemic framework, we appreciated the interactional nature of the refugee condition and understood how the 'specialist care industry' inadvertently may contribute to the refugee's disorientation. Although, admittedly of a different nature, to some the trauma of settling in a receiving country may be equal in intensity to (if not more severe than) the trauma of leaving the country of origin. However unbelievable it may sound, we heard repeatedly from refugees that the way they felt they were treated here by services, officials and people was far worse than their experiences in Bosnia. Characteristically, one said 'at least in Bosnia we knew we were tortured; here we are tormented by people in velvet gloves and we have to keep on thanking them on top of it'.

Finally, returning to the title of our chapter, the home has proven to be a highly complex construct and there are at least two homes refugees are torn between: the home in the country of origin and the home in the receiving country. Moreover, it seems that the home is as much as where the heart is as the heart is where the home is.

## Postscript

We are most grateful to everybody we interviewed. Their generosity was not limited to giving their time and sharing their painful thoughts and feelings, but also included their hospitality and tolerance of our intrusion. To this extent, this chapter is a joint endeavour between our interviewees (the refugee families) and ourselves. We also wish to thank the Tavistock Foundation for their grant which enabled us to complete this study.

## References

Arredondo, P. et al. (1989) 'Family Therapy with Central American War Refugee Families', *Journal of Strategic and Systemic Therapies*, 8: 28-35.
Baker, R. (ed.) (1983) *The Psychosocial Problems of Refugees*, London: The

British Refugee Council and the European Consultation on Refugees and Exiles.

Bell, M. (1997) 'The Truth is Our Currency: the role of the media in reporting war', a series of four talks on BBC Radio 4 (May-June, 1997).

Bowlby, J. (1988) *A Secure Base: clinical implications of attachment theory*, London: Routledge.

Bruner, J. (1990) *Acts of Meaning*, Cambridge: Harvard University Press.

Cohon, D. (1981) 'Psychological Adaptation and Dysfunction Among Refugees', *International Migration Review*, Vol 15, No.1: 255-75.

—— (1985) 'Internal Change Following Uprooting', in *Cambodian Mental Health*, New York: Cambodian Women's Project, pp. 31-42.

Cole, E.; Esprin, O.M. and Robinson, E.D. (1992) *Refugee Women and Their Mental Health: shattered societies, sheltered lives*, The Haworth Press.

de Jong, J.T.V.M. and Clarke, L. (eds) (1996) *Mental Health of Refugees*, Geneva: WHO in collaboration with the UNHCR.

Eisenbruch, M. (1990) 'Cultural Bereavement and Homesickness', in S. Fisher and C. Cooper (eds) *On the Move: the psychology of change and transition*, Chichester: Wiley.

—— (1991) 'From Post-traumatic Stress Disorder to Cultural Bereavement: diagnosis of Southeast Asian refugees', *Social Sciences and Medicine*, 33: 673-80.

Epston, D. and White, M. (1992) *Experience, Contradiction, Narrative and Imagination*, Adelaide, Australia: Dulwich Centre Publications.

Evdokas, T. (1976) *Refugees of Cyprus: a representative research among the 200000*, Nicosia: Research Group.

Friedman, M. and Jaranson, J. (1994) 'The Applicability of the PTSD Concept to Refugees', in A.J. Marsella et al. (eds), *Amidst Peril And Pain: the mental health and social well-being of the world's refugees*, (pp. 207-28), Washington, DC: American Psychological Association.

Geertz, C. (1986) 'From the Native's Point of View', on the nature of anthropological understanding, in Shweder, R. and LeVine, R.A. (eds), *Culture Theory: essays on mind, self and emotion*, Cambridge: Cambridge University Press.

Goderez, B.I. (1987) 'The Survivor Syndrome; massive psychic trauma and post traumatic stress disorder', *Bulletin of the Menninger Clinic*, 51(1), 96-113.

Hirschon, R. (1989) *Heirs of the Greek Catastrophe: the social life of Asia Minor Refugees in Pireaus*, Oxford: Clarendon Press.

Hitch, P. (1983) 'The Mental Health of Refugees: a review of research', in Baker 1983 ICIHI (1986), *Refugees. The Dynamics of Displacement: a report for the independent commission on international humanitarian issues*, London: Zed Books.

Hoffman, E. (1989) *Lost in Translation: a life in a new language*, London: Minerva.

Holtzman, W. and Borneman, T. (1991) *Mental Health of Immigrants and Refugees*, Austin, TX: Hogg Foundation.

Joly, D. (1996) *Haven or Hell? asylum policies and refugees in Europe*, London: Macmillan.

Knox, K. (1997) *Credit to the Nation: a study of refugees in the United Kingdom*, London: The Refugee Council.

Loizos, P. (1981) *The Heart Grown Bitter: a chronicle of Cyprus war refugees*, Cambridge: Cambridge University Press.

Marris, P. (1996) *The Politics Of Uncertainty: attachment in private and public life*, London: Routledge.

Marsella, A.J. (1994) 'Ethno-cultural diversity and international refugee. Challenges for the global community', in Marsella A.J. et al. (eds), *Amidst Peril and Pain: the mental health and social well-being of the world's refugees*, Washington, DC: American Psychological Association.

Marsella, A.J. et al. (1996a) 'Ethnocultural aspects of PTSD: An overview and issues and research directions', in A.J. Marsella et al. (eds), *Ethnocultural Aspects of Post Traumatic Stress Disorder: issues, research, and clinical applications*, Washington, DC: American Psychological Association.

Marsella, A.J. et al. (1996b) 'Ethnocultural aspects of PTSD: Some closing thoughts', in A.J. Marsella et al. (eds) *Ethnocultural Aspects of Post Traumatic Stress Disorder: issues, research, and clinical applications*, Washington, DC: American Psychological Association.

Mollica, R. et al. (1989) *Turning point in Khmer Mental Health: immediate steps to resolve the mental health crisis in the Khmer border camps*, Cambridge, Mass.: Harvard School of Public Health.

Mollica, R. et al. (1987) 'Indochinese Versions of the Hopkins Symptom Checklist-25: a screening instrument for the psychiatric care of refugees', *American Journal of Psychiatry*, 144: 497-500.

Mollica, R.F. and Jalbert, R.R. (1989) *Community in Confinement: the mental health crisis in site two*, The World Federation for Mental Health.

Mollica, R.F. et al. (nd) *Repatriation and disability: a community study of health, mental health and social functioning of the Khmer residents of Site Two*, Vols 1 & 2, Cambridge, Mass.: Harvard Program in Refugee Trauma.

Muecke, M. (1992) 'New Paradigms for Refugee Mental Health', *Social Sciences & Medicine*, 35, (4), 515-23.

Papadopoulos, R. (1996) 'Therapeutic Presence and Witnessing', *Tavistock Gazette*, (Autumn, 1996).

—— (1997a) 'When the Secure Base is No longer Safe: experiences of working with refugees', The Fourth Annual John Bowlby Memorial Lecture, (February 1997), London: The Centre for Attachment-based Psychoanalytic Psychotherapy.

—— (1997b) 'Individual Identity in the Context of Collective Strife', in *Eranos Yearbook*, Vol 66, edited by James G. Donat and Jay Livernois, Woodstock, Connecticut: Spring Journal Books.

—— (in press) 'Working With Families of Bosnian Medical Evacuees: therapeutic dilemmas', *The Journal of Child Psychology and Psychiatry*, (1998), Vol 39.

Parry, A. and Doan, R.E. (1994) *Story Re-Visions: narrative therapy in the postmodern world*, New York: The Guilford Press.

Reichelt, S. and Sveaass, N. (1994) 'Therapy with Refugee Families: what is a "good" conversation?', *Family Process*, 33: 247-62.

Riessman, C.K. (1993) *Narrative Analysis,* London: Sage.

Rutter, J. (1994) *Refugee Children in the Class Room,* Stoke-on-Trent: Trentham Books.

—— (1996) *Refugees: we left because we had to,* London: The Refugee Council.

Shotter, J. (1993) *Conversational Realities: constructing life through language,* London: Sage.

United Nations (1960) *The Social and Economic Aspects of Refugee Integration,* Stockholm, UN.

UNHCR (1993) *The State of the World's Refugees: the challenge of protection,* London: Penguin.

—— (1994) *Refugee Children: guidelines on protection and care,* Geneva.

van der Veer, G. (1994) *Counselling and Therapy with Refugees: psychological problems of victims of war, torture and repression,* Chichester: Wiley.

Vernez, Y. (1991) 'Current Global Refugee Situation and International Public Policy', *American Psychologist,* 46: 427-631.

White, M. (1989) *Selected Papers,* Adelaide, Australia: Dulwich Centre Publications.

White, M. and Epston, D. (1991) *Narrative Means to Therapeutic Ends,* New York: W.W. Norton.

Williams, C. and Westermeyer, J. (1986) *Refugee Mental Health in Resettlement Countries,* Cambridge, Mass.: Hemisphere Publishing Co.

Woodcock, J. (1994) 'Family Therapy with Refugees and Political Exiles', *Context,* No. 20.

Wortman, C.B. and Silver, R.C. (1989) 'The Myths of Coping With Loss', *Journal of Consulting and Clinical Psychology,* Vol. 57, No. 3: 349-57.

Zur, J. (1996) 'From PTSD to Voices in Context: from an "experience-far" to an "experience-near" understanding of responses to war and atrocity across cultures', *International Journal of Social Psychiatry,* Vol 42, No. 4: 305-17.

# Index

239